Black Farm Boys

Rural Studies

Kai A. Schafft and Jennifer Sherman, editors

Rural Studies publishes books on a wide range of social issues with the goal of advancing the scholarly, political, and public discourse on rural spaces and the people in them. The titles in this series seek to foreground important experiences and processes concerning rural life, communities, and the environment in an effort to improve the lives of rural people at the local and global levels.

A complete list of books published in Rural Studies is available at https://uncpress.org/series/rural-studies.

BLACK FARM BOYS

The Untold Story of the New Farmers of America

BOBBY J. SMITH II

The University of North Carolina Press

CHAPEL HILL

*This book was published with the assistance of the
John Hope Franklin Fund of the University of North Carolina Press.*

Designed by Lindsay Starr
Set in Warnock Pro, Scala Sans, Cutright WF,
and Archive Roundface Script
by codeMantra

Portions of the introduction and chapter 5 were previously published in
essay form in "In Search of the New Farmers of America: Remembering
America's Forgotten Black Youth Farm Movement," *Journal of Agriculture,
Food Systems, and Community Development* 11, no. 4 (2022): 9–12.

Cover art: Randolph NFA Annual Livestock and Poultry Show, 1962–1963.
Courtesy of Lorenza and Myrtle Crosby Collection, La Grange, Texas.

Library of Congress Cataloging-in-Publication Data
Names: Smith, Bobby J., II, author.
Title: Black farm boys : the untold story of the
New Farmers of America / Bobby J. Smith II.
Other titles: Rural studies series (Chapel Hill, N.C.)
Description: Chapel Hill : The University of North Carolina Press, [2026] |
Series: Rural studies | Includes bibliographical references and index.
Identifiers: LCCN 2026015741 | ISBN 9781469696928 (cloth) |
ISBN 9781469696935 (paperback) | ISBN 9781469695792 (epub) |
ISBN 9781469696942 (pdf)
Subjects: LCSH: New Farmers of America—History. |
African Americans—Vocational education—History—20th century. |
African Americans in agriculture—History—20th century. |
Agricultural education—United States—History—20th century.
Classification: LCC LC2780.2 .S65 2026
LC record available at https://lccn.loc.gov/2026015741

For product safety concerns under the European Union's General Product
Safety Regulation (EU GPSR), please contact gpsr@mare-nostrum.co.uk
or write to the University of North Carolina Press and Mare Nostrum
Group B.V., Doelen 72, 4831 GR Breda, The Netherlands.

For Black farm boys—past, present, and future

Contents

Illustrations

MAPS

Abbreviations

AES-USOE	Agricultural Education Service of the United States Office of Education
BYFM	Black youth farm movement
FFA	Future Farmers of America
FIS	Farmers' Improvement Society
HBCU	historically Black college or university
LGCC	land grant college complex
MANRRS	Minorities in Agriculture, Natural Resources, and Related Sciences
MTIS	New Jersey Manual Training and Industrial School for Colored Youth
NAACP	National Association for the Advancement of Colored People
NCNFA	North Carolina Association of the New Farmers of America
NCTA	North Carolina Teachers Association
NFA	New Farmers of America
NHA	New Homemakers of America
NJNFA	New Jersey Association of the New Farmers of America
OKNFA	Oklahoma Association of the New Farmers of America

PFT Progressive Farmers of Texas

PVAMU Prairie View A&M University

TXNFA Texas Association of the New Farmers of America

Black Farm Boys

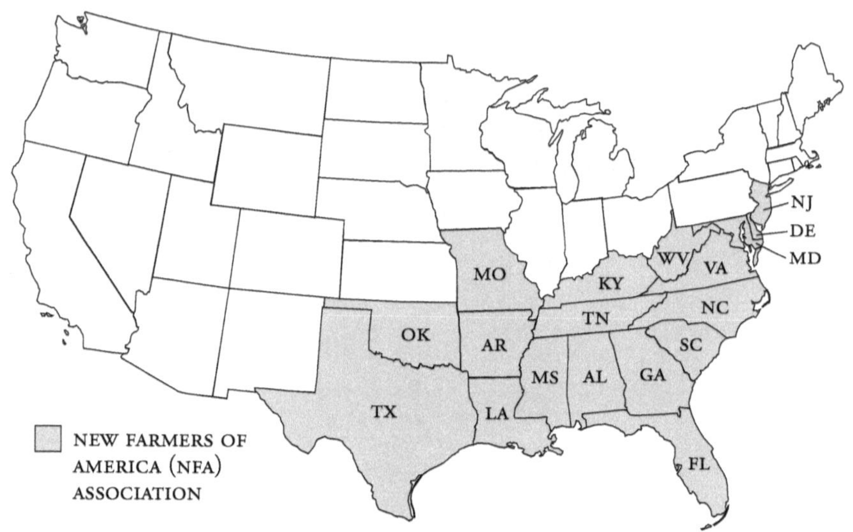

National landscape of the New Farmers of America:
Eighteen state associations.

THE UNTOLD STORY OF THE NEW FARMERS OF AMERICA

An Adventure Through the Shadows of Black Agricultural History

New Farmers of America exposed me to a different way of think-ing. It exposed me to not just the practical side of agriculture, but the educational side. . . . I don't think enough is said about it, writ-ten about it, and the contributions that it made. Few of my friends that are still living, we talk about that, but we need someone like you to tell the story. . . . I don't want the NFA to be forgotten.

—**Alfred L. Parks,** Wallace NFA chapter, Fordyce, Arkansas

The New Farmers of America (NFA) was founded in August 1935 as the first youth organization in the United States exclusively for Black farm boys studying vocational agriculture at public high schools across the South and as far north as New Jersey. For three solid decades, the NFA grew to an annual membership of more than 55,000 active members across eighteen state associations of local chapters, vehemently challeng-ing racialized exclusion in American agriculture through agricultural education. Each state association (except New Jersey's) established its headquarters at the state's 1890 land grant institution, all of which are known today as historically Black colleges or universities (HBCUs). Under the advisement of Black agriculture teachers in high schools, local NFA chapters inspired Black farm boys to practice self-actualization through agricultural advocacy and to reject their presupposed subservient identities linked to systems of slavery and sharecropping. In the face of systemic racial segregation in the education of Black people across the nation, the NFA operationalized a global and national platform to develop, motivate, and empower generations of rural Black boys to become farmers and pursue careers in agriculture to produce a livable future for themselves, their communities, and the nation. Yet, by the end of 1965, the NFA had somehow disappeared and merged with the predominantly white Future Farmers of America (FFA) organization, the NFA's untold story forced to remain in quiet obscurity, orbiting the shadows of Black agricultural history in the American memory.[1]

On the evening of March 17, 2019, the story of the NFA resurfaced in the most unlikely of places: a large gray storage bin in my mother's garage. The bin, tucked away under a dusty shelf, contained some old books and materials from my sister's college days as an agriculture major at our alma mater, Prairie View A&M University (PVAMU). It had been at least fifteen years since my sister had seen the container and finally made the time to go through it. As she carefully examined its contents, my sister stopped abruptly when she stumbled upon two rare, out-of-print books: Ernest M. Norris's *Forty Long Years* and Cecil L. Strickland's *New Farmers of America in Retrospect: The Formative Years, 1935–1965*. Overcome with excitement and nostalgia about finding the books, as she had received them from Strickland—her beloved professor—my sister immediately pulled out her phone, snapped a picture of them, and sent it to me via text message: "Going through old books and came across these gems." I must admit that I wasn't familiar with either book, but my sister's tone intrigued me as she described the books as "gems," so I decided to look into the titles more.[2]

A quick Google search later revealed that the books in the picture were the only two ever written about the NFA, which at the time I had never heard of. Both were published in the 1990s as efforts to preserve the history of the NFA by two former leaders in the organization. However, as I continued to explore the world's largest search engine for information about the NFA, it yielded sparse details about the organization, covering only minimal topics surrounding the NFA's founding in 1935 and dissolution in 1965. The two books were virtually the only sources that existed—at the time—that provided any considerable engagement with this forgotten organization. So, like a detective working a cold case, I responded to my sister's text and asked her to mail the books to me for further investigation. Once I received them, I became rather obsessed with the NFA and read both volumes within a week's time. As I delved deeper into the history of the NFA, my obsession turned into admiration for the NFA, and I embarked on a rather unexpected intellectual adventure through the shadows of Black agricultural history.

Six years into this adventure, *Black Farm Boys* represents my first effort in telling the remarkable untold story of the NFA. Despite its rich history, the NFA is gravely understudied. To date, only three books have been written about the organization: the documentary accounts of Norris and Strickland and *The Legacy of the New Farmers of America* by Antoine J. Alston, Dexter B. Wakefield, and Netta S. Cox, a pictorial history of the organization published in 2022. A review of research across multiple disciplines, including Black studies, rural sociology, and agricultural education, underscores that the scarcity of scholarly engagement with the NFA is symptomatic of a much larger issue: Decades of scholarship on Black people's historical relationship to agriculture have predominantly framed agriculture as a domain of exploitation, subjugation, and racial exclusion.[3]

For instance, a microscopic look at research in Black studies clarifies this symptom as scholars often portray agriculture as an oppressive facet of Black existence—something to be overcome or rejected in the pursuit of freedom. Consequently, organizations like the NFA, which represent a story of empowerment and agency, are often written out of these narratives and are antithetical to the consensus in the literature. While scholars such as Valerie Grim, Monica White, Cherisse Jones-Branch, and others have studied Black people's historical relationship to agriculture beyond its oppressive dynamics, this research has not fully examined Black youth agricultural organizations or Black youths as subjects.[4]

Accordingly, how scholars in the tradition of rural sociology take up the issue of race complicates how rural sociologists and related social scientists study relationships between Black people and agriculture. For example, race has most often been historically treated by them as a variable instead of a lens through which to examine those relationships in rural communities. This level of thinking severely limits the sociological analysis and understanding of the agency of rural Black communities in general, and Black farming communities in particular, rendering Black farmers as just another demographic group of producers in comparison to other groups. Such ways of knowing relegate groups like the NFA—which were a key feature of rural Black communities—to the periphery of rural sociology, hiding them in plain sight.[5]

Even in agricultural education, more specifically, the NFA has not received sustained attention. This is evident in the fact that the *Journal of Agricultural Education*—the leading publication for agricultural education scholars and professionals since its founding in 1961—has published only five articles on the NFA. The problem with these works, as I have written about elsewhere, is that they often frame the NFA in relation to the FFA, which has dominated the literature in agricultural education. As a result, this literature locates the NFA along the FFA's timeline, reducing the NFA to a supporting role—a mere footnote—in the story of agricultural education in America. This view of the NFA is rooted in the widely accepted idea that the NFA was simply the FFA's Black counterpart during the days when the FFA was segregated in the South. Such a view of the NFA distorts the organization's profound impact on the historical relationship between Black people and agriculture, perpetuating intellectual blind spots that sideline the agricultural innovation of the NFA in Black communities.[6]

That being said, what I grapple with in *Black Farm Boys* is an overwhelming paradox: the NFA's very significant existence and its near total absence from our nation's historical memory. This paradox renders the NFA virtually invisible to scholars and the public, muting the stories and voices of the thousands of Black boys who participated in the organization. How did the NFA mobilize thousands of Black youths to consider agriculture as a viable career pathway? Who were the individuals and what were the ideas, forces, and institutions that shaped the evolution of the NFA? How did it carve out spaces of empowerment in the face of a shifting national agricultural landscape configured by segregation? What can we learn from the NFA that can expand our understanding of Black people's historical relationship to agriculture? And more broadly: How is it possible that the NFA escaped the attention of scholars and researchers, especially those who study the Black experience? How does the NFA's existence reshape how we think about Black history and American agriculture? How does the story of the NFA speak to the current state of agriculture in rural and urban Black communities? What blueprints did the NFA leave behind for Black youths today who are considering a life or career in agriculture?

As the first book of its kind, *Black Farm Boys* provides a critical space to think through these questions. It does not claim to be a comprehensive study of the NFA. Rather, it is a modest exploration of the existence, significance, and legacy of the NFA that will hopefully provide the basis for further research and public engagement. Rooted in Black studies, rural studies, agricultural history, agricultural education, rural sociology, and sociological theory more broadly, this book reckons with the absence of knowledge on the NFA, recasting the organization as a site for serious scholarly analysis of Black people's historical relationship to agriculture. *Black Farm Boys* makes clear that the NFA was much more than just a singular national organization—it was part of what I theorize as the "Black youth farm movement" (BYFM) that emerged in the 1870s and declined in the 1960s. As a social movement, following sociologist Mario Diani and historian Robin D. G. Kelley, the BYFM represents a dynamic constellation and ecosystem of actors, activities, ideas, institutions, and organizations that mobilized rural Black children, teenagers, and college students to reimagine and redefine agriculture as a site of social, political, economic, and environmental vitality in their lives.[7]

The mere existence of the BYFM and its ability to help rural Black youths carve out their own space in the story of American agriculture should receive more attention in the many pages of histories of Black life, narratives about Black education, the study of the rural Black experience, Black agricultural research, and studies of Black youth participation in Black social movements. As a theoretical, empirical, and analytical movement framework, the BYFM alters the way we study Black people's historical relationship to agriculture by considering how formal and informal Black social networks empowered Black youths to mobilize around agricultural production. Despite limited visibility in the public sphere, such mobilization efforts forged new relationships to agriculture in the rural South at a time when thousands of Black people were abandoning agriculture and rural life for different futures promised by the Great Migration. By locating the NFA within the lineage of organizations that were part of the BYFM, *Black Farm Boys* shows how the NFA produced what social scientists call "social movement scenes" to contribute to the wider BYFM. According to social scientists Sebastian Haunss and Darcy Leach, a social movement scene is "a network of people who identify as part of a group and share a certain belief system or set of convictions, that is also necessarily centered around a certain location or set of locations where that group is known to congregate." Put simply, social movement scenes are dynamic networks of social movement actors that are embedded geographically.[8]

Black Farm Boys tells the untold story of the NFA through five distinct scenes—the opening scene, the convention scene, the camp scene, the community scene, and the final scene. Taking a multisited approach, each scene was produced through the rubric of the BYFM and represents a case study. When read together, each case study is part of an instrumental collective case study that illuminates key aspects of the untold story of the NFA. In a broader sense, the scenes reflect what sociologist Rinaldo Walcott theorizes as "glimpses of Black freedom" that exist alongside conditions and circumstances that perpetuate myriad inequities in Black life. Through these scenes, NFA members configured a new plane of existence within an alternate world where Black people celebrated and engaged in agriculture without oppression being a preoccupation. This alternate world was built around organized community, statewide, and national activities, including conventions, banquets, fairs, on-farm training demonstrations, livestock judging contests, and summer youth camps.[9]

In this alternate world, Black high school boys in the NFA proudly referred to themselves as "Black farm boys," taking on new agrarian identities by promoting a positive self-image. Black high school girls also embraced their agency in this world through a similarly forgotten organization called the New Homemakers of America (NHA). Founded in 1945 as a national organization, the NHA operated until 1965 when it merged with the predominantly white Future Homemakers of America. The NHA was viewed as the sister organization of the NFA in most rural Black communities, often collaborating with the NFA on local programming. Although the NFA and NHA promoted gender roles that framed men as farmers and women as homemakers, the realities of rural life ruptured this division: Women routinely engaged in agricultural labor, and men participated in domestic work in the home. The scenes produced in *Black Farm Boys* do not document the NFA's work with the NHA, but the organization's impact on the lives of Black girls was integral to the NFA's broader vision of an emancipatory Black agricultural world. The NHA, as a parallel and collaborative institution, rightfully deserves its own book-length treatment—one that extends beyond the scenes documented in this book.[10]

Black Farm Boys brings the untold story of the NFA to life through a creative interpretive research design that integrates a wide range of primary and secondary sources—including archival records, digital materials, organizational records, newspapers, oral histories, interviews, and governmental records. In telling this story, the book makes at least five significant scholarly contributions. First, it provides a new framework—the BYFM—for studying Black people's historical relationship to agriculture, amplifying, recovering, and mapping the liberatory dynamics of this relationship. The existence of the BYFM provides an intellectual space to expand the purview of sociological, cultural, and historical research on Black youths, bringing into focus how organizations like the NFA encouraged them to produce their own visions of an emancipatory Black future through agriculture. The BYFM also captures how they wrestled with conflicting agricultural identities, recalibrating agricultural production as an essential dimension of Black freedom. This recalibration process provides a blueprint for Black activists and community leaders today who are concerned about the future of Black agriculture in movements for food justice, food sovereignty, and land justice. By incorporating this process into their work, Black activists and related stakeholders can use the BYFM and the NFA as models for discussion, debate, and organizing activities.[11]

Second, *Black Farm Boys* sheds light on the critical ways that rural Black youths reconfigured rural Black spaces while navigating Black people's historical relationship to agriculture. Scholarship on rural Black experiences often highlights the underdevelopment of the communities in which these experiences occur. Scholarly conversations on Black agriculture have been concerned primarily with how adult Black farmers have approached this relationship, obscuring the ways in which Black youths took center stage in many historical struggles around agriculture. By extending the theory of a social movement scene and applying it to the story of the NFA, *Black Farm Boys* shows how the NFA created a set of scenes to exert its agency in addressing the agricultural needs of rural Black communities. These scenes expand the narrative of struggles surrounding Black people's historical relationship to agriculture.

Third, *Black Farm Boys* foregrounds the crucial role of rural Black male youths in social movement activism as realized in the BYFM, which offers a fresh perspective on the role of Black young people in social movements between the late 1800s and the civil rights era. Whereas existing research on historical Black youth activism in social movements has largely focused on urban Black youth organizing in the civil rights and Black Power movements between the 1930s and 1970s, this book clarifies how rural Black youths engaged in and created their own organizing efforts that were not directly associated with mainstream historical Black movements. This is not to suggest that urban Black youth organizing during the civil rights and Black Power movements was disconnected from Black agrarian struggles. In fact, early iterations of the National Association for the Advancement of Colored People (NAACP) Youth Councils in the 1930s, such as the council in Cleveland, Ohio, participated in rural Black advocacy efforts, collaborating with the labor movement to address the plight of Black sharecroppers. While these efforts aligned with the goals of the BYFM, they remained outside its purview. In contrast, proponents of the BYFM explicitly and exclusively engaged Black agrarian struggles as a pathway to building a more democratic society through agricultural production and science.[12]

Fourth, *Black Farm Boys* sheds light on an underexplored aspect of HBCU history. As scholarly and public discourse and interest in HBCUs increases, this book extends those discussions in relation to HBCUs that are designated as 1890 land grant institutions. As mentioned earlier, 1890 land grant institutions provided an administrative headquarters for the NFA. The institutions were also breeding grounds for the development and training of Black agriculture teachers who were members of collegiate NFA chapters and who would go on to be NFA advisors and leaders, which was integral to the NFA pipeline from high school to college to a career. As such, the NFA was an important enterprise in HBCU culture, and in many respects the organization wouldn't exist without HBCUs.

Fifth, *Black Farm Boys* documents an overlooked high school experience led by Black farm boys in rural Black communities in the South between the 1920s and 1960s. During this time frame, the only major sociological study to center and document the lives of rural Black youths in relation to the agricultural economy in the South was Charles S. Johnson's groundbreaking *Growing Up in the Black Belt: Negro Youth in the Rural South*. Published in 1941, this study was authorized by the American Youth Commission and concluded that the relationship between rural Black young people and agriculture was largely negative. This negative relationship encouraged them to abandon agriculture, stirring their desire to migrate to urban centers in and outside the South. But not all rural Black youths in the South wanted to escape agriculture. While Johnson gave some attention to those who saw agriculture in a positive light, what is not clear is what mechanisms helped them see agriculture this way. *Black Farm Boys* argues that the NFA was one of those mechanisms, offering rural Black boys an opportunity to develop their social and leadership skills and exposing them to new kinds of thinking with agriculture at the center. For local NFA chapters, the rural Black high school was more than just an educational setting—it was an incubator for cultivating NFA trainings and community programmatic efforts and events. Rural Black high schools were also the staging ground for Black farm boys to administer NFA meetings, agricultural competitions, and special events. The agricultural workshop at the schools served as the staging area.[13]

Beyond its scholarly contributions, *Black Farm Boys* speaks in opposition to public discourses that focus solely on harmful stereotypes associated with agriculture, further perpetuating long-standing stigmas surrounding agricultural production in Black communities. Compounded by the current plight of Black farmers and the underfunding of agricultural programs at HBCUs, stigmas of agriculture fuel a strong disinterest in agriculture and a lack of Black representation in agricultural academic programs and careers. This exacerbates a national problem concerning the alarming shortage of agricultural specialists and professionals needed to sustain the nation's agriculture industry, directly impacting US food systems and the production of necessary goods for human life. *Black Farm Boys* offers a critical space for considering the NFA as a historical organizational model for capturing, igniting, and maintaining the interest of Black youths in agriculture, highlighting how the NFA can be used as a site to produce new discourses that show how the emancipatory dimensions of Black people's historical relationship to agriculture can shape national and community-based conversations about the future of American agriculture.

. . . .

Black Farm Boys proceeds through five chapters and concludes with a postscript reflection. The first chapter, "1935: The Making of the NFA and the Black Youth Farm Movement," rewinds back to the opening scene of the NFA by locating its birth story within the historical arc of the legislative landscape of the BYFM. Chapter 2, "A Black Advantage Vision of Agriculture: The Fifth National NFA Convention in New Jersey," examines the convention scene of the NFA through the prism of the historic 1939 national NFA convention at the New Jersey Manual Training and Industrial School for Colored Youth in Bordentown, New Jersey. Chapter 3, "Camping While Black: The S. B. Simmons NFA Camp in North Carolina," provides an in-depth look at the camp scene of the NFA by probing the history of the iconic S. B. Simmons NFA Camp, where thousands of Black farm boys engaged in recreational activities to enhance social skills and leadership capacities. Chapter 4, "Black Agriculture Teachers Matter: The Randolph NFA Chapter in Texas," centers the role of Black agriculture teachers in the NFA by exploring the community scene of the Randolph NFA chapter in Texas. Chapter 5, "1965: The Mysterious Disappearance of the NFA," recounts the years and days leading to the final scene of the NFA, which is characterized by the peculiar conditions and circumstances along the historical timeline of the NFA between 1941 and 1965. The concluding postscript reflection fast-forwards to the present, making clear that the NFA's untold story does not end with these pages, as I am still actively uncovering aspects of the story as I continue to travel through the shadows of Black agricultural history.

Chapter 1

1935

The Making of the NFA and the Black Youth Farm Movement

The New Farmers of America forced us to believe that anything is possible and dream. . . . It was one of the best models of student development in a rural Black community. Let the story of the NFA tell the story.

—**Freddie L. Richards,** Henry County NFA chapter,
Abbeville, Alabama

Tangled in the warped threads of the beautifully complex tapestry of Black world history, the origin story of the New Farmers of America has long been misunderstood and overlooked. If the story is told at all, it is severely reduced to a reactionary footnote suggesting that the NFA was created in 1935 as a response to the exclusion of Black farm boys from the Future Farmers of America in the South. But the NFA did not appear out of thin air. It was not a spontaneous creation, nor was it the result of a single event, individual, or institution. Instead, the NFA was the culmination of decades of deliberate and strategic efforts that are best understood within the legislative arc of what I defined in the introduction as the "Black youth farm movement." As an analytical, theoretical, and empirical framework, the BYFM captures how rural Black youth from the 1870s to the 1960s worked collectively to create new Black agrarian futures—that is, a future for Black people where they can decide and define the terms by which they interact with agricultural practices. Such futures were drafted on the farms and in the laboratories, seminar rooms, and classrooms located at Black land grant universities (known today as 1890 land grant institutions)—the institutional foundation of the BYFM.

To be clear, the BYFM was much more than an educational project engineered by legislative gains—it was a mechanism designed to protest and undermine the presupposed subservient agricultural identities of rural Black people and their children who were linked to systems of slavery and sharecropping. The protests took the form of various agricultural activities, including agricultural fairs, livestock judging contests, farm business management trainings, leadership training programs, and rural community development schemes. On the surface, such activities seem passive. But reading deeper into the historical context of these activities reveals that these activities were designed to disrupt and remedy the underdevelopment of rural Black communities. Together, the protests created a pathway for Black youths to confront what I refer to as the "Black agrarian question" taken up by sociologist W. E. B. Du Bois in his 1913 paper "The Last Word in Caste": What is the current condition of Black people in terms of agricultural land in the American South? Focusing on how the relationship between race, agriculture, and power impacted access to land for Black farmers, Du Bois posed this Black agrarian question in light of a swiftly shifting Southern agricultural environment with racial segregation at the center. This environment manufactured what Du Bois described as the "color line" and perpetuated the development of segregated systems of agricultural education that reconfigured Black agricultural colleges, vocational agricultural programs at secondary schools, and community-based educational spaces.[1]

At the heart of the BYFM were unsung educators and visionaries who dreamed fiercely in the face of such inequities, transforming agriculture into a tool for liberation rather than subjugation. The NFA represented their wildest dreams—a formalized expression of the BYFM that empowered Black farm boys through education, agricultural training, and leadership development. The formation of the NFA operationalized a new template of Black agricultural education that never existed before, ushering in a new system of beliefs and customs surrounding the role of agriculture in Black life. This template promoted new ways of knowing and being that repositioned Black farm boys to the center of a grand experiment in Black agricultural education that cultivated Black self-determination, uplifted their communities, and authorized them to pursue careers in agriculture. Such an experiment was conducted through an analysis of Black participation in agricultural education as a legal and necessary route to Black freedom.

So, what is the origin story of the NFA? How did the organization come into existence? In what ways do the origins of the NFA speak to the history of the organization, and why it has been forgotten? In this chapter, I take up these questions by sketching out the three eras of the BYFM's development: (1) foundational, (2) grassroots, and (3) systematic. The foundational era involved the establishment of a Black agricultural education infrastructure, including Black land grant colleges and programs in rural Black communities, which served as the institutional base of the BYFM. The grassroots era was characterized by community-based initiatives, grassroots organizing, and the empowerment of Black youth through agricultural programs like Negro 4-H clubs. The systematic era represents the culmination of legislative efforts to formalize agricultural education at rural Black public high schools, solidifying the structure and institutional posture of the BYFM, which would later manifest as the NFA.

In the following pages, I relocate the origins of the NFA within the BYFM—at the intersection of legislative victories, institutional infrastructure, and community organizing surrounding the BYFM. Locating the NFA along the contours of the BYFM not only challenges the idea that the NFA was solely a reaction to exclusion from the FFA but also shows that it was the result of visionary thinking among Black farm boys and their adult advocates. This line of thinking, as this chapter will show, undergirds the opening scene of the NFA's untold story and establishes a crucial entry point for understanding the four vivid scenes that appear later in the book—the convention scene, the camp scene, the community scene, and the final scene—produced by the NFA in alignment with the BYFM. But this overture is more than just a starting point for the NFA's origin story. It compels us to expand the archive of Black life—capturing the historical conditions and circumstances that collided in the BYFM to birth the NFA.

Legislating the BYFM: A Grand Experiment in Black Agricultural Education

The development of the BYFM was shaped by the legislative landscape of what investigative reporter Jim Hightower calls the "land grant college complex" (LGCC), a massive system of institutions and programs that collectively define the structure of agricultural education, research, and extension services in the United States. Rooted in the confiscation of Indigenous land and racial segregation, this legislative landscape was made up of five landmark legislative acts: the Morrill Acts of 1862 and 1890, the Hatch Act of 1887, the Smith-Lever Act of 1914, and the Smith-Hughes Act of 1917. The Morrill Act of 1862 established the 1862 land grant college system, which provided each state with land to construct a college focused on scientific agriculture as a means to improve American agricultural practices. The Hatch Act of 1887 allocated federal funds for agricultural research through the establishment of experiment stations at the land grant universities. The Morrill Act of 1890 provided additional federal funds to the land grant colleges under the Morrill Act of 1862 and authorized the establishment of the Black land grant college system. The Smith-Lever Act of 1914 established the US Cooperative Extension Service: a system of community-based education programs associated with the land grant universities that promoted and supported agricultural and rural development in each state. The Smith-Hughes Act of 1917 allocated federal funding for vocational education in agriculture, home economics, and trades in public schools, ushering in vocational agriculture programs in public schools.[2]

Together, the interplay between these historic laws that built the LGCC paved the way for a grand experiment in Black agricultural education that framed the three eras of the BYFM, culminating in the birth of the NFA. Interestingly, the three eras of the BYFM began with a solid base of institutional backing before transitioning to the grassroots level. This is significant since most movements begin at the grassroots level; however, the BYFM began with the establishment of Black land grant institutions in rural Black communities that would drive national agricultural initiatives in the United States. The systematic era, which marked the BYFM's ultimate stage of growth, allowed the dimensions of the foundational and grassroots eras to coincide. This confluence of legislative groundwork and institutional growth intersected with a systems-level approach to the BYFM, allowing supporters of the NFA idea to establish a national body of leaders as well as state-level organizations. The strategic integration of the key elements of each era caused the BYFM to go through several iterations that not only enhanced movement growth but also propelled the NFA to the forefront, ushering in a new generation of Black farm boys.

The Foundational Era: Reading the Black Side of
the Land Grant College Complex

The foundational era in the development of the BYFM was characterized by the interaction between the Morrill Acts of 1862 and 1890 in the American South. At the time of the signing of the 1862 Morrill Act, approximately 90 percent of Black people in America were identified as slaves. As such, the 1862 Morrill Act made no reference to race, enabling the land grant colleges in the South and border states to operate on the principles of racial segregation through custom and law. Even though Black youths were prohibited from attending these land grant colleges, some states created Black land grant colleges under the Morrill Act of 1862. For example, Alcorn State University in Mississippi was founded in 1871 as the nation's first Black land grant college under provisions from the 1862 act, providing a separate educational space for Black youths in Mississippi to obtain an education in agriculture and related sciences. Twenty-eight years later, Congress passed the Morrill Act of 1890. This legislation provided additional federal funds to the land grant colleges under the Morrill Act of 1862 and included a "separate but equal" clause that authorized the establishment of a system of seventeen Black land grant colleges, which laid the foundation for what I call the Black side of the LGCC.[3]

When examining the text of the Morrill Act of 1890, it becomes clear that the Black side of the LGCC was the product of the idea that educational equity could be achieved through separate but equal education systems—predating the *Plessy v. Ferguson* decision of 1896 that legalized the "separate but equal" doctrine that shaped public education in America until the 1950s. Section 1 of the text includes this passage: "Provided, That no money shall be paid out under this act to any State or Territory for the support and maintenance of a college where a distinction of race or color is made in the admission of students, but the establishment and maintenance of such colleges separately for white and colored students shall be held to be a compliance with the provisions of this act if the funds received in such State or Territory be equitably divided as hereinafter set forth." In his examination of the 1890 Morrill Act, historian Leedell Neyland observed that the legislation "did not demand the creation of black institutions outright, but it provided for the loss of funds in those states in which blacks were not receiving land-grant education. . . . So while there was a definite injunction against discrimination in the allocation and use of federal funds, there was also a provision which enabled states to freely establish separate land-grant institutions for white and black citizens." In response to the Morrill Act of 1890, the Black side of the LGCC transformed rural Black communities into critical sites for the development of a new generation of educated Black youth, ushering in the BYFM.[4]

Historically, the development of rural Black communities in the South was largely dependent on the formal educational infrastructure and community-based programs facilitated by the Black side of the LGCC. This educational infrastructure trained a generation of Black youths who would become rural public school teachers and develop a tailored curriculum in agricultural education for the next generation of Black youths, creating a pipeline of Black agricultural education that funneled up to the Black land grant college system. One of the chief architects of this pipeline at the college level was Booker T. Washington, the founding principal and first president of Tuskegee University in Alabama and a prominent leader on the Black side of the LGCC. Known as the father of Black agricultural education, Washington was a graduate of what is now Hampton University, the Black land grant college of Virginia, until 1919. He began his tenure at Tuskegee in 1881 at the recommendation of his mentor and Hampton's founding principal, Gen. Samuel C. Armstrong, a former white Union soldier and prominent educator.[5]

In many respects, Washington's philosophy for Tuskegee was shaped by General Armstrong's vision for Black education at Hampton. This philosophy, as noted by historian James D. Anderson, "urged Afro-Americans to remain in the south and seek their fortune, primarily in common agricultural and domestic labor." Agricultural education figured prominently in Washington's agenda for Tuskegee's vocational and industrial education portfolio, influenced by his belief that agriculture could be a pathway to freedom for Black people and their communities. As he put it in his book *Working with the Hands*, "It is my conviction that the great body of the Negro population must live in the future as they have done in the past, by the cultivation of the soil, and the most hopeful service now to be done is to enable the race to follow agriculture with intelligence and diligence." Washington's beliefs about agricultural education in Black life sent shockwaves throughout the South and became a model for both Black land grant colleges and historically Black high schools that offered practical training in agriculture.[6]

To be sure, Washington's philosophy of Black agricultural education extended beyond the South. This philosophy became known among social scientists as what sociologist Ira De A. Reid observed as the "Tuskegee

Idea" movement. Reid writes that the Tuskegee Idea movement "generated a Negro pseudo-economy based on small business, agricultural enterprise, vocational training, and philanthropy." In many respects, the Tuskegee Idea movement set the pace for the community focus of the BYFM. This community focus empowered leaders on the Black side of the LGCC to use the complex as the institutional base of the BYFM. They envisioned how the agricultural training of Black youth and their communities could enhance the economic vitality of rural Black communities that were inextricably linked to the land, community, and education. The grassroots era of the BYFM's development extended the movement beyond the gates of the Black land grant colleges and expanded the Black side of the LGCC into rural Black communities across the South.[7]

The Grassroots Era: Community Formations and the Role of Negro 4-H Clubs

The grassroots era of the BYFM that transported the movement from Black land grant colleges to rural Black communities was located at the intersection of the inequities in the Hatch Act of 1887 and the Smith-Lever Act of 1914. While the Black side of the LGCC was legislatively denied access to funds from the Hatch Act to establish experiment stations for agricultural research on Black land grant college campuses, Tuskegee University and Prairie View A&M University accessed these funds at the state level and produced research that would benefit rural Black communities. The groundbreaking research conducted by the research arm of Tuskegee, known as the Tuskegee Institute Agricultural Experiment Station, created an environment conducive to this kind of research. Led by prominent Iowa State University–trained scientist Professor George Washington Carver, who was hired by Washington in 1896 as head of the Tuskegee Department of Agriculture, the experiment station consisted of a team of Black agricultural scientists, students, farmers, and community stakeholders. The arrival of Carver to Tuskegee reshaped the research productivity of the university and its role in creating a curriculum in agricultural education for Black youths in rural communities. Across his storied career at Tuskegee, Carver published an impressive research portfolio on Black farming communities. A central component of this portfolio was the study of the relationship between Black youths and agriculture.[8]

For instance, Carver's portfolio included several bulletins designed to awaken and cultivate a new agricultural spirit in Black youths who were making sense of the aftermath of the system of enslavement and how it shaped the role of agriculture in their lives. In this body of research, Carver urged Black agricultural educators to embed garden spaces within the geography of rural Black public schools. He envisioned garden spaces as key sites for "the awakening of a greater interest in . . . a few of the cardinal principles of agriculture" among Black children and encouraged rural Black teachers to present agriculture "in an attractive way." As seen in chapter 4, many Black teachers took seriously the work of Carver and agreed with him that agricultural education "stimulates thought, investigation, and encourages originality" among Black children, providing them a space to reshape themselves and their communities.[9]

Moreover, Carver's ideas and research on the relationship between Black youths and agriculture were used not only to promote agriculture in rural Black public schools but also to support the development of community-based programs for young people in rural Black communities. Such programs began shortly after the passage of the Smith-Lever Act and were organized under the banner of Negro 4-H clubs within the Negro Extension Service component of the Black side of the LGCC: the segregated component of extension programming that served counties in the South that had a Black extension agent. While Negro Extension has origins in the work of Booker T. Washington's Tuskegee Negro Farmers' Conference and Carver's concept of the "Jesup Agricultural Wagon" that extended Tuskegee's research program into rural Black farming communities, the first Black extension agents were Thomas M. Campbell, who was based at Tuskegee, and John B. Pierce at Hampton. Negro Extension as a federal program was born out of the NAACP's efforts to include a racial component of the Smith-Lever Act of 1914. Such efforts did not result in race being included in the legislation, but it did place race at the center of the debates about the cooperative extension service, as historian Carmen V. Harris found.[10]

Consequently, these debates influenced states that practiced segregated land grant systems to create the severely underfunded and under-resourced Negro Extension Service. The Black side of the land grant college complex provided a statewide administrative base for Negro Extension, enabling it to translate and transfer the knowledge produced at Black land grant colleges to rural Black communities. The network of Negro 4-H clubs extended this knowledge to rural Black youths from ages ten to twenty, creating a new community space for them to explore and experiment with various forms of agriculture, modern farming techniques, home economics, and leadership skills.[11]

In a larger sense, Negro 4-H clubs were modeled after earlier manifestations of community-driven Black youth farm organizations that were created in places like Texas but have long gone unacknowledged. For example, in 1890, prominent Black political leader and educator Robert L. Smith created the Farmers' Improvement Society (FIS) in Texas for Black farmers and developed a statewide network of youth branches of the organization for young people ages six to seventeen. By 1901, the FIS was chartered by the state, and the youth branches represented the lifeblood of the organization. Smith believed that Black youths were a crucial resource in the eradication of problems associated with the social, political, and economic development of rural Black communities configured around an agricultural economy. The philosophy of the FIS was rooted in the idea of self-reliance, given that the organization rose to prominence as a direct result of Black exclusion from state policies designed solely to enhance the lives of white farmers and their communities. Smith ensured that this philosophy spilled over into the communities that housed FIS youth branches as well as into the FIS School, also known as the FIS College, which he founded in 1906 and focused on vocational agricultural training and rural community development. At its peak in the early twentieth century, the FIS boasted and claimed over twenty thousand members in Texas and surrounding states, including Oklahoma and Arkansas.[12]

At the same time, Negro 4-H clubs were the first cross-geographic organizational expressions of the BYFM located at the community level, and by 1924, a decade after the Smith-Lever Act became law, the Negro 4-H had an enrollment of over 45,000 Black boys and girls—a significant increase from the roughly 2,500 enrolled in 1916. The Black county extension agents who led the clubs were trained at Black land grant colleges and operated as a bridge between the Black side of the land grant college complex and rural Black youth. Oftentimes, the county agent was a Black man who worked with farmers, and his counterpart would be a Black woman who was classified as a home demonstration agent who worked with rural Black women and girls on how to enhance their homemaking skills. Together, these agents would cooperate with Black agriculture teachers to connect their community-based leadership programming to curriculum-based training in agriculture and home economics, emphasizing Negro 4-H clubs as an important feature of rural Black life. Although both Black boys and girls engaged in farmwork in their communities, Negro 4-H clubs organized local fairs and livestock judging contests along gender lines characterized by programmatic efforts that suggested that boys should practice agriculture and girls engage in homemaking activities. These gendered restrictions created a robust space for agricultural education that profoundly impacted Black boys and empowered them to lead the agricultural pursuits of their communities. This emphasis on Black boys participating in agriculture in 4-H clubs cascaded into local public schools, and in the wake of the Smith-Hughes Act of 1917, the BYFM was institutionalized.[13]

The Systematic Era: Black Agricultural Science Clubs and State-Based Formations

The systematic era in the development of the BYFM was supported by the Smith-Hughes Act of 1917 and translated the work of the Black side of the LGCC in Black public high schools in the rural South and parts of the East Coast. This legislative act created a formal system of Black vocational agricultural education departments at the schools. At the federal level, this system was under the direction of northern Alabama–raised Dr. Harvey Owen Sargent (known by his contemporaries as H. O. Sargent), a white government official and graduate of Auburn University and George Washington University, who was appointed in October 1917 as the federal agent for Negro and Special Groups in the Agricultural Education Service of the US Office of Education (AES-USOE) (also referred to as the Agricultural Education Branch). Between 1917 and 1936, Dr. Sargent advocated tirelessly for the advancement of Black agriculture teachers and played a crucial role in the establishment of over six hundred Black vocational agricultural education departments at public schools. He was also instrumental in the development of a standardized curriculum in agricultural education at Black land grant institutions. Many of these teachers worked closely with Sargent to ensure that they had access to the resources needed to produce rigorous programs for Black youths in agriculture.[14]

While these resources were not equitable in relation to what white agriculture teachers received, they still made a difference. For example, Dr. Sargent co-organized a summer school program in 1919 at Hampton University for Black agriculture teachers who had been hired across the South under the Smith-Hughes Act. Sargent's summer school program was the first of many that were designed as professional development opportunities for Black agriculture teachers. To be sure, the creation of professional development programs at the federal level by Sargent for Black agriculture teachers provided the teachers with the skills needed to build high-performing agricultural education programs at their respective schools. Sometime in the early 1920s, influenced by such professional development programs, Black agriculture teachers across the South worked collectively to transform Black vocational agriculture departments into ideal spaces for formal agricultural science clubs that emphasized leadership, community uplift, educational excellence, and farm management among Black boys.[15]

At the state level, Black agricultural science clubs somewhat replicated the work of the Negro 4-H in a public school setting, operating as a network, and many Black agriculture students participated in both activities in their rural communities. For some Black farm boys who were in 4-H, the Black agricultural science clubs offered them additional opportunities to expand their agricultural knowledge from their communities to the classroom in a high school setting. It also positioned them within a rural Black community leadership pipeline, which enabled them to discover their ability to navigate their racial and locational identities as rural Black men in a changing society that witnessed a new generation of Black agricultural leaders. But for some of the other rural Black boys who were not in 4-H, the agricultural science clubs exposed them to an educational space that was explicitly devoted to producing a new generation of Black leaders through agriculture. Both demographics of Black boys worked collectively with their adult mentors to assemble state-based formations and networks of the clubs.

For instance, the network of clubs in Texas was known as the Progressive Farmer organization and focused on farm management and training. In Louisiana, the club network operated as the Louisiana Colored Boys' Vocational Club and specialized in farm demonstrations, contests, and recreational activities. In South Carolina, the clubs emphasized camping experiences and livestock judging contests through a state organization known as the Junior Farmers of South Carolina. Other states had their own variations of Black youth farm club activities, such as Arkansas's state organization that placed a strong emphasis on fairs and exhibitions and Kentucky's emphasis on judging competitions. But the development of agricultural science clubs known as the New Farmers of Virginia at segregated Black public high schools in Virginia served as the basis for what would become the national concept of the NFA. The inspiration for the formation of these organizations in Virginia came from a man named George Washington Owens, who was the first Black graduate of Kansas State University.[16]

Born in 1875 on a farm in the Flint Hills of Kansas, just forty miles west of the state capital of Topeka, Owens was the son of formerly enslaved

Africans who had migrated from Tennessee to Kansas to become farmers in the wake of Black emancipation. He spent his early years helping out on his family farm, and as a teenager he began working on multiple farms in the area, developing a passion for agricultural production. This passion was complemented by Owens's desire for educational pursuits. As he wrote in his autobiography, "As a boy, I was very apt and ambitious, eager to learn, ready to read any literature I could find, even old books, newspapers, or journals. I was particularly good at spelling, and I won most of the spelling bees I participated in around the community. I also read all the histories I could secure, ancient, medieval, or current." Both his agricultural training and educational experiences empowered him to pursue higher education at Kansas State University, where he was accepted in 1896, becoming the university's first admitted Black student.[17]

While attending Kansas State, Owens worked as a janitor, for the railroad, and on a variety of farms, including the university farm and dairy, to help pay for his educational expenses. His farm experiences, especially in the dairy, solidified his admiration for agricultural education, and when he graduated in 1899, he secured an internship opportunity that August in

George Washington Owens. From New Farmers of America, *N.F.A. Guide for New Farmers of America* (2nd ed.), 7.

H. O. Sargent. From New Farmers of America, *N.F.A. Guide for New Farmers of America* (4th ed.), 9.

the Iowa State University creamery, working on butter production, cheese making, and dairy science and business management. Prior to his internship, Owens had received a letter from Booker T. Washington that contained a job offer as an assistant to George Washington Carver at Tuskegee. He accepted the position and started his agricultural career one month after his internship. It is not clear how he landed on Tuskegee's radar, but his work as Carver's assistant and the first head of the dairy program in Tuskegee's Department of Agriculture provided him with the skills needed to become a leader in Black agricultural science. For eight years he worked under Carver, leading all efforts surrounding Tuskegee's dairy cattle.[18]

In 1908, Owens was recruited by Virginia State University to establish its Department of Agriculture, where he focused on developing and training the next generation of Black youths who would become professional educators in agriculture. This focus was likely cultivated by Owens during his time under the guidance of Carver, as the Tuskegee Department of Agriculture produced its first set of publications for Black youths while Owens was on staff. Between 1908 and 1927, he served as the first head of the Department of Agriculture at Virginia State. In this role, Owens led the university in replacing Hampton University as Virginia's Black land grant college. He also coordinated the state's annual conference of Black agriculture teachers, which offered opportunities for teachers to come together and learn new methods for teaching agricultural education in rural Black communities. In fact, Owens presented his blueprint for the New Farmers of Virginia to the 1926 delegation at the annual conference, and they voted to support the creation of the organization under the auspices of the Smith-Hughes Act. One year earlier, the "Future Farmers of Virginia" was created exclusively for white farm boys, serving as the foundation for what would become the national FFA organization that was established in 1928. This exclusion of Black farm boys from Future Farmers of Virginia clubs, due to racial segregation in agricultural education in the South, provided the necessary context by which the New Farmers of Virginia emerged.[19]

Even in the face of such exclusion, Owens worked closely with his fellow Virginia State University colleague James R. Thomas, Dr. Sargent, and the AES-USOE to carve out a space in the world of agricultural education in Virginia for Black farm boys. At some point during the 1926–27 academic year, Owens moved from his position as department head to director of the university's teacher trainer program, where he stayed until his retirement in 1945. In this new role as head teacher trainer, Owens traveled around the state spreading the gospel of the New Farmers of Virginia

and enlisted the help of Thomas to write the organization's first constitution and bylaws. As the architect of the New Farmers of Virginia, Owens
used the organization as the foundation for the creation of many Black
vocational agriculture programs at segregated public high schools across
the state. Within a matter of months, the New Farmers of Virginia was
composed of four hundred Black farm boys across eighteen local chapters.
This tremendous start to the New Farmers of Virginia catapulted the organization to the forefront of efforts to build a national program for Black
agricultural education through the Smith-Hughes Act, becoming a model
for other states and increasing the demand for Black agriculture teachers
to lead such efforts at the local level.[20]

In May 1927, the New Farmers of Virginia held its first state meeting
at Virginia State University. This event was a watershed moment in the
BYFM, bringing into focus a transformative pathway for the national idea
of the NFA. Participants agreed that the organization, with its agricultural
activities and competitions, was the future of Black life. Financial literacy,
agricultural initiatives, community-based programs, and leadership training would all contribute to this future. This inaugural meeting, borrowing
the words of Mr. N. B. Beanis, a Black agriculture teacher from James City
County Training School in Williamsburg, marked a "new era" in the history
of Black agricultural education. Speaking on behalf of meeting participants,
Beanis concluded, "We sincerely believe that the future success of the race
lies to a large extent in their ability to become better farmers, hence the
name of the organization." These comments were validated and picked up
by the staff at the prominent Black newspaper the *New Journal and Guide*,
which ran a story on the New Farmers of Virginia in its July 30, 1927, edition. The article stated, "That belief [put forth by Beanis] is shared by the
Journal and Guide, and the idea of encouraging young men of our group to
take to the farms and become better farmers once they have chosen agriculture as their life's vocation should be given race-wide support." By publicly
declaring their support for the New Farmers of Virginia, the staff at the *New
Journal and Guide* set the stage for coverage of the organization as national
Black newspapers such as the *Chicago Defender* and the *Afro-American*
began to print frequent commentary on Black youth farm efforts.[21]

In addition to the organization's growing national prominence in Black
newspapers, the New Farmers of Virginia's framework quickly expanded
throughout the South after its first meeting, setting off a sequence of
events from 1928 to 1935 that would cement the national NFA organization's existence. During the 1927–28 academic year, George Washington

Owens and H. O. Sargent widely circulated the organization's constitution and bylaws to other states that expressed interest in building on the New Farmers of Virginia model. Alabama, Georgia, Florida, North Carolina, and South Carolina were early states that adopted the model. To signify this organizational arrangement, the advisors of preexisting statewide variations of Black youth farm club activities in those states changed their names to align with the New Farmers of Virginia's model: for example, the Junior Farmers of South Carolina organization became the New Farmers of South Carolina. As more states adopted the New Farmers idea, they began to operate interdependently and organize annual sectional meetings through the prism of three sections: Washington, Sargent, and Almmot. The Washington section, named for Booker T. Washington, was created in 1928 and included the states of Virginia, North Carolina, South Carolina, Maryland, West Virginia, New Jersey, and Delaware. Named for H. O. Sargent, the Sargent section was made up of Alabama, Florida, Georgia, Kentucky, and Tennessee. The third section, which included Arkansas, Louisiana, Mississippi, Missouri, Oklahoma, and Texas and took the first letter of each state name, was referred to as the Almmot section (formerly the Almot section before the Missouri NFA was founded in 1949).[22]

Against the backdrop of the development of the sectional formations of the New Farmers, state advisors from the Washington and Sargent sections gathered in Orangeburg, South Carolina, in 1929. At this meeting, the advisors agreed that the time was right for a national structure for the New Farmers idea, and they appointed a committee to take up this issue. Sidney Britton Simmons (known as S. B. Simmons by his contemporaries), a pioneer in the development of Black agricultural education in North Carolina and director of the teacher training program in agricultural education at North Carolina A&T State University, was selected as chair of the committee. Under the leadership of Simmons, the committee was charged with providing recommendations for the national structure of the New Farmers idea and designing appropriate pins, medals, keys, badges, and other forms of symbolic and material paraphernalia for the proposed national organization. Two years later, in 1931, the Washington section assembled in Washington, DC, for a meeting to discuss and vote on the recommendations and terms put forth by Simmons and the committee. Participants also discussed favorable and supportive reports from the Sargent and Almot sections. By the end of the meeting, the Washington section adopted the terms of the potential national NFA organization, clearing the path toward the birth of the NFA.[23]

1935: The Birth of the NFA

After a couple of years of extensive discussions at the local and regional levels about the New Farmers concept, the dreams of Black farm boys, George Washington Owens, H. O. Sargent, and many other visionaries were made real when the NFA officially emerged as a national organization on August 4, 1935. This historic announcement took place during what would be recognized as the first NFA convention, held at Tuskegee University from August 4 to 7. This gathering marked a significant turning point, not only for the NFA but also for the BYFM. The convention brought together Black farm boys, vocational agriculture teachers, professors, and federal agents who shared a vision for improving agricultural practices and supporting Black farm boys in their pursuit of agricultural education as a way to enhance themselves and their communities. Black farm boys in attendance represented an estimated nine thousand new NFA members. Discussions focused mostly on developing a national constitution and bylaws that would be used to govern the new national body of the NFA, which comprised four units: local chapters at high schools, federations of local chapters, state associations, and the national organization. Such discussions were separated by committee work that ranged from national contests and budgetary concern to membership levels and a host of other issues spread across eleven appointed committees. The enthusiasm and commitment displayed at this event set the tone for further development of both the NFA and the BYFM, positively impacting the lives of many Black farm boys, their communities, and the nation.[24]

To be sure, the choice of Tuskegee for this national meeting was profoundly symbolic, paying tribute to Booker T. Washington's pivotal role in advancing Black education in general, and Black agricultural education in particular. The choice was also an ode to his beloved institution that he used as a laboratory to produce a new pathway in the struggle for Black freedom. His influence was felt throughout the existence of the NFA through annual events. For instance, every April 5—Booker T. Washington's birthday—was designated as National NFA Day. In the eyes of NFA members, NFA Day was a national holiday and was to be commemorated by a week of activities under the banner of "NFA Week" that included the crowning of Miss NFA (sometimes referred to as Miss NFA Sweetheart or NFA Sweetheart) and an annual program. Each program, held by a local NFA chapter, began with a public discussion about Washington and his contributions to vocational and agricultural education. The program also included the highlighting of outstanding achievements of the local chapter

NFA emblem. Courtesy
of the Lorenza and Myrtle
Crosby Collection,
La Grange, TX.

that year, which was likely a recruitment opportunity as well. Visually, the
location of the NFA Day program would be decorated in black and old
gold, the official colors of the NFA, and the emblem would be present as
well. The NFA's emblem featured the words "NFA" and "Vocational Agriculture" along with five symbols: (1) a plow, which symbolized the tillage
of the soil and modern agriculture; (2) an owl, which symbolized wisdom;
(3) the rising sun, which represented progress; (4) an open boll of cotton, which represented the crop and the economic interests of many Black
farm boys in agriculture; and (5) an American eagle, which represented the
organization's national reach. In later years, National NFA Day expanded
to National NFA Week, which occurred the week of Washington's birthday. [25]

Structurally, each unit of the NFA was expected to have a copy of the
national *N.F.A. Guide* and adhere to the guidelines and recommendations
put forth in it. As the official organ of the NFA, the *N.F.A. Guide* was first

published in 1938 with an initial print run of five thousand. It featured the NFA emblem on its cover, and its contents covered a range of topics for NFA compliance, such as the constitution and bylaws, organizational history, officer designation, levels of membership, meeting procedures, ceremonial guidelines, and the NFA creed, which served as the philosophical underpinnings of the NFA. Cecil Strickland Sr. wrote that "the founding of the NFA can best be expressed in its Creed." This foundational statement consisted of six declarations, each beginning with the words "I believe," which all NFA members proudly recited, affirming publicly their devotion to the work of the NFA:

> I believe in the dignity of farm work and that I shall prosper in proportion as I learn to put knowledge and skill into the occupations of farming.
>
> I believe that the farm boy who learns to produce better crops and better livestock; who learns to improve and beautify his home surroundings will find joy and success in meeting the challenging situations as they arise in his daily living.
>
> I believe that rural organizations should develop their leaders from within; that the boys in the rural communities should look forward to positions of leadership in the civic, social, and public life surrounding them.
>
> I believe that the life of service is the life that counts; that happiness endures to mankind when it comes from having helped lift the burdens of others.
>
> I believe in the practice of cooperation in agriculture; that it will aid in bringing to the man lowest down a wealth of giving as well as receiving.
>
> I believe that each farm boy bears the responsibility for finding and developing his talents to the end that the life of his people may thereby be enriched so that happiness and contentment will come to all.[26]

As a transformative space to prepare Black farm boys to actively incorporate the principles and values stated in the NFA creed, Black land grant institutions served as administrative hubs for the organization at the state and local chapter levels. This administrative space was crucial and enabled the NFA to empower Black male youths to organize eighteen state associations of local chapters at its height, as well as to cultivate a national

N. F. A.
GUIDE

FOR

THE NATIONAL ORGANIZATION FOR NEGRO STUDENTS STUDYING VOCATIONAL AGRICULTURE

Prepared and published by the New Farmers of America in cooperation with U. S. Office of Education, Federal Security Agency

REVISED 1946

Cover of the 1946 *N.F.A. Guide.* From 1946 New Farmers of America, *N.F.A. Guide for New Farmers of America* (4th ed.).

program of work that would shape the organization. The program of work comprised an eleven-point platform of activities: (1) supervised farming, (2) community service, (3) cooperative activities, (4) publicity, (5) thrift, (6) meetings, (7) membership recruitment, (8) leadership training, (9) scholarship, (10) character building, and (11) recreation.[27]

In a larger sense, this national program of work clarified the vision of the NFA and led to its rapid development. S. B. Simmons recorded that by 1940, the organization had "increased from a few members and chapters to the present number of 916 chapters, 55,000 active and associate members; and has the distinction of being the largest national incorporated Negro farm group in the world." During these early years, until 1941, the NFA operated independently of the AES-USOE. Its founding advisor, Professor Church H. Banks of Prairie View A&M University (PVAMU), and Executive Secretary-Treasurer S. B. Simmons worked collectively to set the tone for the organization. Banks was in his position for only two years because of his untimely death, but he was instrumental in the creation of collegiate chapters of the NFA, which would act as a pipeline for future Black agriculture teachers who would advise local NFA chapters. PVAMU was one of the first Black land grant universities to start one of these chapters. Due to the dual role of Simmons, the founding headquarters of the national NFA was North Carolina A&T State University.[28]

Without question, such tremendous growth provided a platform for Black farm boys to unite, share resources, and advocate for their rights. It also allowed Black agriculture teachers to invest time in promoting unity among the boys, empowering them to challenge the long-standing inequalities faced by their communities. Undoubtedly, the impact of the NFA aligned the BYFM with other social movements of the time, highlighting the importance of cohesion, resistance, and resilience. As the world's largest Black farm organization at the time, the NFA's formation was crucial not just for the BYFM but also for world history. On a worldwide scale, the NFA reconstructed the BYFM and associated it with the greater continuous Black fight for equality and justice in society, carving out a social space that emphasized farming and related activities as fundamental to rural development and community life.

Overture

This chapter has served as an overture to the larger untold story of the NFA and its profound role within the BYFM. It argued that the birth of the NFA must be understood as an integral aspect of the broader BYFM—reframing it not simply as a reactionary footnote in relation to the FFA but as a vital volume in the encyclopedia of Black life. Although in the eyes of the AES-USOE the NFA was considered the FFA's counterpart and was required to work with H. O. Sargent to administer its programs and access limited federal funds for travel expenses, its existence extended beyond this arrangement. In many ways, the presence of the NFA disrupts the organization's invisibility in American memory and expands the archive of Black agricultural history. By traveling along the legislative landscape that shaped the development of the BYFM, this chapter examined the movement's three eras—foundational, grassroots, and systematic—to reveal how the contours of this movement space made room for the NFA to emerge. Said differently, the BYFM represented a grand experiment in Black agricultural education, blending institutional innovation, grassroots organizing, and systematic thinking to empower Black youths and rural communities. Its most notable result was the NFA.

As the next four chapters show, however, the NFA was much more than the culmination of the BYFM. Each chapter depicts a specific scene produced by the NFA in the spirit of the BYFM, even as it faced an uncertain future in the early 1960s in the context of its relationship with the FFA. Black farm boys—alongside their agriculture teachers, Black land grant college professors, and communities—take center stage to celebrate Black agrarian identities, foster physical spaces for social development, and amplify rural Black culture through community transformation. They engage in agricultural education as a means to redefine themselves as leaders and cultivate strategies for self-actualization. Such strategies offered a pathway not only for them to become farmers or pursue professional careers in agriculture but for them to reclaim their agricultural heritage on their own terms. For far too long, the recognition of these terms has been muted. A deeper look into the untold story of the NFA through the scenes it produced illuminates the significance of the organization and showcases the ingenuity of Black farm boys in using natural, human, and technological resources to change their communities and, by extension, the world. Let's begin.

A BLACK ADVANTAGE VISION OF AGRICULTURE

The Fifth National NFA Convention in New Jersey

We are indeed happy to be in New Jersey because we feel that contact with you will serve to strengthen and revitalize our effort and dreams of "Better Days through Better Ways." New Farmers means new ways of doing things. . . . A meeting of the N.F.A., national in scope, must certainly provide a rare opportunity for growth through a liberal exchange of ideas.

—**Jethro Hill,** 1939–40 national NFA president

Claude A. Barnett traveled from his home in Chicago to the New Jersey Manual Training and Industrial School for Colored Youth (MTIS) in Bordentown, New Jersey, to address the fifth national NFA convention in August 1939. Barnett was a journalist and founder of the Associated Negro Press, the pioneering Black news service of the early twentieth century. A prominent figure in Black media and a key leader in the creation of national and global news outlets for Black reporters and writers, Barnett had been asked by the NFA to speak at the convention alongside other important Black leaders, including Walter White, executive secretary of the NAACP. As he took the stage in the assembly hall at MTIS, the headquarters of the New

Jersey Association of the NFA (NJNFA), Barnett was shocked to see nearly one thousand Black farm boys seated in the audience. "I had no idea that there would be so many of you at this convention, and I want to congratulate you, first, upon having the vision and opportunity of belonging to such a fine organization as the New Farmers of America. It is mighty good to know that you are but representatives of hundreds of other boys," Barnett stated. Speaking in admiration of the massive crowd, he declared, "I am not afraid of the future of Negro farm life in America when enough boys can be persuaded to learn its fine points and are willing to appreciate the fact that life on a farm is . . . *where one can do more than just exist*, where one can grow to be independent and carve out a career."[1]

Barnett's address set the tone for the convention, and he later became special assistant to the US secretary of agriculture in 1942, serving under Presidents Franklin D. Roosevelt and Harry S. Truman, where he championed efforts to improve the lives of Black farmers. His sentiments that the farm was a place "where one can do more than just exist" captured how NFA members envisioned their relationship to American agriculture. Instead of focusing on the negative aspects of the Black agricultural experience, Black farm boys in the NFA promoted a new vision of agriculture that reconfigured the farm as a portal to a successful career in farming or farm-related industries. Theoretically, the NFA's new vision of agriculture can be understood through the rubric of what sociologist Mary Pattillo calls "Black advantage vision." Pattillo argues that Black advantage vision emphasizes the strengths, achievements, and unique perspectives of Black people in shaping their own realities, recognizing how Black people contribute to the production of equitable futures. In other words, the NFA sought to provide its members with the tools to recast the farm as an incubator for a Black advantage vision of agriculture where Black people could create their own agricultural systems that addressed their social, economic, political, and environmental realities. Such systems would authorize Black people to lead agrarian lives of dignity, abandoning a life of mere survival in pursuit of opportunities to thrive.[2]

From the first national convention in August 1935 at Tuskegee University to the final convention in October 1965 in Atlanta, Georgia, the NFA constructed the organization's convention scene as what anthropologist Jeffrey Juris observes as an "intentional space" to set up a national platform to equip its membership to cultivate and operationalize a Black advantage vision of agriculture. Juris explains that an intentional space is a deliberate and targeted social movement building strategy designed to produce "a platform for expressing a particular kind of grassroots identity and politics." The platform is an interactive plane of discourses built on strategic commitments that ensure that "the communities that are most directly affected by prevailing structures of exploitation and inequality are viewed as the principal agents of social change." By reading the NFA convention scene as an intentional space, I assert that this scene provided an annual, geographic-specific site to activate a Black advantage vision of agriculture as a source of energy for Black farm boys who were seen as the principal agents of social, economic, political, and environmental change in their communities. Through a widespread emphasis on building the educational and leadership capacity of Black farm boys, the NFA convention scene was curated to intentionally prepare them to lead the nation in addressing the most pressing problems along the contours of America's agricultural and rural terrains.[3]

Given the thirty years of national NFA conventions, why is the fifth national convention so important? What can this particular convention teach us about the untold story of the NFA that other conventions cannot? How did NFA organizers produce such an exemplary convention? In this chapter, I take up these questions through a case study of the fifth national NFA convention in New Jersey with a focus on the location, organizational structure, and key features of the convention, demonstrating how geographic-specific convention scenes represent intentional spaces to operationalize a Black advantage vision of agriculture. This case shows how New Jersey, as the site for the national convention, exposed Black farm boys—who were primarily from the South—to new ways of farming that promoted new relationships with agriculture. The organizational structure of the convention allowed Black farm boys to interact with multiple actors across local, state, national, and global levels in the context of agricultural and food systems. Such interactions allowed convention attendees to develop their own systems-level analysis to address rapidly shifting farm problems. The structure also strengthened the impact of the NFA on alumni members through the launch of the prestigious H. O. Sargent Award. Key features of the fifth national convention included NFA participation in the Seventh World's Poultry Congress and Exposition in Cleveland, Ohio, and the 1939–40 New York World's Fair in New York City. The fifth national convention of the NFA also revealed the national

NFA program of work that guided the state and local activities of the organization for the remainder of its history.[4]

The National NFA Convention Scene: A Brief History

The idea for the first national NFA convention at Tuskegee University in August 1935 evolved out of prior discussions at sectional and state meetings concerning the creation of a national NFA organization. Between 1928 and 1935, sectional and state meetings of Black farm boys collectively used these discussions as active sites to publicly grapple with what I referred to in the previous chapter as the "Black agrarian question," taken up by sociologist W. E. B. Du Bois. In many ways, this question was at the center of the first forms of meeting spaces designed to facilitate the growth of the NFA. The proposal to arrange meeting spaces in the context of the idea of a national organization of the NFA was put forth in 1929 at the meeting of advisors in both the Washington and Sargent sections in Orangeburg, South Carolina. By 1935, H. O. Sargent, S. B. Simmons, and representatives from all three NFA sectional organizations—Washington, Sargent, and Almot—had laid the groundwork for the development of a national organization, and the first convention inaugurated the national NFA.[5]

On Sunday, August 4, 1935, Black farm boys and their advisors from thirteen states traveled to Tuskegee, Alabama, to form the national body and cultivate the national NFA convention scene. NFA leaders chose Tuskegee as the institutional host due to the college's prominent role in the story of Black American agriculture and the NFA's roots in the school's agrarian traditions initiated by Booker T. Washington. For four full days, wrapping up on August 7, attendees worked efficiently and tirelessly to set up the national NFA organization. The convention program was structured around several sessions and contests, including a preliminary session, business session, public speaking contest, judging contest, committee work session, banquet, and awards ceremonies. David Simmons, president of the Alabama Association of the NFA, who was later elected as the first national president of the NFA, opened the convention with a general session in Logan Hall. Simmons appointed eleven committees, ranging from the Constitution and Bylaws Committee to the Alumni Organization Committee. As a result of Simmons's critical leadership, convention attendees formally adopted the tentative constitution and bylaws, providing a shared governance structure for the national NFA organization.[6]

In addition to the convention's sharp focus on business and organizational logistics surrounding the national NFA, the meeting also provided a space for Black farm boys to collectively learn firsthand about the importance of Tuskegee to the story of Black agriculture. A brief look at the first convention's proceedings reveals that the meeting included tours of the Booker T. Washington Monument, the Tuskegee farm, and the agricultural building. The convention also included a "Self-Help Project," a community-based program designed to help Black farmers reestablish themselves in farming through agricultural trainings. On the last day of the convention, participants attended an inspiring lecture by George Washington Carver, prominent Black agricultural scientist and director of the Tuskegee Agricultural Experiment Station. The convention proceedings report that Dr. Carver "urged the farm boys to prepare themselves to give society a most useful service." Carver's lecture was the perfect way to end the convention, as Black farm boys were encouraged to think about the role they would play in helping not only their communities but also the world.[7]

In many respects, the first NFA national convention was a test run for producing a national platform for Black farm boys to meet and learn from and with each other. This convention became a template and set the stage for the national NFA convention scene that served as the nucleus of the organization. The national NFA convention scene became the site where major decisions—beyond the purview of the state convention scene—were discussed and decided upon. In 1936, for example, the second national NFA convention was held at Hampton Institute (now Hampton University), where the constitution and bylaws were modified and formally adopted. In 1941, the decision to formally reorganize the NFA under the US Office of Education was made at the seventh national convention in Tallahassee, Florida, at what is now Florida A&M University. One year later, in 1942, at the eighth national convention in Orangeburg, the NFA creed song was adopted as the national NFA creed song. Beginning in 1949, the Municipal Auditorium in Atlanta, Georgia, became the permanent national convention headquarters for the rest of the NFA's history, enabling the organization to grow to over fifty-five thousand members annually and adapt to changing social, political, and economic conditions. In 1950, the National NFA Chorus was organized at the sixteenth national convention. Two years later, the official NFA jacket was standardized at the eighteenth national convention. Prior to the NFA's dissolution in 1965, these successes persisted in the national NFA convention scene into the early 1960s.[8]

When considering the history of the national NFA convention scene, the fifth national NFA convention is instructive and stands out for a number of reasons. First, it was the only convention to be held outside the South and at a high school, requiring Black farm boys to travel and experience a different Black cultural experience. Second, the fifth convention catapulted the NFA onto the global stage of agriculture, which allowed Black farm boys to show the world that they could exist on an international platform. Third, the convention ushered in a new phase of the national NFA that shaped the organization's history. When read together, these reasons not only illustrate the importance of the fifth national NFA convention but also provide us with the necessary understanding of the NFA convention within the larger story of the NFA. This particular scene becomes clearer as we examine the place, structure, and key features of the fifth national NFA convention.

The national NFA convention scene, 1938–57. From Fields,
New Farmers of America: 25 Years of Accomplishment, 12–13.

Black Agricultural Education and Place(making) in New Jersey: Setting the Scene

The fifth national NFA convention not only was a significant event in the organization's history, but it also marked a turning point in the development of agricultural education at the Manual Training and Industrial School for Colored Youth, the New Jersey NFA's headquarters and host institution. Founded in 1886, the MTIS was a coed boarding high school devoted to the vocational education of Black youths. It was the dream of its founder and first principal, Rev. Walter Allen Rice, a minister in the African Episcopal Methodist church. The MTIS, also known as the Ironsides Normal School or colloquially as the Bordentown School, was conceived by Reverend Rice as a vocational school for Black youths in New Jersey aligned with a vision of Black education established by Black conventions and organizations, including the African Education Society of Newark in northern New Jersey. Historian Marion M. Thompson Wright asserts that such groups had long "advocated the establishing of schools which would combine training along academic and industrial lines" for Black people. Reverend Rice brought this vision of Black education to life through the founding of MTIS, which was the result of what some social scientists refer to as Black placemaking—the practice of Black Americans to "create sites of endurance, belonging, and resistance through social interaction"—with agricultural education at the center.[9]

During the first eight years of its existence, the MTIS was supported by private funds. It was located in two frame buildings in the city of Bordentown in Burlington County, New Jersey, with a curriculum designed to build a class of Black people who would be economically self-sufficient. In 1901, under the direction of the New Jersey State Board of Education, the school relocated to four hundred acres along the Delaware River on the outskirts of Bordentown. This new location allowed the MTIS to develop a master plan for the new campus that included a state-of-the-art farm and agricultural buildings. In many respects, the school's early agricultural education program was aligned with Booker T. Washington's philosophy of agriculture as a pathway to freedom for Black people and their communities in the South. This pathway was rooted in the same soil where rural Black people negotiated their agrarian identities, collectively transforming their relationship to agriculture through emancipatory thinking. For Washington, this kind of thinking was clarified through agricultural education in Black life. His beliefs extended beyond the South, becoming a model for other Black institutions like MTIS.[10]

In fact, Washington was invited to visit the MTIS in 1913 by Calvin Kendall, then New Jersey state commissioner of education. During his visit, Washington was amazed by the breadth of educational instruction at the school and recommended that its agriculture and domestic service programs receive funds to expand their offerings. He also endorsed an extension component to the school modeled after the annual Tuskegee Negro Farmers' Conference that started in 1892. "I would also suggest that a farmers' conference, that would meet at least once a year, be organized as soon as possible," Washington proclaimed in his recommendations, "that the leading and successful farmers be invited to come to Bordentown and tell how they have succeeded. I believe that this conference would grow from year to year in power and strength."[11]

In 1915, the state board of education hired William R. Valentine, a Harvard graduate and classmate of future US president Franklin D. Roosevelt, to lead the school. Valentine's tenure as principal of the MTIS gave birth to a world-class vocational, agricultural, and cultural education program that not only exposed students to vocational training but invited esteemed guests of the time—including Mary McLeod Bethune, Albert Einstein, Paul Robeson, Benjamin Mays, R. R. Moton, and Eleanor Roosevelt—who gave lectures at the school. Such educational programming attracted Black students from all over the nation, which increased enrollment from about ninety students to over four hundred under the leadership of Valentine. The programming also provided the basis for an expansion of the building spaces needed for the school. The 1943 MTIS *Bulletin of Information* boasted that the MTIS was comprised of "some thirty buildings—including dormitories, trade and academic buildings, assembly and dining buildings, farm structures, and private residences. . . . All school buildings and dormitories are of red brick and colonial style architecture, and are equipped with modern conveniences." This infrastructure enabled the MTIS to become a Black cultural center for Black people across New Jersey and the nation that organized annual ministers' conferences, community outreach programs, and a host of other programming for Black communities.[12]

In 1918, heeding Booker T. Washington's advice, Principal Valentine operationalized a statewide Black farmers conference in New Jersey as a northern version of the Tuskegee Black farmers conference. Beginning in 1918, the MTIS Black farmers conference began as a series of local meetings of Black farmers organized by J. R. Fugett, an agriculture teacher at the school. Fugett, a graduate of the Department of Agriculture at Cornell

University, farmer, and former professor of agriculture at Tuskegee, worked with the faculty in the MTIS agricultural department in building the curriculum for students and served as an "extension agent" for Black farmers in New Jersey. Transplanting the Tuskegee model of agricultural education and extension activities to New Jersey—although the state had no Black people in the state extension service—Fugett planned a series of local meetings with Black farmers to discuss topics that ranged from tomato growing to farm business and infrastructure management. The meetings were attended by representatives from the New Jersey Department of Agriculture and Principal Valentine, who assisted Fugett with presentations and the dissemination of agricultural knowledge. The presentations were designed as conversations instead of lectures, which Fugett hoped would enhance methods employed by Black agricultural workers and farming operations across the state, exposing Black communities to farming as a viable and profitable career option. These local meetings were extremely successful and set the stage for the manifestation of the larger state conference held at the institution.[13]

Throughout the 1920s, the conference grew tremendously, and the MTIS provided a critical space for Black farmers to gather safely and exchange best practices on the land; the school also used its farm as demonstration plots. A February 1939 article in the *Ironsides Echo*, the MTIS school newspaper, stated that the central purpose of the conference was to "acquaint the many Negro agriculture workers of this state with the problems and questions which might confront them; and at the same time to suggest ways and means of remedying or curing them." With this purpose in mind, the New Jersey Black farmers conference peaked in the 1940s when over one hundred farmers, workers, and emerging farmers attended the conference in 1941. What also made the 1941 conference memorable was that it included the address "Woman's Part in an American Farm Program," given by Jennie Booth Moton, then field agent for the Agricultural Adjustment Administration and widow of Tuskegee President Robert Moton. The profile of the Black farmers conferences, in tandem with the world-class education taught by impressive Black faculty and cultural activities for students, contributed to the school being known as the "Tuskegee of the North." In fact, likely due to this moniker, the MTIS was the only Black secondary school that held associated membership in the Conference of the Presidents of Negro-Grant Colleges, the group of seventeen Black land grant college presidents who worked together to build institutional power.[14]

National affiliations, state funds, and the support of Black communities in New Jersey placed the MTIS in a unique position to access resources that tremendously grew its agricultural education and Black farming program. Under the long tenure of Principal Valentine, faculty and staff included Benjamin Jones, Gerard N. Low, Harrison Jacobs, Ira Godwin, Benjamin F. Bullock, Clarence Banks, John Urquhart, J. R. Fugett, and S. A. Haley, the father of Pulitzer Prize–winning writer Alex Haley. The credentials of the faculty included degrees from Howard University, Hampton University, Michigan State University, Cornell University, and the University of Minnesota. These distinguished faculty members provided students with training in vocational, scientific, and practical agricultural methods. They taught classes ranging from dairy science and farm management to animal husbandry, meat processing, and methods in crop production. In addition to teaching classes, historian Ezola Bolden Adams found that instructors in the MTIS agriculture department "would teach farming, gardening, maintained the campus, conducted farmers' conferences among black farmers, had charge of the creamery, kept farm records, maintained the greenhouses, and cared for the livestock which included cows, pigs, horses, and poultry." This list of responsibilities reveals that faculty in the MTIS agriculture program went beyond the classroom to provide students with a well-rounded, state-of-the-art agricultural education.[15]

The efforts of the faculty and staff in agriculture were recognized in 1926 when the state granted the school permission to offer courses toward a high school diploma. This move by the state enabled the school to establish a Department of Agriculture and institutionalize a vocational agriculture program for male students through curriculum and supervised farming practices on the MTIS farm. The mission of the faculty emphasized the training of students to be specialists in vocational agriculture and farming who would become educators, farmers, and extension workers. Between 1928 and 1932, students in the department organized an agricultural club linked to the NFA. Likely influenced by the school's close ties to Black land grant colleges in the South, the MTIS NFA became the New Jersey NFA in 1935. What was unique about the NJNFA being part of the national NFA was that it was the only association to have headquarters at a high school, it was a single local chapter, and it was the only NFA unit in a Northern state. Yet, the NJNFA contributed greatly to the agricultural life of the MTIS and its surrounding communities, playing an important role in training the next generation of Black farmers in New Jersey and across the nation.[16]

Indeed, the history and expansion of Black agricultural education at the MTIS, in and outside the classroom, made the institution a unique site for the fifth national convention of the NFA. NFA organizers of the convention most likely knew that, due to the reputation of the MTIS, it would be a great place to host the convention and highlight the Black agricultural history of New Jersey. What also made the MTIS an ideal location for the convention was that the 1939–40 World's Fair would be in New York during the convention and would provide Black farm boys with a world view of agriculture. Relatedly, the Seventh World's Poultry Congress and Exposition in Cleveland, Ohio, would serve as a preconvention activity for NFA members traveling to New Jersey from the South. Such considerations were an important part of the planning process that shaped the structure of the fifth national convention of the NFA.

An Intentional Structure: Designing the Scene

In his brief remarks at the opening ceremony of the fifth national convention of the NFA, Jethro Hill of Fordyce, Arkansas, made clear what he hoped the convention would achieve. Hill was the first vice president of the NFA and the president-elect for the following 1939–40 academic year. A key leader in the early years of the national NFA, Hill was deeply committed to the mission of the organization. Speaking with a profound sense of the state of US agriculture, Hill argued that the NFA should lead the nation in addressing the looming problems of America's "unbalanced agriculture" that threatened the livelihoods of all people. "We are faced with new plant and animal diseases, injurious insects, soil erosion, decreasing home and foreign markets, and new relationships with industrial and economic problems with which we must cope and solve," he observed. What must be added to Hill's words is that unbalanced agriculture impacted Southern Black farmers in particular ways, producing a number of problems. Agricultural economist Frederick A. Williams, writing in 1939, stated that unbalanced agriculture was instigated by different forms of government neglect and compounded by numerous problems for "Negro marginal farmers," including "racial prejudice, unfavorable farm legislation, [and] local administrative policies," to name a few. Williams argued that groups like the NFA "must coordinate their programs in conserving Negro humanity, which is as important as conserving natural resources . . . in order to promote a definite or well-established program that will improve [the] socio-economic status of the Negro marginal farmer."[17]

Considering the words of Williams, Hill envisioned the convention scene as the site for a collective discussion on how Black farm boys would produce solutions to such problems associated with an unbalanced agriculture. As Hill put it: "A meeting of the NFA, national in scope, must certainly provide a rare opportunity for growth through a literal exchange of ideas. I hope that this convention will make it possible for each delegate to take an active part so that the convention may share your thinking on these vital farm problems." In Hill's eyes, the new solutions needed to address the nation's farm problems would come from a new generation of farmers led by the NFA. This new generation would think differently about farming and put forth a new vision of American agriculture that would eradicate unbalanced agriculture. As Hill declared, providing meaning for the NFA name, "New Farmers means new ways of doing things." In many ways, Hill's point of view captures the ethos surrounding the intentional planning process and structure that brought the fifth national convention of the NFA to life.[18]

PRECONVENTION PLANNING

As the host of the fifth national convention of the NFA, the NJNFA began the planning process for the meeting in January 1939. While the NJNFA was the smallest chapter by design, it was active on the national conference platform. NJNFA member Valdimir Pitts was the sole NJNFA delegate at the first national NFA convention. Accolades and awards received by the NJNFA included three national officers and two superior farmers' degrees, and at least three faculty and staff members, including Principal Valentine, were awarded the "N.F.A. key," which entitled them to honorary membership in the organization. Such accolades reveal how invested the NJNFA was in contributing to the sustainability of the national NFA, and the opportunity to host the fifth national convention cemented the NJNFA in the history of the national NFA.[19]

Building on their emerging legacy in the national NFA, convention organizers in the NJNFA met with officials from the national NFA, the federal government, and the New Jersey Department of Agriculture to discuss the process. Mr. Harrison D. Jacobs, NJNFA advisor and head of the MTIS Department of Agriculture, was the chief organizer of the convention.[20] As department head, Jacobs had coordinated the annual New Jersey Black Farmers Conference and worked tirelessly to assist the NJNFA in developing skills to promote leaders in its community and on the farm.

While little is known about Jacobs, he was a key figure and role model in the NJNFA. One member of the NJNFA described Jacobs as "an able one who has the whole-hearted confidence and cooperation of the fellows" in the NJNFA.[21]

Accordingly, Jacobs used his previous planning experiences to work with Principal Valentine to make local convention arrangements, securing spaces to host the various conference contests. For seven months, Jacobs worked with NJNFA members to prepare the campus for the convention. Rutgers University in New Brunswick was selected for the highly anticipated agricultural judging competition. As New Jersey's only land grant college, Rutgers had the agricultural infrastructure and facilities to host the NFA. All other contests (including public speaking and quartet singing), conference activities, and business meetings were to be held at the MTIS.[22]

DEVELOPING RURAL TALENT THROUGH THE NFA

On Sunday, August 6, 1939, nearly a thousand Black male high school students—representing seventeen NFA state associations—arrived at the MTIS for the fifth national convention of the NFA. The theme of the convention was "Developing Rural Talent Through N.F.A.," and organizers curated a convention scene focused on how the NFA would address issues in rural Black communities. NJNFA officers led the opening ceremony, and Lester Albert of the Florida Association of the NFA, the national NFA president at the time, presided over all business-related meetings at the convention. According to the conference program, Walter White, NAACP executive secretary, delivered the keynote address, sharing the program with esteemed guests including Leon R. Harris, cofounder and president of the National Federation of Colored Farmers Inc.; Mrs. Frances L. Murphy of the Baltimore-based *Afro-American* newspaper; and John C. Wright, US assistant commissioner for vocational education.[23]

Throughout the convention, speakers tailored their comments to a specific area of the Black youth experience of the NFA at the intersection of social, economic, environmental, and political contexts of Black communities. For example, the main point of Walter White's keynote address was that NFA members should actively participate in Black communities' civic life by joining groups like the NAACP and working to find answers to issues that affected their lives and communities. Frances Murphy discussed Baltimore's "Clean Block Campaign," a program designed to bring better living conditions to urban Black communities, and how NFA members could use the campaign as a model for their communities. Speaking directly to the Black farming experience, Leon R. Harris encouraged NFA members to be leaders in the building of Black rural cooperative models in their neighborhoods and communities. "The practice of cooperation has succeeded and has brought untold blessings to some Negro rural communities, but these communities are few and far between," Harris stated. "This is a new field for the plow of the New Farmers of America. It is a rough and rocky field, but for New Farmers, the soil is abundantly fertile. It will produce a thousand-fold." Such rural cooperative models Harris spoke up for were linked to a larger wave of Black cooperative movements across the nation and the world.[24]

While convention speeches encouraged the youths to continue in their pursuit to reshape Black farm life against the backdrop of a rapidly changing US agricultural landscape, participants were excited to compete in the annual contests, which were the highlight of the conventions. Three main contests shaped the NFA national conference: quartet singing, public speaking, and the coveted agricultural judging. Each year, students would prepare for these contests at the local and state association levels to see who would represent each state at the national level. Final contest results from the convention indicate that the quartet from the Florida Association of the NFA won the quartet singing contest; William Hopkins from Eastover, South Carolina, won the public speaking contest for his speech, "Do We Want to Be Farmers?"; and the Arkansas Association of the NFA won first place in the agricultural judging contest. The highest score across

Group picture from the fifth national NFA convention, Bordentown, New Jersey, 1939. From Hargraves, "Fifth National FFA Convention Held at Bordentown, N.J.," 19.

all convention activities was obtained by the Tennessee Association of the NFA.[25]

In addition to the three main contests, the H. O. Sargent Award was introduced at the fifth annual convention and slated to be given out at the sixth annual convention held at the University of Arkansas at Pine Bluff. According to the 1946 *N.F.A. Guide*, the award was designated for "the most successful" NFA alumnus "who has been out of public school at least three years and not more than ten years and who has completed four years of instruction in day-unit, all-day, or part-time classes." The award was created by the family of Sargent, who passed in 1936, in honor of his efforts in shaping Black agricultural education as he oversaw Black vocational agriculture in the US Office of Education for nineteen years. The honor was supplemented by a gift of up to fifty dollars, and the award plaque was passed down from recipient to recipient at the annual national convention.[26]

Beyond contests and award ceremonies, convention attendees were able to attend other activities and special programs. For instance, the first day of the convention began with a special radio program by the NFA produced by S. B. Simmons, then national executive secretary-treasurer of the NFA, called *Wings over Jordan*, the first religious radio program to be produced and hosted by African Americans through a national broadcast network in affiliation with CBS. In the radio program, Simmons spoke about the critical need for NFA chapters to install radios in churches in rural Black communities to raise public awareness of issues impacting those communities and to spread the agricultural gospel of Black farm boys. At the same time, the program also served as a recruitment tool for the NFA to increase membership. The radio broadcast was followed by a concert put on by the Alabama Association of the NFA band, represented by the Snow Hill Institute NFA Band from Snow Hill, Alabama, which was designated as the official NFA band for their sixth national convention. This concert was followed by a tour of nearby Princeton University, where attendees spent time learning about the campus.[27]

After the Princeton visit, NFA members traveled to Plainsboro to tour the laboratories and production facilities at the leading Walker-Gordon Dairy Farm, an innovator in the scientific production of safe raw milk. After visiting the dairy farm, they returned to the MTIS and convened on the campus lawn for an outdoor concert by the North Carolina Association of the NFA band, represented by the Laurinburg Institute NFA Band from Laurinburg, North Carolina. On the second day of the convention, the NJNFA held a livestock show, exhibiting the impressive herds of different animals. The livestock show included another concert by the Snow Hill Institute NFA Band. While all these activities provided educational programming, entertainment, and social interactions, the key features of the convention enabled Black farm boys to make their presence known on a global platform for agricultural innovation and scientific progress. The key features also allowed the NFA to decide on a course of programming that would guide the organization throughout its history and establish a process to honor the efforts of NFA alumni.[28]

Black Worldmaking and Agriculture: Black Farm Boys in Cleveland and New York City

Rather than a singular public sphere of interactions at the MTIS through convention meetings, contests, and area tours, the fifth national convention of the NFA operated across a multiplicity of spaces: the Seventh World's Poultry Congress and Exposition and the 1939–40 New York World's Fair. These two events served as major features that expanded the scene of the NFA's fifth national convention. Beginning on July 28 and concluding on August 7, the Seventh World's Poultry Congress was the first poultry congress to ever be held in the United States and was designated as a preconvention activity for NFA state associations traveling to New Jersey. The New York World's Fair ran from April 30, 1939, to October 27, 1940, and was part of the concluding activities of the fifth national convention. These two events marked the start and finish of the convention, respectively, and provided a worldwide platform for NFA members to contribute to the historical process of what some scholars call "Black worldmaking": a practice engineered by Black people who sought to imagine new ways of existing in the world while creating a new world of emancipatory possibilities. As literary scholar Judith Madera writes, Black worldmaking is a "modal possibility for vibrant Black life," and NFA members saw agriculture as the vehicle to produce such vibrancy in their lives and surrounding communities.[29]

To be sure, convention organizers strategically planned the convention with these two events in mind. They saw them as an opportunity for Black farm boys in the NFA to learn about agriculture from a world perspective that would expand their minds to consider how they could be part of this world. For many NFA members, their world perspective of agriculture was nonexistent as they thought about agriculture only from the vantage point of their rural Black communities. Yet, the mere presence of the NFA at these global events enhanced their purview of Black worldmaking in the context of the global conditions of agriculture. Simultaneously, the NFA provided a glimpse of how Black agriculture could be utilized to improve global prospects on this international platform.

THE SEVENTH WORLD'S POULTRY CONGRESS AND EXPOSITION

From August 3 through August 5, 1939, delegates from ten state NFA associations attended and participated in the Seventh World's Poultry Congress and Exposition in Cleveland. World Poultry Congresses are triennial meetings of the World's Poultry Science Association and related organizations. Founded in 1912, the World's Poultry Science Association held the first poultry congress in 1921 in the Netherlands. The purpose of the poultry congress was to stimulate worldwide interest in poultry at the intersection of education, scientific research, industry, production, marketing, and public media. The Seventh World's Poultry Congress program was composed of a general assembly, association meetings, scientific conferences, national and state exhibits, consumer meetings, and youth programming, among other features. The NFA, along with other youth groups including the Future Farmers of America and 4-H clubs, attended the convention as part of the public program and national meeting designed for youth to spark the interests of young people in the poultry industry. This program was located in the Hall of Youth—in the Armory Building in downtown Cleveland—where young people engaged in dialogue, live poultry show exhibits, and commercial demonstrations.[30]

In the Hall of Youth, the NFA displayed an educational exhibit booth, and its members participated in competitions for enterprise demonstration and poultry judging. This exhibit provided a different approach to world agriculture, illustrating how vocational agriculture could be used as a tool to better the social and economic livelihoods of sharecroppers and tenant farmers in poor rural Black communities. According to the *Cleveland Call and Post*, the city's major Black newspaper, the NFA's exhibit illustrated "the poverty stricken conditions of sharecropper and tenant farmers, and how through the application of instruction received in vocational agricultural classes, the young Negro farmer is gradually bettering his conditions." Vocational agriculture classes, according to the exhibit, would benefit not only the lives of sharecroppers but also other marginalized farming communities across the world.[31]

During the agricultural competitions, NFA delegates from Louisiana earned superior ratings in both judging and poultry enterprise demonstrations. Delegates from Texas and Oklahoma earned superior ratings for their abilities in judging. NFA member teams from Arkansas, Florida, North Carolina, Tennessee, Virginia, and West Virginia were ranked excellent, while representatives from the Delaware Association of the NFA received a rating of good in judging. For the poultry enterprise demonstration contest, Virginia was ranked excellent, while Texas and North Carolina received good ratings. Participation in these events offered NFA delegates the opportunity to compete on a global stage and contributed to the momentum surrounding their fifth national convention.[32]

THE 1939–40 NEW YORK WORLD'S FAIR

On the morning of the last day of the fifth national convention, several buses filled with Black farm boys departed from the MTIS at 7:30 a.m. for the iconic New York World's Fair. Located in Flushing Meadows–Corona Park in Queens, New York City, the fair was one of the largest world expositions in the history of world fairs. The official guidebook stated that the fair was generated in part as an effort to celebrate the 150th anniversary of George Washington's inauguration as the first US president. The theme of the fair, "Building the World of Tomorrow," was to celebrate the advancements made by humanity and to usher in a new era marked by freedom, progress, and peace. Organizers saw it as an "everyman's fair," signaling that it was a space for all people to display their "most promising developments of production, service, and social factors of the present day in relation to their bearing on the life of the great mass of the people." Through the fair, "the plain American citizen will be able to see here what he could attain for his community and himself by intelligent coordinated effort and will be made to realize the interdependence of every contributing form of life and work." For NFA members, the fair was a chance for them to see the world of agriculture and then translate it into their communities.[33]

On this global platform, the NFA offered a range of entertainment and educational content. For example, the Laurinburg Institute NFA Band gave a concert at the fair's Court of Peace, and the Snow Hill Institute NFA Band played for visitors at the Equitable Garden of Security on the fairgrounds.

Snow Hill Institute NFA Band of Alabama at the Equitable Garden of Security,
New York World's Fair, 1939. Courtesy of the S. B. Simmons Collection,
ncatsbs13033, NCATSBS.

Throughout the day, NFA members interacted with George Washington
Owens, a key founder of the organization, who spoke to the group in the
garden. They also observed many exhibits devoted to life around the world,
especially as it related to farming. For instance, NFA members were drawn
to the Ford exposition that housed the Ford tractor and daily demonstrations surrounding American farm life. The NFA boys took turns driving
the tractor in the demonstrations with the Ferguson plow and other tools
attached to it. Such exposure to modern farming machinery and the latest
agricultural technologies of the time was an important part of the NFA's
trip to the New York World's Fair.[34]

But the NFA's day of programs at the fair included much more than the
students observing exhibits as passive fair attendees. In fact, the trip to the
fair culminated with the organization's program being presented on the
National Broadcasting Company's nationwide radio show *Farm and Home
Hour.* This program at the Equitable Garden of Security was headlined
by C. C. Spaulding, a prominent Black businessman and president of the

North Carolina Mutual Life Insurance Company in Durham. Following an address by Commissioner John C. Wright; the reading of the NFA creed by James Warren, national student secretary of the NFA; and remarks on the accomplishments of the NFA by Executive Secretary-Treasurer S. B. Simmons, Spaulding addressed the fair. "I am very happy to have the privilege to speak a word of encouragement and to express keen appreciation to the New Farmers of America, the national organization of Negro Youth, which is doing so much to make the rural boy have confidence in himself. . . . Their achievements will inspire thousands of Negro farm boys to do likewise," he proclaimed on the radio program.[35]

At the end of his speech, Spaulding presented a one-hundred-dollar check to James W. Smith of Gause, Texas, the recipient of the 1939 "Ranking Superior Farmer" award, which recognized the most outstanding member of the national organization. Smith, who served as president of his local NFA chapter and was a two-time officer in the Texas Association of the NFA, was recognized for his impressive efforts in operating a one-hundred-acre farm. According to the convention proceedings, Smith owned twenty-five of those acres that were used as pasture for livestock. The remaining acres were in partnership, where Smith cultivated cotton, corn, grain, and a small orchard of approximately twenty-seven trees. Smith's accomplishments were attributed to his training in vocational agriculture through the NFA. The radio program concluded with great excitement, and the NFA solidified its space in the history of the 1939–40 New York World's Fair.[36]

The Climax of the Summer

This chapter has offered a case study of the fifth national convention of the NFA held in New Jersey, emphasizing its location, organization, and salient characteristics. It showed how intentionally created spaces inside convention scenes that were distinctive to a certain region served as deliberate places to operationalize a vision of agriculture that benefited Black people. The words of NFA member Jethro Hill and journalist Claude Barnett, as stated at the fifth national convention, provide a way to understand the importance of the convention scene. Hill's words emphasized the need for Black farm boys to recognize their own power in shaping and leading their communities—and by extension the nation—through agriculture. Hill wanted his peers to know that "New Farmers means new ways of doing things," which can be read as a call to action. Barnett's statement validated Hill's words by clarifying the need for this recognition of such power, as the farm was a place "where one can do more than just exist." Together, the sentiments of Hill and Barnett, when placed in both social and geographic context, convey how the NFA convention scene was the site for the exchange of ideas that could be translated into actions.

Although the NFA's radio broadcast on NBC's *Farm and Home Hour* at the 1939–40 New York World's Fair marked the end of the fifth national convention of the NFA, the impact of the convention reverberated throughout the state associations and local chapters. As the hundreds of Black farm boys exited the buses at the MTIS and prepared to head back to their hometowns, they left with a profound sense of how the agricultural world functioned on a global scale. They were also able to share and transmit this knowledge to many of the NFA members and other Black boys in their communities who were unable to attend the convention. Indeed, the NJNFA and other convention organizers put together an unforgettable convention scene, which the *Ironsides Echo* called "the climax of the summer" in Bordentown.[37]

What made this convention "the climax of the summer" was related to the programming offered and the record number of NFA attendees, bolstering the social and cultural scene of the institution. The landscape of the fifth national convention of the NFA was concurrently on local, state, national, and global levels. At the local level, the convention extended the public engagement efforts of the MTIS Department of Agriculture. At the state level, it demonstrated the power of place and scientific innovation through agricultural education. The mere presence of seventeen state associations—all member associations at the time—and the inauguration of the H. O. Sargent Award illuminated how the convention offered a national level of interactions that allowed Black farm boys to build lasting relationships with the national NFA body beyond their own chapters and state associations. At the global level, as realized by NFA participation in the Seventh World's Poultry Congress and Exposition and the 1939–40 New York World's Fair, NFA members carved out their own space in the international arena of agriculture.

But the lasting influence of the fifth national convention of the NFA was the development of the revised 1939–40 program of work, which served as the permanent, standardized rubric for every state association and local chapter of the NFA. In previous business meetings, namely those at the first and fourth conventions, the Program of Work Committee discussed key components of the program but never fully agreed upon them.

At the first convention, the committee offered an eight-point program of work that was broad and focused on the need for increased membership in the organization, local chapter structures, supervised farming activities, and related educational activities. At the fourth convention, the committee put forth a ten-point platform that expanded the program to include a more explicit plan around recreation but did not include any details surrounding membership. In recognizing the need for a complete program, the committee at the fifth convention worked diligently to produce and submit an eleven-point program of work. In the months following the convention, the new program of work was approved.[38]

In many respects, the NFA's comprehensive eleven-point program set the stage for the expansion of the organization, demonstrating a unified body of members and expectations surrounding the business of the organization. Every NFA guide printed after the convention included a section devoted to outlining activities that contributed to the program of work. To be sure, the activities suggested in the program of work provided NFA state associations and the local chapters a foundation to build on. At the same time, the program of work also allowed NFA units to be creative in planning additional activities that served both the organization and their communities.

As the next chapter shows, the NFA summer camp scene was one of those activities that emerged out of the plan of work and brought together many of the points of the program, including recreation, leadership, community service, publicity, and cooperative activities. Specifically, I focus on the NFA camp scene in North Carolina and argue that it serves as an important camp to study in order to understand how this scene shaped the lives of Black farm boys in the NFA. While the convention scene offered a national view of the NFA's story, the camp scene provides an in-depth look at how state associations operationalized a regional-localized geographic campsite that brought together members of NFA local chapters—and other Black youth groups—through a week-long program of outdoor activities designed to expand the minds of NFA members beyond just agricultural training. In many ways, the NFA summer camp scene served as a way to cultivate a new generation of Black farm boys who would become community leaders who understood agriculture and the other needs of their communities.

Chapter 3

CAMPING WHILE BLACK

The S. B. Simmons NFA Camp in North Carolina

The NFA Camp takes a boy away from his home environment and places him in an environment where everybody is the same. . . . This will remove the feeling of inferiority that a boy might have; increases his ability to get along with others; and teaches him how to become well-liked by other boys. . . . It gives a boy a chance to meet other boys who will inspire him.

—**Alexander Dawson,** 1961–62 state president,
North Carolina Association of the NFA

In honor of the twentieth annual National NFA Day, the WFMY-TV station in Greensboro, North Carolina, aired a special live segment, called the "NFA Day TV Program," on its morning show on Friday, April 6, 1956. Those who tuned in to the local station learned about the history and significance of the NFA from Sidney Britton Simmons, widely known as S. B. Simmons, one of the founders of the national NFA who served as the longtime state advisor of the North Carolina Association of the NFA (NCNFA) and a key player in the development of vocational agriculture programs at Black public schools in the state. Simmons was joined in the studio by two eleventh-grade NFA members, Jimmie Bond and Dallas Cornelius of the Catawba-Rosenwald School NFA chapter, who talked about their involvement in the organization. While Bond spoke about the tremendous accomplishments of their award-winning local chapter, Cornelius shared his experiences participating in the NCNFA camp located at Hammocks Beach in Onslow County. "The camp program was a great surprise to me. I thought it would be only playing and fishing, but it was different," Cornelius explained to the audience. "In the morning, we had classes in nature study, safety measures, leadership activities, and arts and craft work. We learned the real purpose of the camp is to build better youth, to teach them leadership, cooperation, sportsmanship, and citizenship, all of which will prove helpful in adult life." Cornelius concluded his part of the segment by discussing other characteristics of the camp, which further illustrated how the experience influenced his outlook on life.[1]

Two years later, in the summer of 1958, hundreds of guests gathered on Hammocks Beach at the newly constructed NCNFA camp for a naming and dedication ceremony in honor of Simmons, who passed away in 1957. The ceremony was held in the recreational hall, and Dr. Ernest M. Norris (known by his peers as E. M. Norris), then national NFA executive secretary and professor at Prairie View A&M University, delivered the dedicatory address. Norris had been a close friend of Simmons and worked with him in the formative years of the NFA. Speaking to a packed house of guests and others who were listening through loudspeakers outside the recreation hall, Norris paid tribute to his friend and spoke about the importance of vocational agriculture in the lives of Black farm boys. "In Vocational Agriculture, it must ever be our dual concern to make of men farmers who are efficient and proficient, in the art of production and management, and to make of farmers men who are noble, true, and happy in the art of living with themselves and others," Norris proclaimed. Yet, for "too long, we have preached produce, produce, produce with greater efficiency and too seldom have we injected live, live, and live in this outlook series for life abundant." As if he were echoing the words of Dallas Cornelius from the WFMY-TV's NFA Day program two years earlier, Norris envisioned the NFA camping scene in North Carolina, known as the S. B. Simmons NFA Camp, as a natural physical site for Black farm boys to practice how to live an abundant life.[2]

In thinking with Cornelius and Norris, this chapter asks: How did the NFA conceptualize campsites as part of producing a new generation of Black farm boys? What were the experiences of Black farm boys who

S. B. Simmons. From New Farmers of America, *Guide for New Farmers of America* (12th ed.), 2.

participated in NFA camps? In what ways did the NFA camps use nature to empower Black farm boys to develop new social meanings with land? To answer these questions, I explore a case study of the Simmons NFA Camp. I argue that the natural world of the camp—and the entire NFA camp scene— provided the ideal setting for testing ideas aimed at improving the lives of Black farm boys beyond the farm gate and in service of their communi- ties. Specifically, I situate the camp within what historian Dianne D. Glave refers to as the "African American environmental heritage" by emphasizing nature as a central part of the architecture of the NFA camp scene. Glave writes that "African Americans have long envisioned the environment in luminous and evocative ways . . . and applied both preservationist and conservationist ideologies and practices—a preservation-conservation for lack of a better term." Preservation-conservation characterizes the heritage of the African American experience with the environment—from enslave- ment to today—and is helpful in thinking about the NFA camp scene. The concept emphasizes how Black people preserve nature as a mechanism of conservation and care for it as a means of preservation, building on the work of Black environmental thinkers such as George Washington Carver, Ned Cobb, and Thomas Monroe Campbell.[3]

Black farm boys and their advisors in the NFA camp scene used camps as natural recreational areas to convert preservation-conservation into an essential site for Black youth development. The goal of the scene was to enhance the ability of Black farm boys to grow as individuals and future community leaders in hopes of redefining the Black agricultural experience. Put differently, the NFA camp scene was a stage for the practice of camping while Black, which amplified the ways in which Black communities saw camping as a form of recreation for Black youth empowerment, advocacy, and resilience. Such crucial investments in the lives of Black farm boys represent what social scientist Shawn Ginwright calls an "ecologically responsive approach to working with black youth." In *Black Youth Rising*, Ginwright notes that this approach "build[s] the capacity of young people to act upon their environment in ways that contribute to well-being for the common good." NFA leaders and members envisioned the NFA camp scene as a laboratory to test out particular capacity-building efforts, emphasizing the transformative potential of investing in Black farm boys and placing them in nature as a way to empower them to improve their own communities.[4]

Black in the Wilderness: A Brief Look
Inside the NFA Camp Scene

Emerging in the 1930s, the NFA camp scene was important to the state associations, offering an outdoor learning experience for Black farm boys at the intersection of physical activities, educational programming, and community leadership training. "As an extension of the classroom," NFA member Clinton V. Turner from the Carver-Price NFA chapter in Appomattox, Virginia, recalled, the camp scene "was perfect for developing leadership skills, problem-solving skills, and social skills." Turner further commented that NFA summer camps "developed component, aggressive, agricultural, and rural leaders who went to their home counties and improved their communities." The Black men and women who brought the NFA camp scene to life—state advisors, community leaders, families, and hundreds of agriculture professors and teachers—were part of a new chapter in the history of the African American environmental heritage. This new chapter was cultivated by Black community leaders and civic groups like the Urban League and the NAACP who envisioned the wilderness as a site of organized summer camping for Black youth. Architecturally, the wilderness provided these early Black leaders and communities with a canvas for the staging of what architectural historian Elizabeth Cromley has called "activity arenas." Cromley describes activity arenas as dynamic three-dimensional systems of human action, tasks, and spaces that are not confined to the physical layout and landscape of a particular site.[5]

The early proponents of Black recreational camping in the NFA produced such activity arenas in order to think seriously about the interaction between the environment, physical structures, and the social capacity of Black youth. Writing about the NFA camp scene in the May 1962 edition of *Agricultural Education Magazine*, Walter T. Johnson, the national NFA executive treasurer at the time, argued that "camping offers experiences that will aid youth to become desirable citizens, personally broadening experiences which will develop self-reliance, poise and maturity . . . geared to give youth additional training in educational, recreational, and leadership activities that will help them in life, but in such a way that it seems like play." The NFA camp scene was built on a thought process that advocated for what historian Marcia Chatelain has called the "politics of play," using the idea of camping as a space to make broader claims about how a curated outdoor experience could promote a new generation of Black citizens and provide Black youth with time and space to practice democratic values and self-actualization. At the same time, camping grounds offered a natural world to tend to the sociocultural and emotional needs of Black youths who were growing up in a segregated world where they would be deemed inferior due to the color of their skin.[6]

Prior to the creation of the NFA camp scene, though, this kind of thinking had already come into focus in the decades between 1900 and 1930 when Black thinkers considered how camping could be used to socialize Black families and young people who were part of the first Great Migration. Such thinking was made real in the 1920s when Camp Atwater was founded in Brookfield, Massachusetts, in 1921. Located on the shores of Lake Lashaway, Camp Atwater represents one of the nation's oldest Black-owned camps (if not the first) for Black youths. The creation of the camp initiated this new chapter in the African American environmental heritage and set the stage for the rise of youth camps owned and facilitated by Black people. Camp Atwater was developed by Dr. William DeBerry and operationalized by the Urban League in Springfield, Massachusetts. Upon its founding, the camp's purpose was to socialize rural Black children who migrated to Springfield from the South, and it evolved over the years as a critical development in the arc of Black Life.[7]

Ten years after the founding of Camp Atwater and some 1,600 miles away, the Oklahoma Association of the NFA (OKNFA) organized the first statewide NFA camp in the summer of 1931. While other NFA state associations had hosted camping trips for select local chapters as far back as 1927, the OKNFA was the first to host an NFA camping experience at the state level. From 1931 to 1941, the OKNFA camp was hosted by a local chapter of the organization every year in August. Each year, the camp was filled with Black farm boys who spent time together engaging in various recreational activities, including swimming, horseshoe pitching, and team-building exercises designed to increase their social capacity through supervised work and play. While Black farm boys had a relationship with the wilderness in places like Oklahoma, camping experiences enabled them to negotiate their relationships with nature. The camp was facilitated by camp advisors and volunteers from across the state who worked diligently to create a memorable summer for all participants and help Black farm boys think through their relationships with nature and community.[8]

In his study of the OKNFA, James Roy Johnson wrote that the OKNFA "summer camps served as a means of getting the boys from all over the state to learn to work and play together and at the same time to accomplish something." In 1942, the OKNFA secured a permanent campsite at Lake Murray in the southern part of the state but halted the camp in response to the onset of World War II. In 1946, the OKNFA camp was reactivated at Lake Murray, and by 1950 it expanded its operations to provide two weeks of camping for different chapters across Oklahoma. In 1953, the state association was gifted the deed of eighty acres and used it for the purpose of building its own permanent campsite and farm from the ground up. To support the development of the camp and the preservation of the land, the OKNFA state committee required local chapters to donate fifty dollars to aid in the purchasing of materials for the camp's infrastructure. Additionally, each chapter would be involved in the construction of the camp by working at least half a day at the site during the 1953 camping season. This first summer on its own campsite yielded tremendous results for the OKNFA in that the campers built a pond, dug a well, installed pumps, cleared the land where the main OKNFA camp building would be located, and erected a summer playground.[9]

During the summer of 1954, the campers laid concrete for the foundation of the main building and oversaw the installation of the structure with the support of their adult mentors, who had specialized skills in construction. The NFA campers saw their participation in the building of the camp not only as fun but also as a learning experience. This experience taught the campers new skills that would be helpful for their communities as well and would support the development of rural Black communities across the state. "Several members expressed their feeling about what they were doing in these words." Johnson wrote: "We feel that we are actually accomplishing something, making a contribution to ourselves and humanity." Such feelings among NFA members captured the ethos of the camp and how it provided a space for Black farm boys in Oklahoma to feel like they mattered in society. Throughout the rest of the history of the OKNFA camp, participants would make use of something that their organization built, recognizing the power of community-building from within.[10]

The OKNFA efforts in creating its own statewide camp served as a model for other state associations as they constructed their own camps, building up the NFA camp scene. In 1932, the NCNFA hosted its first state camp. The South Carolina Association of the NFA launched its camp, Camp Pewilburwhitcade, three years later in 1935. Camp John Hope, the Georgia Association of the NFA's camp, opened in 1938. In the 1940s and 1950s, NFA state camps could be found in other states, including Texas, Mississippi, and Virginia. The Texas Association of the NFA never had a permanent statewide campsite; instead, many of the camps were run in conjunction with the annual Negro 4-H club summer forestry camp or at the local level in different parts of the state. The Mississippi Association of the NFA camp was built by Black farmers in Holmes County near the city of Lexington in the Yazoo–Mississippi Delta region of the state. The J. R. Thomas NFA-NHA camp in Virginia opened in the 1940s and was unique in that it was created to accommodate both the NFA and its sister organization, the New Homemakers of America, which was an important group in the lives of rural Black girls in the South devoted to vocational home economics.[11]

Even though some state associations did not have an NFA state camp, the NFA camp scene was crucial to the development of the organization's history and the experiences of its members. The story of the S. B. Simmons NFA Camp is helpful in understanding how the scene made a difference in the lives of Black farm boys and is the focus of this chapter for a number of reasons. First, the Simmons NFA Camp was the dream of S. B. Simmons, reflecting how the founders of the NFA worked tirelessly to create experiences for Black farm boys. Second, the NCNFA was known for its camping program and established its own specialized model of outdoor recreation for Black youth, which included a focus on forestry and training in rural electrification. Third, the Simmons NFA Camp stimulated the leadership potential of Black farm boys, providing them with a natural space to test out new ideas that could be used to enhance not only their lives but also the social, political, economic, and environmental realities of their own communities.

Such characteristics of the Simmons NFA Camp speak to the ways in which the NFA camp scene made a difference to Black farm boys in the states where it existed. They also reflect how the transformative power of vocational agriculture in Black communities reconfigured the act of camping while Black, illuminating a new pathway for the process of development among Black farm boys. A closer look into the history of the S. B. Simmons camp illustrates these points. This history of the camp includes the history of the first NCNFA camping experience prior to the establishment of a permanent campsite at Hammocks Beach on the Atlantic Ocean and its renaming in honor of S. B. Simmons in 1958. The evolution of the Simmons NFA Camp occurred through the prism of three phases: formative, transitional, and operational.

The Formative Phase: S. B. Simmons and the NCNFA Camp

The origins of the Simmons NFA Camp can be traced back to the visionary thinking of S. B. Simmons, who imagined the NFA camp experience in North Carolina as "an introduction to democracy in action" for Black farm boys. As Simmons told a reporter for the *Greensboro Daily News*, "The main function of the camp is to provide leadership training. Leadership training has been interpreted to cover all activities in which a farm boy might participate and which will help him to develop a well-rounded personality and character. American leadership is based on democracy. This philosophy is the basic philosophy of the camp." This social experiment in democracy through camping was conducted to develop leadership, citizenship, sportsmanship, and moral values in NFA members. It was first tested during the 1926–27 academic year at the Pitt County Training School in the town of Grimesland and continued until 1965 at Hammocks Beach in Onslow County. The experiment was shaped by early recreational efforts for Black farm boys at various camping sites that evolved into the NCNFA camp in 1953 before its renaming as the S. B. Simmons NFA Camp in 1958. The significant growth of the NFA camp experience predated the configuration of the national NFA and paralleled the development of the NCNFA, originally established by S. B. Simmons in 1928 as the Future North State Farmers organization. The role of S. B. Simmons in the creation of the NCNFA and its NFA camp cannot be overstated and represents just how far he would go to ensure that Black farm boys had the tools to be leaders in their communities and productive citizens in society.[12]

Born Sidney Britton Simmons in 1894 in Mecklenburg County, North Carolina, Simmons was raised in Fayetteville by his father, Rev. Robert H. Simmons, a presiding elder, and his mother, Julia A. Simmons, who was affectionately known as "Mother Simmons" in their local community. The early years of Simmons's life were built around church and education, which shaped his outlook on service to his community and devotion to the pursuit of education. He started formal schooling in Fayetteville and later attended Lincoln Academy, a Black boarding school in Kings Mountain, just west of Charlotte. After Lincoln Academy, Simmons was one of the first students to attend what is now Fayetteville State University and earned a degree in agricultural education from North Carolina A&T State University in 1914. He also earned another degree in agricultural education from the University of Illinois at Urbana-Champaign and completed further studies in California, Kansas, and Colorado. While finishing this additional academic training, he held several teaching positions in Downingtown, Pennsylvania, and Topeka, Kansas, and worked at Tuskegee University as a teacher trainer in vocational agriculture, providing training, mentoring, and ongoing support to Black agriculture teachers across Alabama.[13]

In 1924, at the age of thirty, Simmons returned to his home state to work at his alma mater, North Carolina A&T State University, where he would spend the rest of his life in vocational agricultural education until his death in 1957. Throughout his career in North Carolina, Simmons held two positions: itinerant teacher trainer (1924–30) and assistant state supervisor of agricultural education in Negro schools (1930–57). As an itinerant teacher trainer, Simmons worked with Black agriculture teachers in North Carolina and expanded the statewide purview of social and educational activities for Black farm boys. This expansion set the stage for what would become the Future North State Farmers, the precursor to the NCNFA. Founded in 1928, the Future North State Farmers was modeled after the state's tradition of community-based Negro 4-H clubs and livestock judging contests for Black vocational agriculture students at the Negro State Fair. As assistant state supervisor of agricultural education in Negro schools, Simmons reconfigured the Future North State Farmers as the NCNFA, cofounded the national NFA organization, and served diligently as national NFA executive secretary (1935–41) and executive treasurer (1935–55). Indeed, Simmons was a giant in the NFA and remained committed to ensuring that the organization performed at full capacity.[14]

But the project that occupied the mind of Simmons for most of his career was the NCNFA camping program. He first conceived the idea for the camp in 1927 when he visited the Pitt County Training School in Grimesland. Founded in 1917 as a Black vocational agricultural school, the Pitt County Training School was one of the first schools of its kind in the state within the public school system under the Smith-Hughes National Vocational Education Act of 1917. By 1920, the Pitt County Training School was providing evening adult classes in agriculture for Black men and women who were interested in learning new farming methods to improve their current operations. Seven years later, Simmons selected the Pitt County Training School as the site of the first local camp for Black farm boys in vocational agriculture departments. While it is unclear why he chose Pitt County, it is likely that the programmatic efforts and agrarian traditions of the school made it an ideal location. This first camping programing was described as a "weekend outing" and was attended by thirty-five Black farm boys who spent time on the grounds of the Pitt County Training School engaging in various activities designed to empower the boys to translate skills learned into meaningful action in their communities. It also placed Simmons on a long yet rewarding journey to building a permanent NFA camp in North Carolina.[15]

The Transitional Phase: From Pitt County to Hammocks Beach

Between 1927 and 1953, Simmons organized several NCNFA camping programs in different locations across the state. The 1927 camping weekend at the Pitt County Training School had been a success, and he wanted to keep building on the momentum. As he organized the founding meeting of the Future North State Farmers in 1928, he continued the camping program under the banner of this organization. Due to his efforts, the camping program received coverage from national Black newspapers. For instance, the September 6, 1930, edition of the *Afro-American* ran a story about the camp program, reporting that the camp was attended by sixty Black farm boys and their vocational agriculture teachers from seven high schools in the eastern region of the state. When Simmons relocated the camp to Vance County at the all-Black Kittrell College in 1932, he offered the first statewide camping experience for the Future North State Farmers. The August 13, 1932, edition of the *New Journal and Guide* reported that the camp was attended by over three hundred Black farm boys. A. H. Peeler, then principal of Price High School in Greensboro, served as the camp's director and worked with A. J. Taylor, a pioneer in the Boy Scouts movement in Black communities, to build the first statewide NFA camping program in North Carolina.[16]

The statewide camp remained at Kittrell College for three years until the Future North State Farmers became the NCNFA, marking a growth in the participation of Black farm boys in the NFA in other parts of the state. Given that many Black farm boys were unable to travel due to distance and the state's inadequate rural road infrastructure, Simmons recognized that housing them at a single campsite for a single weekend would be challenging given this rapid expansion in membership. As a result, Simmons established two district summer camps, one in the state's western region and one in its eastern region. The district camp in western North Carolina was held at multiple locations near Kings Mountain, including a Boy Scout camp and Lincoln Academy, where Simmons had attended. In eastern North Carolina, the camp was held near Winton at Chowan Beach. While both camps served a crucial purpose in the lives of Black farm boys, the NCNFA decided that one permanent campsite would be manageable and selected the Chowan Beach camp as the site. But before they could break ground on the camp, World War II started and seriously delayed the project. During this time, Simmons also served in the war effort and was honored with certificates and medals by Presidents Franklin D. Roosevelt and Harry S. Truman for his service.[17]

After the war, Simmons continued to pursue his dreams of locating and building a permanent campsite for Black farm boys in the NCNFA to call their summer home. These dreams came true when Simmons joined with his colleagues in the all-Black North Carolina Teachers Association (NCTA) to manufacture a Black coastal wilderness at Hammocks Beach in Onslow County, just south of Swansboro. This Black coastal wilderness comprised 4,600 acres of beachfront property on the Atlantic Ocean that had previously been owned by Dr. William Sharpe, a prominent white brain surgeon in New York City who played a major role in the development of modern neurosurgery. In Sharpe's eyes, the Hammocks was "a peninsular wonderland on the east coast of North Carolina" that served as a vacation spot for him and his family. He first encountered the land during a hunting trip in 1914 in Onslow County and immediately fell in love with the area.

During this trip, he met a local Black resident by the name of John Hurst, who served as Sharpe's assistant and guide. Sharpe asked Hurst to help him locate a permanent vacation spot in Onslow County, and Hurst found the Hammocks. Sharpe purchased the property and selected Hurst and his wife, Gertrude, an educator and NCTA member, as the managers of the property.[18]

For nearly thirty years, the Hursts were caretakers of the Hammocks and maintained a close friendship with the Sharpe family. In the early 1940s, as an expression of gratitude, Sharpe offered the Hammocks to the Hurst family, but they declined, and Mrs. Hurst suggested that he gift the land, which was valued at over half a million dollars at the time, to the NCTA. Given the social and racial context of nearby Swansboro, which was considered a "sundown town," the Hursts understood how owning the Hammocks would make them a target of racist tactics. However, they saw strength in the land being controlled by the NCTA, which consisted of approximately eight thousand members and represented the educational initiatives of Black schools, teachers, and groups like the NFA. Sharpe respected their decision and in 1945 initiated the process of gifting the land to the NCTA with two stipulations: (1) The NCTA executive board was required to create a separate board of directors, which became the Hammocks Beach Corporation, to handle all affairs associated with the property, and (2) the NCTA would have to raise $100,000 to support construction on the property, with the Sharpes matching these funds. Additionally, Sharpe also arranged for his family, as well as the Hurst family, to have a space on the land. After four years of meetings and negotiations the NCTA agreed to the terms, and in 1949 Sharpe transferred the Hammocks to the organization under the management of the Hammocks Beach Corporation.[19]

But before the ink dried on the signed agreement between Sharpe and the Hammocks Beach Corporation, Simmons applied for and successfully secured a fifty-year lease on twenty-seven acres of Hammocks Beach to build a permanent NCNFA camp. This move by Simmons and his status in the state as assistant state supervisor of agricultural education in Negro schools undoubtedly earned him access to the exclusive group of persons involved in the planning of Hammocks Beach during the project's early phases. In this capacity, Simmons worked with his colleagues to bring to life the Hammocks Beach Resort that opened in 1952, anchored by the state-of-the-art Gertrude Hurst Assembly Hall that housed a four-hundred-person auditorium, office, kitchen, snack bar, and restrooms.[20]

In 1953, Simmons invited Dr. Harold L. Noakes, director of the Oswegatchie FFA Camp in New York, to assist him in selecting a suitable location on the newly leased twenty-seven acres for the NCNFA camp. Based at Cornell University, Noakes managed the New York State FFA camping program, which comprised nearly one thousand acres of forest land and represented one of the nation's finest FFA camps in terms of logistics, planning, and programming. Simmons saw this program as a model and consulted Noakes for help in locating a site for the camp. They selected land on the banks of Queens Creek on Hammocks Beach, just a little over one mile from the Atlantic Ocean, as the site for the camp. This site was ideal for the NFA, and Noakes was then asked by Simmons to conduct a workshop for 115 Black vocational agriculture teachers who would serve as the camp's first counselors. The training workshops included actual camping in army tents so that the teachers would be familiar with the potential experiences of future NFA campers. Teachers who participated in the workshops also engaged in recreational activities like boating and deep-sea fishing, as well as a supervised camping activity that future NFA campers would engage in.[21]

To be sure, Noakes believed these types of workshops were beneficial, as he put it, because "the effectiveness of any camp in meeting the needs of its campers is dependent largely upon the counselors. A camp can be no better than its counselors." Simmons also believed this philosophy, and the workshops proved to be extremely informative, contributing to the development of an infrastructure of teachers who would be the first counselors at the NCNFA camp. More importantly, the workshops were integrated into the formal NCNFA camping program and occurred prior to each camping season for counselors. Such early workshops and the selection of Queens Creek as the campsite set the stage for the first camping season of the permanent NCNFA camp.[22]

The Operational Phase: A Summer Home for Black Farm Boys

When the NCNFA camp opened for its first camping season at Hammocks Beach in the summer of 1953, the land was still in its natural state. The campgrounds had not been developed, and the twenty-seven acres of the camp along Queens Creek offered a refuge of forests for Black farm boys to create a world beyond their rural communities. The camp ran Monday through Friday, and the housing for NCNFA campers was army

The Camp

The New Farmers of America Camp is located in Onslow County, near Swansboro, North Carolina, at Hammocks Beach. It's directly on the banks of Queen's Creek, a little bit more than a mile from the Atlantic Ocean. It was established in 1953 on property mode available for this purpose by Dr. William Sharp. A 4,500 acre tract of land is under the direct control of Hammocks Beach Corporation and a Board of Directors.

The camp itself is under the management of the New Farmers of America of North Carolina, with headquarters at A. and T. College, Greensboro, N. C.

Facilities are available for housing and feeding 150 campers. Equipment and buildings are constructed to meet the standards of the American Camping Association.

The camp is operated under efficient management and well trained camp counselors for the months of June, July and August. One of these months is used exclusively by NFA members. Provisions are made whereby other campers and youth organizations may use the facilities.

The staff is well qualified to render the type of program most helpful to campers. Senior counselors are teachers; Junior counselors are competent, experienced campers in camp activities.

Every effort is made to keep the cost at a minimum fee.

Page from the *NFA Camp Booklet*, North Carolina NFA. Courtesy of the S. B. Simmons Collection, ncatsbs11055, NCATSBS.

Activities

FISHING   TRACK AND FIELD

CRABBING   GROUP GAMES

BOATING   ARTS AND CRAFTS

BASEBALL   FIRST AID

HORSESHOES   CONSERVATION

CAMP PAPER   OVERNIGHT HIKES

CAMPFIRE PROGRAMS

VESPERS

CAMP COOK-OUTS

SWMMING   MOVIES

LEADERSHIP ACTIVITIES

Page from the *NFA Camp Booklet*, North Carolina NFA. Courtesy of the S. B. Simmons Collection, ncatsbs11055, NCATSBS.

tents. For meals, they traveled about one mile to the NCTA's dining hall each day. Simmons wanted these first campers to experience this natural world as the counselors had during their workshops. But he also saw the untouched physical environment of the new campsite as a blank canvas on which to build a massive camping operation that would serve as a week-long summer home where Black farm boys could learn, play, and dream. This operation would enable NFA campers to recharge while gaining skills that would help them and their families during the summer growing season and beyond.[23]

In order to accomplish this vision, Simmons launched a statewide NFA camp fund drive during that first camping season. The sole purpose of building the fund was to support the construction of an administration building and a bathhouse. By the next camping season, Simmons, local NFA chapters, and other supporters had donated and raised enough money to build these structures. Due to the success of this initial fund drive, Simmons planned additional fund drives in 1954 and 1955, which allowed him to work with an architect and other stakeholders to create a

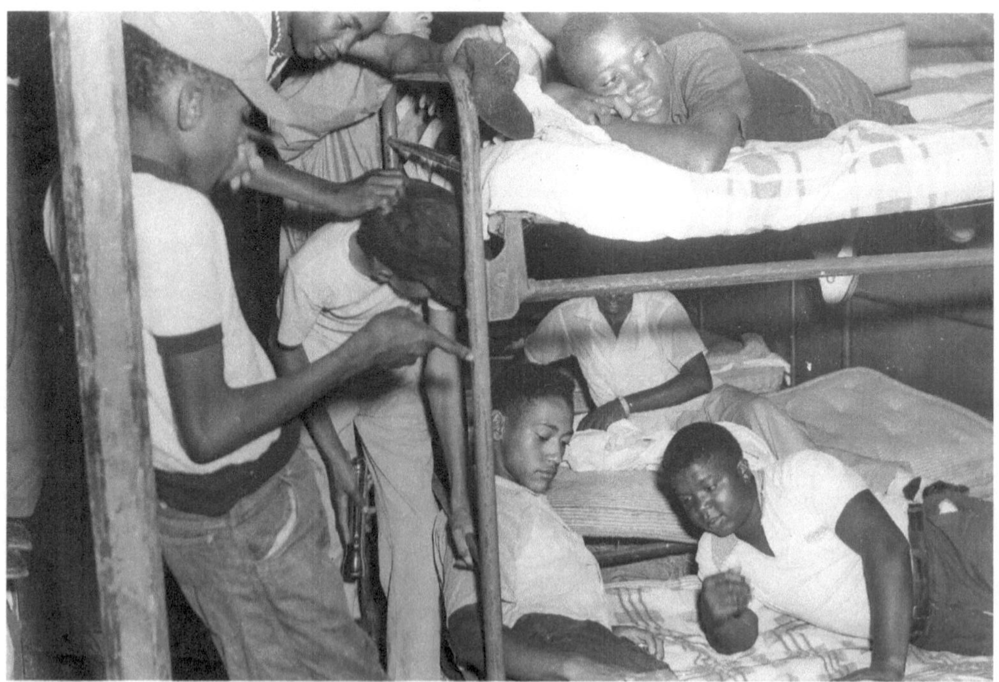

North Carolina NFA campers lounging around on bunk beds in a tent.
Courtesy of the S. B. Simmons Collection, ncatsbs11016, NCATSBS.

master plan for the camp's infrastructure that included a dining hall and concrete cabins to replace the army tents as the primary camp housing. This infrastructure would also include amenities to support various recreational activities. As part of this plan, local NFA chapters would provide most of the labor to erect these essential buildings, demonstrating the construction expertise of Black farm boys.[24]

By the fifth camping season in 1957, the NCNFA camp had expanded greatly. The geography of the campsite was made up of an assembly hall—which included a main assembly and recreational room, dining hall, commercial kitchen, offices, a lodge for camp officials and guests, and restrooms with shower stalls—a recreational hall, eight cinder block cabins, a pier, a fleet of four boats, bathhouses for boys and girls, a flagpole, a shop building, a pavilion, two incinerators, a playground, and courts for tennis, basketball, and volleyball. All this infrastructure was configured around a new main road that was paved, providing safe access to the campsite. During the off-season of the NFA camp, the site was used by other groups, including the NHA, the NFA's sister organization; Boy and Girl Scouts; and other youth organizations. In observing the developed NCNFA camp, one school principal said, "It is quite difficult to find words that will adequately express my first impression as I arrived on the camp scene. . . . The location and structure of the eight cabins, the bath house, and Assembly Hall are truly marvelous. The cabins are systematically located on each side of a beautifully graded roadway." While the principal had "the good fortune to visit many types and kinds of camp," he stated, "My hat is off to the New Farmers of America Camp at Hammocks Beach." This principal's impression of the camp reflected how numerous others encountered it when they drove into the NFA campsite.[25]

The visionary thinking of Simmons that brought the NCNFA camp into existence was cut short as he passed away less than two weeks after the fifth camping season. An obituary published in the *Atlanta Daily World* reported that Simmons had suffered a heart attack prior to the season and never fully recovered. The absence and death of Simmons devastated the NCNFA. At the start of the sixth camping season in 1958, however, the camp was renamed the S. B. Simmons NFA Camp in honor of Simmons and his commitment to the empowerment of Black farm boys in North Carolina and to the NFA. As Warmoth T. Gibbs, then president of North Carolina A&T State University, put it, "I believe the Camp represents one long-time dream of the late S. B. Simmons, and I am hopeful that it will play an important part in developing our farm boys into good farmers and good citizens." D. C. Jones, executive advisor to the Oklahoma Association of the NFA, added, "S. B. will always be remembered as the one person who gave so much to so many. Not only did he convene a National NFA organization, but he also knew and did take the right steps to create it. We not only depended on him for leadership, but accepted it and expected it. No greater tribute could the North Carolina Association make than to perpetuate his memory by naming its Camp for him." But the memory of Simmons remained not only in the naming of the Simmons NFA Camp. His legacy endured in the camp's three core areas: leadership training, educational instruction, and recreational programming.[26]

LEADERSHIP TRAINING

In his 1940 article in the *Journal of Negro Education*, S. B. Simmons wrote that one of the many advantages of the NFA was that "it teaches the members to cooperate because there are many activities in the organization which are group activities and cannot be accomplished except through the work of the group as a whole." The leadership training area of the Simmons NFA Camp offered a critical platform to illuminate this advantage and shaped each week of the camp. Beginning on the first day of camp, leadership training began after all the campers arrived and got registered. Counselors were tasked with dividing the boys into a system of camp chapters in cabins to prevent local NFA chapters from bunking together, cultivating a method for NFA members from all regions of the state to meet and form new relationships. Each camp chapter unit comprised two counselors and about eighteen to twenty campers, operating as its own community. One of the first tasks of the camp chapter was to nominate a candidate for camp chief and hold elections and vote for the following officers: president, vice president, secretary, treasurer, and reporter. These officers worked in tandem with the camp director, counselor, and chief to produce a safe living and learning camp experience alongside storekeepers, camp inspectors, class instructors, cabin counselors, and a news staff. The election process for the officers was facilitated by one camper who was designated as an election commissioner, who worked with the counselors to ensure a fair election. This process was designed to teach the campers democratic values that emphasized respect for one another and the freedom to shape one's own community. The process also promoted public speaking skills as those who were interested in leadership positions were required to prepare and give speeches, with the assistance of the counselors.[27]

During the first camp chapter campfire on Monday evening, the speeches were delivered, and in some cases the chapter would hold elections that night. In other cases camp chapters held elections the following morning. After elections were complete, the camp chapter program was collectively drafted and approved by the camp director. The camp chapter program was the ultimate camper guide for the week and structured each day of the camp. It included specific details related to flag raising and lowering, mealtimes, cleaning duties, educational and recreational activities, campfire programming, social hour, and vesper services. The creation of the camp program required the entire camp chapter to work together and provided many of the boys with training in how to generate a schedule of activities. This skill would benefit their local NFA chapter as the campers could go back and lead their respective chapters, cultivating their own program of work. On the surface, these types of activities may have seemed routine or mundane, but they were an integral part of the leadership training area of the camp.[28]

As the week progressed, the camp chapter units also established committees, including committees devoted to books, history, campfire arrangements, and safety procedures. These committees contributed to building camaraderie among campers and connected cabinmates around specific issues or opportunities. The committee work also allowed boys who weren't part of the formal election process to still play an important role in the design of their camping experience. As one camper put it, the "leadership activities give the fellows a chance to become leaders. . . . They are encouraged to become leaders. . . . At camp a boy feels wanted, and he knows he is eligible to participate in the many activities offered." The Camp Court, which represented the various levels of leadership at the camp, believed in this view of the Simmons NFA Camp's leadership activities and recognized the boys for their involvement. This recognition was part of the selection of campers who would receive various superlatives, such as the highly coveted Best Camper or Best Leadership awards. Other awards were also given out at the camp chapter level. At the end of the week on Friday morning, these superlatives and awards were announced at the camp-wide assembly, and the winners were celebrated. This final event was organized by the campers and allowed them time to publicly reflect on what they learned and accomplished during the week. They also were able to discuss ways to improve the camp for future seasons and received a printed bulletin and program of their camping experience that they could share with their local chapters, which was likely used as a recruitment tool to inspire other Black farm boys to attend the camp. To be sure, while there was a specific leadership training area of the Simmons NFA Camp that benefited the campers, leadership skills were gained in the camp's other two core areas as well.[29]

EDUCATIONAL INSTRUCTION

The Simmons NFA Camp's educational instruction area offered Black farm boys a variety of courses designed to stimulate their minds. In the spirit of S. B. Simmons, this area helped Black farm boys to discover "hidden abilities which perhaps would never have been brought out except through activities" sanctioned by the NFA, such as the camping experience. Such hidden abilities were brought to the surface through a project-focused curriculum and program that would leave campers "educationally refreshed" by the end of camp, as one former camp chief put it. Beginning on every Tuesday morning of the camp week, camp instructors transformed the natural environment of the camp into a set of outdoor classrooms for experiential learning and supplemental training in various topics, including highway safety, practical electricity, conservation and forestry, arts and crafts, rural leadership, citizenship, agriscience, and natural resources. The formal course schedule varied from week to week and would begin at 8 a.m. and conclude by noon for lunch. It was organized by topics, and campers were separated into groups for the courses, enabling boys from different cabins to learn alongside one another. This co-learning process emphasized hands-on training taught by experts in the fields associated with the topics presented to the campers.[30]

For example, one of the week's most popular classes was on natural resource conservation and forestry. This course was a collaborative effort between the NCNFA and the North Carolina Forest Service. Each year, a forest ranger or designated official provided instruction on subjects such as soil and water conservation, wildlife management, tree identification, wildfire prevention, tree measurement, and related conservation techniques and practices. What made this course so fascinating was that it allowed the campers to connect the science of natural resources conservation and forestry with the practical side of preservation-conservation that was rooted in the historical relationship between Black children and the broader idea of nature study—a systematic curriculum ranging from elementary school to higher education that stressed environmental awareness. Historian Dianne D. Glave argues that environmental awareness among Black children was built on their particular experiences in nature that allowed them to use science as a way to improve their lives and their communities. At the same time, such awareness allowed Black children to redefine their relationship with nature. The Simmons NFA Camp provided this level of instruction so that campers would be enriched through learning and the application of these skills in their communities, with the hope that they would go on to pursue careers in natural resources conservation and forestry. At some point during the camp week, the campers participated in a forestry contest, which allowed them to showcase their learned skills and be rewarded for various levels of conservation competency.[31]

Another popular course among campers was the practical electricity class. This class provided campers with intensive instruction in the manufacturing of electrical products, electric meter inspection, and the use of electricity in the home and on the farm. The course emerged out of unique partnerships between the NCNFA and the Duke Power Company, the Carolina Power and Light Company, and the Virginia Electric Power Company. Representatives from these companies met with the campers and guided them in projects focused on rural electrification that increased their understanding of the consequences of access to electricity on a population's quality of life. The projects likely addressed earlier manifestations of the rural-urban divide surrounding the lack of energy sources in isolated areas that could disrupt the livelihoods of the communities in which campers lived. At the same time, the projects exposed students to an untapped career pathway in the energy companies that could provide them with a source of economic security. This level of training also included demonstrations of energy generation, transmission, and distribution, with an emphasis on safe usage of power. Such an emphasis was important, providing campers with knowledge on the electrical infrastructure needed to adapt to shifting conditions in rural areas where energy grids were expanding. For the Simmons NFA Camp, knowledge of electricity was beneficial in developing a generation of Black farm boys who would go on to lead their rural communities in all aspects of life.[32]

During some camping seasons, experiential learning was explored through educational activities such as budgeting, the basics of planning and designing meetings in the context of parliamentary procedure, the art of networking, extemporaneous speech writing and delivery, and organizational leadership—which provided campers with lessons that could enhance the function of their local chapters. Experiential learning also occurred in the daily camp improvement project and the production of the *Mosquito Express,* the camp's official publication. The camp improvement project was a one-hour activity tailored around team-building exercises that gave campers skills in applied conservation practices that they could explicitly take back to their farms. This was important since many of the NFA campers would leave their farms at a crucial time of the growing season, and such skills could show their communities that the camp was a worthy endeavor for all. Campers who worked on the staff of the *Mosquito Express* were trained in news literacy, acquiring critical thinking and journalistic writing skills surrounding the design and mass production of a community-based publication. Such skills in developing the *Mosquito Express* provided staff members with the tools to communicate effectively through news writing for the public good.[33]

Group of North Carolina NFA campers preparing to start their camp improvement project. Courtesy of the S. B. Simmons Collection, ncatsbs11030, NCATSBS.

Educational instruction at the Simmons NFA Camp was achieved in many ways, and the campers looked forward to taking courses and co-learning with their peers. In fact, many campers agreed with the 1960–61 NCNFA state reporter James Eaton, who, after taking courses at the Simmons NFA Camp, concluded that "there is no better place for young boys to spend a summer." Each camping season, the camp agenda was created by and for Black farm boys under the supervision of caring adults, teachers, and mentors who had one goal in mind: to enhance the lives of all campers through a strategically curated program of activities. The educational instruction area of the Simmons NFA Camp ignited a passion for organized education in the minds of Black farm boys, allowing them to remain connected to intellectual pursuits during the summer. After educational instruction was completed, campers prepared for recreational programming, which taught them the importance of leisure as a form of community and self-care.[34]

RECREATIONAL PROGRAMMING

The afternoon component of each day during the Simmons NFA Camp week was devoted to the area of recreational programming. Based on a camp chapter's schedule, this area also spilled over into other parts of the day when leisure or athletic activities were permitted. According to several annual Simmons NFA Camp reports, recreational programming was "safe, enjoyable, educational, and designed to develop health and leadership." This programming consisted of numerous activities, including, but not limited to, water recreation, fish fries, barbecues, hiking, worship services, campfire bonding, sports, physical workouts through calisthenics, talent shows, archery, games, and arts and crafts. Together, these activities exposed Black farm boys to the joys of outdoor living and how it could be a source of fun. The activities also promoted another advantage of the NFA in that it "develop[ed] a love of country life by furnishing recreational activities," borrowing the words of S. B. Simmons. This love for country life would be realized as campers completed each activity, discovering how leisure was an important part of daily life.[35]

Water recreation was what most campers looked forward to. The location of the camp on an inland waterway with direct access to the Atlantic Ocean created a natural beachfront environment for swimming, swim lessons, boating, and other water-related activities. In the late 1950s, a pier was built on the ocean to facilitate trainings in water safety, provide a space for small boats to dock, and allow campers to enjoy the view of the ocean. At a time in the Jim Crow South when racial segregation shaped water recreation and public beach access, the Simmons NFA Camp and the larger Hammocks Beach resort property were critical sites for Black people to access water activities on their own terms. Due to this context, the Simmons Camp offered Black farm boys who were not from coastal North Carolina their first opportunity to see the ocean and play in it. The same ocean that carried their enslaved ancestors to the very land in which they sought to farm and uplift their communities was now being used as a source of fun and adventure for Black farm boys.[36]

During the camping week of June 18–22, 1956, for example, fishing and the evening boat cruise on the Atlantic were popular activities. These activities allowed the campers to build community and encounter new experiences together. What made fishing a camp favorite was that it was many of the boys' favorite pastime and contributed to the nightly fish fries that cabins organized around the campfire program. The fish fries required the boys to catch their seafood, clean it, and prepare it to be cooked and served. Seafood was a crucial source of nutrition for the campers, and the fish fries were a crucial component of what made the Simmons NFA

Hammocks Beach pier. Courtesy of the
S. B. Simmons Collection, ncatsbs11018, NCATSBS.

Camp a food-secure environment. One cabin in particular was known for its fish fries, which "was the talk of the whole N. F. A. camp," the camp chapter reported in the *Mosquito Express*. "The smell of fish, shrimps, oysters, and crabs cooking brought boys and advisors from every cabin in the camp." Such opportunities to connect through food and cooking greatly enhanced the camping experience for Black farm boys in North Carolina and showed them that they could survive by taking care of one another through the preparation of food.[37]

The evening boat cruise that week offered a unique water recreational experience that brought campers, camp staff, teachers, and other visitors together to explore the Atlantic Ocean. In reflecting on the cruise, one staff member from the *Mosquito Express* wrote, "While making the trip across, one could see the sandy bottom in places and yet, just a few feet away, the bottom was not to be touched with a fifty-foot pole. The ship was one of beauty, with its coloring of blue and white and the captain and crew gave one the feeling of security, for surely they had made this voyage many times before." Over one hundred people were aboard the ship, and when they arrived at the beach, the staff member further observed "the cool water of the Atlantic with the white surf beating the sand under the feet of happy N. F. A. boys, supervisors, and guests" who were collecting "treasures such as drift wood, and sea shells of all kinds, shapes, and colors." Upon returning back to camp from the cruise, "there seemed to have been a sudden stillness among the boys, for truly, they had one of the many wonderful experiences awaiting each N. F. A. boy" who was able to attend the camp. In many ways, the cruise was therapeutic and gave the NFA campers a space to reflect while having fun. Such moments during the camping week made a difference in the lives of Black farm boys.[38]

Recreational programming at the Simmons NFA Camp complemented both the leadership training and educational areas of the camp's agenda. While such programming was designed for Black farm boys to have fun while learning, recreational activities also taught the importance of working together as a team and building a sustainable living environment. The science behind the Simmons NFA camping experience was built on a particular type of care that operated at the intersection of self and community. This form of care, as social scientist Shawn Ginwright put it, "is more than simply trusting relationships and mutual expectations and bonds between individuals." Instead, this level of care "moves beyond coping and surviving and encourages black youth to thrive and flourish as they transform community conditions." Indeed, the ultimate goal of the Simmons NFA camping experience was to teach this kind of care to Black farm boys in hopes that they would take back what they learned in camp to their communities and transform them. In this way, their communities would also be beneficiaries of the camping experience, which demonstrated the NFA's commitment to using the lives of Black farm boys as a vehicle for community change and development.[39]

A Natural World for Black Farm Boys

After leaving the June 18–22, 1956, camping experience at the Simmons NFA Camp, Principal N. L. Dillard from the Caswell County Training School in Yanceyville, North Carolina, was not only impressed with the camping experience but also inspired by the overall program that took place that week. "The officials and personnel of the N. F. A. are due a real bouquet for the splendid facilities for the High School boys of our state at the Hammocks," Dillard remarked. "They are pioneering an adventure which shows courage, foresight, and vision. . . . I dare say that generations yet unborn will rise up from every nook and corner of our fair State and applaud the move made here by men who have looked into the future and laid the foundation for one of the finest recreational centers in the South." Indeed, S. B. Simmons was a visionary in his pursuit to develop a recreational institution for Black farm boys that would outlive him. This institution was built on the idea of camping while Black, which was realized through a historical relationship between Black people and preservation-conservation. Simmons translated this relationship through the lives of Black farm boys, illuminating a pathway for them to make a difference in society. For many Black farm boys, the rurality of their everyday lives was isolating and perpetuated feelings of inferiority. Yet, the Simmons NFA Camp allowed them to meet boys who were just like them, showing them that they were not alone.[40]

Alexander Dawson, the 1961–62 president of the NCNFA, picked up this line of thinking when he reflected on his own experience at the camp in the early 1960s. "The NFA Camp takes a boy away from his home environment and places him in an environment where everybody is the same. . . . This will remove the feeling of inferiority that a boy might have. . . . It gives a boy a chance to meet other boys who will inspire him," Dawson explained. What must be added to Dawson's reflection is that the Simmons NFA Camp provided a natural world for Black farm boys to draw on their collective strength while learning how to care for themselves and each other. Through its three core areas of activities—leadership training, educational instruction, and recreational programming—the Simmons NFA Camp was built on this strength and represented a critical asset of the NCNFA. This asset was rooted in community and served as a summer incubator for the minds of Black farm boys to be challenged and validated so they could be well-rounded leaders in their communities.[41]

What is also fascinating about the story of the Simmons NFA Camp is that it did not end in the 1960s. The campsite surprisingly survived the NFA's dissolution in 1965, remaining open for twenty-six more years until 1991 as part of the North Carolina FFA Association camp network, which kept the lease on the land. But what was lost in its remaining years after the NFA disappeared has not fully been recovered. Nonetheless, the camp's story is instructive. As others have suggested, recounting the camp's story along the NFA's timeline could be useful in making historical connections to the consistently overlooked lives of rural Black youths today who are still making the most out of the possibilities available to them, as Black farm boys in the NFA did in the past. This story could also provide historical texture to present-day programs aimed at introducing young people to "nature" that frequently target urban areas exclusively, casting a light on the radical and rural roots of such programs that are buried in the untilled soil of the NFA camp scene's past. In a larger sense, the Simmons NFA Camp exemplifies the NFA camp scene and demonstrates how the NFA expanded into the wilderness to create a unique life-altering experience that not every Black farm boy in the NFA had the opportunity to enjoy. For those who didn't experience the camp scene or even the national convention scene described in chapter 2, the NFA community scene made the biggest difference in their lives.[42]

As the next chapter shows, the NFA community scene functioned as the site for local NFA chapters to communicate and translate the vision of the national body of the NFA at the micro level, establishing the organization as a vital part of the rural Black experience in the South. The NFA community scene in places like La Grange, Texas, for example, was tailored to the specific experiences of Black farm boys and their communities, and Black vocational agriculture teachers were at the center of this scene. These teachers devoted their lives to the NFA, working tirelessly to show Black farm boys that agriculture could be a guiding light for the production of a brighter future for all community members within and beyond the farm gate.

Chapter 4

BLACK AGRICULTURE TEACHERS MATTER

The Randolph NFA Chapter in Texas

I remember taking bus trips, doing those contests, we had a good group. But we had a good teacher, Mr. Crosby. . . . Mr. Crosby was a father figure to me. He saved my life. . . . All the Black people that I know respected him and trusted him. That was the key thing: being trusted. . . . I was blessed to be able to be a part of the NFA. It blessed me in more ways than one. And I try to teach some of those skills we learned to my kids today.

—**Jeff Kelly,** Randolph NFA chapter, La Grange, Texas

One hot day in the summer of 1959, twenty-four-year-old Lorenza Crosby Jr. stopped at the Eckel's Grocery & Service Station on Highway 71 in the city of La Grange in Fayette County, Texas. After he pulled into a parking spot, Mr. Crosby turned off his 1956 brown four-door Chevrolet and walked in to ask for directions to the all-Black Randolph High School. He had been invited to the school to interview for the recently vacant position of vocational agriculture teacher and was anxious to meet with Mr. Shellie L. Hatch, the school's principal, and Mr. Charles A. Lemmons, La Grange Independent School District superintendent. Once he finally arrived and got settled, Crosby's itinerary involved a tour of the school—which included all grade levels—and interviews with Principal Hatch and Superintendent Lemmons. During the interviews, Crosby talked about his vision for the Randolph Department of Vocational Agriculture and its award-winning chapter of the New Farmers of America. This vision emphasized agricultural mechanics as an invaluable local asset to Black farm boys, taking the department in a "different direction," as Crosby put it. "I wanted to teach agricultural mechanics: skills the kids could use for the rest of their lives, like how to repair tractors, build steps, mend screen doors, pour concrete, and fix engines." In the face of a shifting rural Black landscape and national agricultural economy that was pushing Black people further away from farming, Crosby wanted to show the boys that there was more to agriculture than just farming.[1]

As Lorenza Crosby's visit to Randolph High School concluded, Principal Hatch and Superintendent Lemmons voiced their admiration for Crosby's innovative thinking in vocational agriculture and offered him the job on the spot. They were also likely impressed with his strong passion for agricultural mechanics that had been fueled at Prairie View A&M University, where he earned his bachelor of science degree in agriculture in May 1956. More importantly, Superintendent Lemmons shared similar interests with Crosby in agricultural mechanics and assured him that he would provide the school with the necessary tools and materials needed to offer this new curriculum. He also worked with other school authorities to secure Crosby's wife, Myrtle, a teaching position in the Randolph Junior High music program, which was slated to begin during the 1961–62 academic year. Mrs. Crosby was also a May 1956 graduate of PVAMU, earning her bachelor of arts degree in music. Such promises put Crosby at ease, and he felt like Randolph High School was the place where he could make a difference in the lives of Black farm boys and their families. He accepted the position and drove away from Randolph that afternoon, excited about the future.[2]

Several weeks later, in the fall of 1959, Crosby arrived at Randolph High School to lead the school's vocational agriculture department and continue its rich NFA tradition produced by his predecessors. This tradition had begun eighteen years earlier, in September 1941, when the school was known as La Grange Colored High School (sometimes referred to as La Grange Negro High School) and the Randolph NFA was known as the La Grange NFA. It was shaped by the NFA community scene, which exemplified a microcosm of the historical rural African American experience. Historian Valerie Grim writes that this experience "was energetic and diverse and included many social, spiritual, and educational activities." Through their own knowledge production practices, rural Black people used this experience to "creat[e] an identity that embraced their expressions and empowered their sense of blackness." These expressions were fashioned from active participation in "local organizations" that "met specific needs, maintained community solidarity, and were important for individuals who wanted to belong but did not have the money or time to participate in national organizations." While the NFA was a national organization, its greatest influence was felt locally, as not every Black farm boy could participate in national activities. For Black farm boys in places like La Grange, as well as their peers in other rural Black communities, the NFA was a local source of empowerment that provided them with new Black agricultural identities based on the emancipatory aspects of American agriculture. Such identities were created under the careful supervision of Black agriculture teachers, who played an important role in directing the NFA's community scene, facilitating a local presence that made a difference in the lives of rural Black people.[3]

This chapter is dedicated to Black agriculture teachers like Lorenza Crosby and those who came before and after him who devoted their lives to the development of the NFA's community scene that was anchored in a particular local chapter. These Black men were not only teachers but also role models and father figures who showed Black farm boys that they could be more than what they imagined. Before the current discussions about the importance of representation in Black communities, Black agriculture teachers were embedded in the community and were the leading image of Black representation in agriculture. Black writer George M. Johnson argues that such representation, in a broader sense, enables Black boys in general (and I would add Black farm boys in particular) to recognize "the fact that you sometimes can't see yourself if you can't see people like you existing, thriving, working." Sociologist E. Yvonne Beauford and agricultural education scholar Wash A. Jones have likewise found that Black agriculture teachers provided a real-life model of what success in agriculture looked like that promoted Black participation in agriculture and related fields. In other words, Black agriculture teachers offered a physical manifestation of what students could be, even if they never even considered a career in agriculture.[4]

Borrowing the words of Beauford, the presence of Black agriculture teachers who advised local NFA chapters in rural communities showed Black farm boys that "their aspirations [could] be achieved in a rural setting or through commitment to an agriculture-related career . . . provid[ing] exposure and experiences which refute the negative image often associated with agriculture." Therefore, the ultimate goal of the Black agriculture teacher was to show Black farm boys—through the NFA—that they could be anything in the world of agriculture and that this could greatly benefit their communities both directly and indirectly. Put differently, Black agriculture teachers activated new ways of knowing agricultural production in the lives of Black farm boys, helping them to identify desires to change their communities through agriculture and locate ways to make real such goals. As one former NFA member in Texas told me, Black agriculture teachers were the "light out of the rural." This light that shined through Black agriculture teachers guided the minds and lives of Black farm boys, empowering them to manifest their dreams of rural community improvement into reality.[5]

This chapter builds on that analysis by raising the following questions: What can we discover about local NFA experiences from the perspective of Black agriculture teachers? How did they contribute to the growth of the NFA at the grassroots level? What initiatives did they organize, and how did they affect Black communities? How did they design an NFA program that addressed the realities of Black farm boys and helped them transform their dreams into realities? I explore these questions through a case study of the community scene produced by the Randolph NFA chapter. This case provides a microscopic look at the three eras that shaped the Randolph NFA chapter, revealing the inner workings of the NFA community scene and how it played out in real time. Each era—that of Collins, Jackson, and Crosby—can be identified by the last name of the Black vocational agriculture teacher who served at the school at the time. To be sure, given the fact that the national NFA was made up of over one thousand community scenes, the scene of the Randolph NFA chapter is by no means typical, as it is impossible to capture the breadth of programming operationalized in the NFA community scene. A case study of the Randolph NFA chapter through the lens of Black agriculture teachers, however, at least demonstrates how this scene was deeply local and had effects on Black farm boys and their communities. This kind of programming was tailored for the benefit of a particular community, and Black agriculture teachers facilitated this process.

Unlocking New Agricultural Pathways: A Brief Look at the NFA Community Scene

As chapter 1 revealed, the origins of the NFA are located in the communities from which the organization emerged. These communities represented a network of activities, initiatives, and institutions that worked together to cultivate the NFA community scene. In this way, the NFA community scene did not begin with the needs of Black farm boys; it began with the needs of the communities that the boys lived in. The early main cast of this scene included Black agriculture teachers who were male and educated in the departments of agriculture at Black land grant institutions. These teachers were an integral part of their communities and trained in vocational agriculture, that is, the systematic study of scientific agriculture in the context of career training. According to Professor Arthur Floyd, itinerant teacher trainer in agriculture at Tuskegee University, vocational agriculture in the classrooms of Black agriculture teachers was built on the process of "learning through environment." This process transformed the students' environment into a laboratory for the testing of programmatic efforts that would provide a source of intellectual stimulation and community improvement. The dual outcome of this process unlocked new agricultural pathways for Black farm boys that created new conditions for their communities.[6]

For example, the learning-through-environment process greatly enhanced rural Black communities in places where the South Carolina Association of the NFA had local chapters. In his August 1950 article in *Agricultural Education Magazine* titled "Needs of Farm Families," Professor William F. Hickson argued that the mission of Black agriculture teachers in the Palmetto State was to create a vocational agriculture program that was "centered around activities designed to meet the needs of farm families." Hickson, who at the time was the itinerant teacher trainer in agriculture at South Carolina State University, strongly believed that "if any agricultural program is of any value, or worthy of praise, it must satisfy the needs of the community." Within this program, Hickson saw the NFA as a weapon in the arsenal of the Black agriculture teachers to address community needs and solve related problems. While he highlighted several exemplary Black agriculture teachers who were involved in this work, Mr. C. H. Thomas stood out. As the vocational agriculture teacher in the Jamison community in Orangeburg County, South Carolina, Thomas led efforts to address food and nutrition insecurity among over 150 Black families in his community. His efforts resulted in the construction of a community cannery that trained the NFA members, their families, and other community members in new technologies in glass canning methods that allowed them to preserve greater volumes of nutritious foods to support and improve their diets. Such efforts were occurring in other communities across the state and in other states, illustrating how rural

Black communities addressed their own problems through vocational agriculture.[7]

Over four hundred miles northwest of the Jamison community, Mr. G. K. Kersey, vocational agriculture instructor at the all-Black Holloway High School in Murfreesboro, Tennessee, worked to make sure that the local NFA chapter at the school reached all parts of the lives of its members and community. Kersey led one of the most active NFA chapters in the Tennessee Association of the NFA. What made Kersey's NFA program different was that his students regularly contributed to the NFA section of *American Farm Youth* magazine, documenting its community scene throughout Rutherford County. This documentation not only highlighted Kersey's robust NFA program but also served to inspire other NFA chapters. In his personal message to the national NFA presented in the October 1939 edition of *American Farm Youth*, Kersey pleaded with his peers to publish in the magazine since there would "never be a time that every student, teacher, and teacher trainer will meet as a group, but it is possible that we can reach our fellow workers, both students and teachers, throughout the United States" every month through the publication. As such, Kersey argued that an important part of the NFA community scene was to document what each chapter was doing as a way to communicate effectively across the massive network of local NFA chapters. Due to his publication efforts, we learn that the Holloway High School NFA community scene comprised many activities, such as poultry and livestock shows, supervised farm projects including animals and crops, judging contests, agricultural exhibits, county and state fair participation, and evening classes in innovative farm methods for Black farmers.[8]

At the state level, the Mississippi Association of the NFA emphasized a statewide activity for its community scene that focused on home improvement, which aligned with the national organization's focus on this particular area. According to a statement released by the Magnolia State's NFA association in May 1941, "The New Farmers of America has come to realize and has pledged to support the belief that a community is built to live in. Some communities are good living places, for the people in them planned them as such. It is the united endeavor of local chapters of the N.F.A. to [d]esign well-planned communities for the needs of all the people and for the future as well as the present." For the Mississippi Association of the NFA, well-planned communities were to be cultivated through improvements in and outside the home. The local advisor of the Amite County Training School NFA chapter in Gloster, Mississippi, for example, focused

on the repair of rural homes in his community as well as on the building of new homes. NFA members received training in brickwork, interior
decorating, painting, rural electrification, and home foundation development through this project. Roughly 230 miles northwest of Gloster, the
Oktibbeha County Training School's advisor taught students landscaping
to improve the outside conditions of their school as well as in the communities where NFA members lived. Such improvements to Black communities in Mississippi ushered in a new era of rural Black living where
neighborhood beautification served as a vehicle for community uplift.[9]

During the 1940s, the national NFA contributed to the country's war
efforts in support of the National Defense Program of World War II—"one
of the greatest accomplishments in the history of the New Farmers of
America," Antoine Alston, Dexter Wakefield, and Netta Cox write—which
resulted in eleven state associations taking part in this initiative. In Louisiana, for example, the state NFA association outlined its war effort plans in
the December 1941 edition of *American Farm Youth* magazine. In the article, the Louisiana Association of the NFA state reporter Otis Hicks noted
that "the Louisiana New Farmers have taken the defense operations as personal responsibilities and have grasped opportunities for rendering service to embattled democracy here in America and surviving democracies
abroad." The services offered by the Louisiana association were centered
on the purchase of war bonds and stamps, the production of staple foods
through supervised farm projects, and the development of shopwork projects focused on carpentry, machining, and related shop skills. "In other
words," Hicks concluded, "the Louisiana Association of the New Farmers
of America is ready and willing to do its share of the job . . . to aid in the
construction of defense for democracy." As a result of the efforts of the
Louisiana Association of the NFA and other states that participated in war
efforts, the national NFA purchased $153,996 in war bonds and stamps,
constructed 383 food conservation centers, and processed 838,726 cans of
food, among many other noteworthy accomplishments.[10]

While the activities that characterized NFA community scenes differed
across the nation, the annual NFA parent-son (sometimes called father-
son) banquets were the premier social occasion of every local chapter. The
banquet was attended by parents, community members, NFA officials,
and other invited guests. It was carefully planned and hosted by the local
chapter and usually occurred at the end of the academic year. Local NFA
members, in consultation with their advisor, designed the menu, which
included only locally grown foods produced by the chapter; decorated the

banquet venue; curated the guest list; and oversaw the entire program. Professor George W. Conoly, itinerant teacher trainer in agriculture at Florida A&M University, was an expert on NFA banquets and argued that the five objectives of the annual banquet were to (1) raise awareness about the NFA, (2) strengthen relations between the NFA and the public, (3) provide leadership training, (4) promote cooperation between chapter members, and (5) create a meaningful experience and social activity for the community. "If we accept the five objectives, then we must decide what . . . committees are used to work out different phases of the [banquet]," Conoly wrote. "The experience gained in cooperation will not only be beneficial on this occasion but will help develop the boys' ability to organize other cooperative activities in their communities." Indeed, this experience allowed local NFA chapter members to tailor their banquets in relation to their communities, keeping community needs at the forefront of the organization.[11]

To be sure, this brief look at the NFA's community scene is by no means exhaustive or complete. What has been shown is that the local NFA presence was driven by the careful advisement, guidance, and leadership of Black agriculture teachers. This presence demonstrated to rural Black people that vocational agriculture could be used to enhance their lives. Black farm boys were seen as the hope of their communities—future leaders who would pursue careers in agriculture not only to better themselves, their families, and their communities but to create a different world for generations to come. As I noted in the introduction of this book, Black girls in the New Homemakers of America were a part of this future, too, and often worked alongside local NFA chapters in community programming. But not all girls wanted to be homemakers. Some Black girls chose to study vocational agriculture at their high school, participating in local agricultural competitions organized by the NFA and related activities in their communities. In rare but notable instances, their contributions were formally recognized. One of the earliest documented examples is Katie Cobbs of Lincoln Academy in Kings Mountain, North Carolina, who studied vocational agriculture throughout all four years of high school. In 1939, she was awarded the honorary modern farmer degree at the North Carolina Association of the NFA state convention—an early and powerful reminder that Black girls also saw themselves reshaping their lives and the world through agriculture.[12]

Viewing the NFA through the lens of its community scene reveals how it made a lasting difference, creating meaningful, place-based opportunities—on and off the farm—for Black farm boys and their peers. As Cecil Strickland Sr. wrote in his book *New Farmers of America in Retrospect*, "The NFA was organized upon the philosophical foundation that young men taking vocational agriculture . . . should be given the opportunity to develop into capable rural leaders, developing their leadership skills, whereby they could better deal with the future problems of their communities and the people with whom they live." Examining the community scene directed by the Randolph NFA chapter results in a backstage view of how the NFA community scene translated this philosophical foundation in rural Black communities. The creation of the Randolph NFA chapter was instigated by the development of the Texas Association of the NFA (TXNFA), marking a turning point in the agricultural history of La Grange Colored High School and paving the way for the three eras of the Randolph NFA chapter.[13]

The Agricultural History of La Grange Colored High School

The agricultural history of La Grange Colored High School can be traced back to the educational foresight and groundbreaking work of Mr. Giles A. Randolph, often referred to as G. A. Randolph, who served as the school's principal and first agriculture teacher from 1910 to 1941. Born in the 1870s in Wharton County, Texas, Randolph graduated from PVAMU in the 1903–4 academic year with a bachelor's degree in education and taught in rural Black schools in Fayette County before assuming leadership over La Grange Colored High School. Randolph is credited with numerous contributions to the school, which include the revamping of the school's curriculum, the development of school sports and extracurricular activities, the construction of a new school building, and the expansion of community education programs. His curriculum in agriculture was part of the industrial and manual education area of the school and transformed the school's garden into a site for training in applied agricultural methods and sciences. The curriculum also involved home projects that allowed students to test concepts learned in class in the context of their own environments. Additional projects focused on how to use agriculture to enhance the vitality of rural Black communities through farm improvement methods and home economics.[14]

Principal Randolph's agriculture curriculum, in many ways, was likely informed by prominent Black agricultural scientist George Washington

Carver's research on the relationship between children and gardening in rural Black public schools. As director of the Tuskegee Agricultural Experiment Station, Carver published several research bulletins about this relationship, urging administrators, teachers, and schools to take seriously the use of gardens as a vehicle for agricultural and environmental education. In his June 1910 Tuskegee Agricultural Experiment Station Bulletin No. 18, *Nature Study and Gardening for Rural Schools*, Carver wrote that the purpose of these publications was to guide Black educators in the "awakening of a greater interest in practical nature lessons in the public schools . . . to bring before our young people in an attractive way a few of the cardinal principles of agriculture, with which nature study is synonymous." Carver concluded that gardening education in rural Black public schools reached beyond the school grounds, offering formal knowledge that students could use to aid in the development of their minds and communities. Such education represented "the only true method that leads up to a clear understanding of the fundamental principles which surround every branch of business in which we may engage. It also stimulates thought, investigation, and encourages originality." As if he were a disciple of Carver's, Randolph engineered a robust gardening component of the agriculture curriculum that transmitted this philosophy to rural Black students and their families whom the high school served.[15]

More importantly, Principal Randolph's Carver-inspired curriculum activated a new way of thinking about agriculture for the students. This new way of thinking positioned agriculture as much more than just the act of farming. It showed the students that agriculture was rooted in scientific principles that could be used to recalibrate rural Black communities and create new mechanisms for them to embrace rurality and thrive on the land. By the 1930s, as Principal Randolph worked to secure a new La Grange Colored High School campus, which opened in 1934, his curriculum in agriculture was complemented by the work of the La Grange Negro Farmers Saw Mill Cooperative and County Council and the Negro 4-H youth programming for Black farm boys and girls in the Fayette County Negro Extension Service. Both the council and the Negro 4-H were under the direction of Randolph's son, Emmett A. Randolph, a graduate of the high school who was hired in 1933 as the county's first Black extension agent. Randolph and his son worked closely together as the same boys who attended the school were also active in the programmatic efforts for Black farm boys in the county. Most of the boys more than likely had family members who participated in the council. One of the first projects the

Giles A. Randolph. From *A School with a Mission: Randolph High School* (La Grange Randolph Alumni Association, 2018). Courtesy of the Fayette Heritage Museum and Archives, Fayette Public Library, La Grange, TX.

Negro 4-H boys completed was the installation of subirrigation systems in community gardens that would promote efficient watering to aid the growth of plants. Principal Randolph remained committed to such projects until his retirement in 1941.[16]

In looking back at his thirty-one years of service to La Grange Colored High School, Randolph wrote that when he arrived at the school, "there were only three teachers employed, including the principal. . . . We have seen the scholastic population double itself, the number of teachers doubled. . . . Through it all, our main concern was to stress the need of spiritual values; to make good citizens of our boys and girls, teaching them how to live among and with neighbors." Randolph's legacy in the agricultural history of La Grange Colored High School was his devotion to raising up a new generation of rural Black leaders who would practice good citizenship in service of their professions and communities. As he stated upon his retirement, "We have carefully checked, and found that 80% of our 200 and more graduates are succeeding in their chosen fields of labor." For those graduates in the agricultural industry, the training at the high school provided an educational platform for them to be successful.[17]

Principal Randolph's educational platform, in many respects, also cultivated a path forward for the NFA to enter the agricultural history of La Grange Colored High School and begin building its community scene.

Randolph's successor, Mr. William M. Collins (known across public circles as W. M. Collins) would become the father of the NFA at the school as he was solely responsible for bringing the organization to the school as part of its newly developed comprehensive program in vocational agriculture. While it is unclear why Principal Randolph did not initiate an NFA chapter at the school, he couldn't have asked for a better heir to his legacy than Collins, who would also serve as the first formal vocational agriculture teacher at La Grange. Prior to his appointments at the school, Collins played a role in the creation of the TXNFA and was known for his work in vocational agriculture in rural Black communities. Such experiences allowed him to hit the ground running when he arrived at the school in July 1941.[18]

The Collins Era

W. M. Collins's main goal as principal and agriculture teacher was to expand the work of his predecessor, G. A. Randolph, and build an impressive educational and recreational program so that his students could learn and thrive. The heart of this program was his vision for a vocational agriculture department that would produce the next generation of Black farmers who would lead their communities. Born in 1908, Collins was raised on his family farm about forty miles north of La Grange in the Lee County town of Dime Box, Texas. Growing up on the farm instilled in him the importance of agriculture to family, community, and society. This experience likely inspired him to pursue higher education in agriculture. In 1935 he earned a bachelor's degree in general agriculture and in 1941 a master of science degree in agricultural education, both from PVAMU. But before he finished undergraduate studies, Collins began his career in 1933 as a part-time teacher at Sam Schwartz High School (the former Hempstead Negro High School) in Hempstead, Texas, the seat of Waller County and a border town of the university.[19]

At the time, Schwartz High School was the exemplary public school for Black agricultural education in Texas and served as the first site of the PVAMU School of Agriculture's vocational agriculture student teaching program, which began in 1926. The program was the dream of Mr. Lawrence A. Potts, who came to the university in 1925 and became the director of the PVAMU School of Agriculture in 1929. Potts, who earned his bachelor's degree in rural education from Iowa State University and his master of science degree in agriculture from Cornell University, was a role model for undergraduates like Collins, who was a student under his leadership. Collins was able to see firsthand how Potts transformed Schwartz High School into a testing site for the development of a new generation of Black agriculture teachers. These new teachers would not only teach the agricultural sciences but also complement their curriculum with activities such as livestock judging, farm management, field crop production, and animal science. Such activities gave birth to a statewide movement of Black farm boys studying vocational agriculture at the high school level under the banner of what Potts called the Progressive Farmers of Texas (PFT) organization, the precursor to the TXNFA.[20]

From 1926 to 1933, the PFT was administered through PVAMU and hosted the organization's annual state agricultural and farming contests. Potts was the convener of the contests and worked with faculty and staff in the PVAMU School of Agriculture to organize the agricultural competitions. Black farm boys looked forward to traveling to PVAMU each year because the PFT contests were, as one article in the April 1930 edition of the *Prairie View Standard* newspaper put it, "eye-openers of what the vocational teachers and students are doing and the effectiveness of their work. The knowledge of farm products by the students engaged in these contests heretofore gives unmistakable evidence not only of a better class of farmers, but also a better class of farms and farming conditions." As a student, Collins witnessed how the PFT annual contests profoundly reshaped Black agricultural education in Texas public schools and increased access to agricultural education for Black farm boys. The PFT competitions— along with the organization's design and structure—laid the groundwork for the creation of the New Farmers of Texas organization in 1933, signaling the PFT's alignment with the growing national idea of the NFA. In 1935, the New Farmers of Texas became the TXNFA. Said differently, the transition from the PFT to the TXNFA linked Black farm boys in Texas to a larger national network of peers devoted to ensuring the sustainability of Black farm life. At the same time, it also cultivated a critical space for Black vocational agriculture teachers in Texas to share skills with other teachers beyond the state and contribute to building the national NFA.[21]

Given his multiple points of exposure to the development of agricultural education in Black public high schools and the formative years of the TXNFA as a student in the PVAMU School of Agriculture, Collins was the ideal person to charter the Randolph NFA chapter. In addition to starting his teaching career at Schwartz High School, Collins had served as a principal at two high schools in Giddings, Texas, and in the dual roles of principal and vocational agriculture teacher at Schulenburg Colored High

School in southern Fayette County. While working in Schulenburg, Collins studied the implications of health conditions of Black households on agricultural education in the town as part of his master's thesis project. His project revealed that the high school's vocational agriculture department, in collaboration with its NFA chapter, could play a major role in enhancing the social, physical, and emotional health of Black communities. From 1936 to 1941, Collins led the Schulenburg NFA chapter to prominence across the state and was the architect of its local chapter band, which was the only one in the state at the time.[22]

Likely considering the success of Collins at Schulenburg Colored High School, the superintendent and board of education in La Grange recruited and appointed Collins to be the principal and vocational agriculture instructor at La Grange Colored High School. Building on the rich legacy of his predecessor, Principal Randolph, and his own experiences, Collins embedded himself in the Black community of La Grange, serving on the Fayette County Negro Health Committee, among other roles. Within a matter of months, he transformed the academic and social life of the school. In his role as principal, Collins commissioned the development of the school's first football team, pep squad, marching band, and school newspaper. He updated the equipment used by the school's championship basketball team and enhanced the track and field program that enabled La Grange Colored High School to win the 1942 state track meet in its Class B division. Collins relentlessly worked with the school district and the Black

William M. Collins. From *A School with a Mission: Randolph High School* (La Grange Randolph Alumni Association, 2018). Courtesy of the Fayette Heritage Museum and Archives, Fayette Public Library, La Grange, TX.

community of La Grange to raise funds to support these extracurricular activities that supplemented the school's academic program. Due to his early efforts that breathed new life into La Grange Colored High School, it continued to produce graduating classes where nearly 100 percent of the students entered college.[23]

As the vocational agriculture instructor, Collins initiated the school's first formal Department of Vocational Agriculture during the 1941–42 academic year. The department's curriculum was designed for both male and female students to understand general agriculture, from livestock management to food production. The department facilitated a student teacher training program in collaboration with PVAMU that enabled college students studying agricultural education to receive on-site training under the supervision of Collins. This student program prepared future Black agriculture teachers not only to teach the agricultural sciences and organize farm activities but also to charter and implement NFA chapters. The department served as the headquarters of the La Grange NFA, which was founded on September 14, 1941. From its inception, the La Grange NFA was destined to change the lives of Black farm boys and their communities. Students worked closely with Collins to codesign a broad program of work that would promote positive self-development among the students while simultaneously addressing the needs of their families, the school, and rural Black communities within and beyond La Grange. In many ways, this first program of work piloted a number of activities organized around three core areas: farming, rural community development and improvement, and organizational leadership.[24]

The early farming activities of the La Grange NFA exposed students to the way farm life could be an incubator for translating coursework in vocational agriculture to everyday practices surrounding livestock care and farm improvement. Three months after the founding of the La Grange NFA, the chapter sponsored its first Southern District Fat Stock Show at the Fayette County fairgrounds on January 1, 1942. Schools from thirteen counties that made up Area 3 of the TXNFA, the birthplace of the organization, participated in this district show. While there are no records available that provide detailed information about the stock show, the show was the La Grange NFA's first public appearance as a chapter at the area level, revealing that the chapter was able to create and operationalize a district-wide stock show that served as the first level of competition among NFA chapters. For many chapters, the district show was a litmus test to foreshadow how the NFA competition season would go. More importantly, the stock show set the stage for the formative years of the chapter that catapulted it to the NFA national arena.[25]

While the first year of the La Grange NFA was focused on district- and area-level contests, the second year of the chapter expanded its programming in farming activities. This expansion contributed to the La Grange NFA making its debut at the TXNFA state competition at PVAMU in February 1943. At the competition, the La Grange NFA won more awards—cash prizes—than any other chapter present. It won first place in tool identification and second place in saw sharpening. In egg judging, members took home first, second, and third place. In potato judging, they placed first and third. They finished in third place in poultry judging and sweep sharpening. In dairy cow judging, they were awarded third and fifth place. Norman Henderson, the first president of the La Grange NFA, was named the third-ranking student in the state. Such accolades at its first state meet positioned the La Grange NFA to be one of the greatest NFA chapters in the history of the TXNFA.[26]

What is even more noteworthy about the La Grange NFA's outstanding results at the 1943 TXNFA state judging contest at PVAMU is that the chapter had been operating for less than fourteen months. In comparison to other chapters that had been around since the 1930s, this impressive record set the La Grange NFA apart, and it was due to the influence and advice of Principal Collins. As a student reporter from La Grange Colored High School put it in the *La Grange Journal* when documenting the 1943 TXNFA state judging contest results, "It may be interesting to know that the school has had the agriculture work going on for 16 months. These boys had possibly 14 months of instruction in agriculture, under the guidance of Prof. W. M. Collins." But the 1943 TXNFA state meet was just the beginning for the La Grange NFA and Principal Collins.[27]

During the 1943–44 school year, Collins left the school temporarily to take over the position of teacher trainer in farm shops at PVAMU, where he supervised all agriculture shops in the state. When Collins returned, he came back with a sense of renewed energy and immediately started working with the La Grange NFA to plan its second livestock and poultry show, which was held in December 1944. As the La Grange NFA prepared for the show, which lasted two days, Principal Collins encouraged the community to support it. "We will be pleased to have the public—which includes everybody—to visit with the boys . . . to show you what they have tried to raise during the year," he stated in an interview about the livestock show with the *La Grange Journal.* "Your presence will encourage the boys, will give them new energy, and will cause them to put forth greater efforts." For Collins, as the interview reveals, the La Grange NFA community scene was an integral part of the high school and a key source of encouragement for Black farm boys in the NFA. He believed that community support would show the boys that they mattered and that their work was important.[28]

In 1946, La Grange Colored High School was renamed Randolph High School in honor of former Principal Randolph, and the La Grange NFA became the Randolph NFA. Although the chapter's name changed, community support for Black farm boys in the Randolph NFA continued and carried them all the way to the state fair of Texas and the national NFA spotlight. For instance, Randolph NFA member Milbrew Davis was one of five recipients of the prestigious TXNFA outstanding achievement award given out at the Texas State Fair of 1946 on Negro Achievement Day, the only day Black people were able to attend and participate in the fair. This award recognized one NFA member from each area who exhibited excellent farm and leadership skills in their chapter and area. That same year, Davis placed second place for his vocal solo in the music contest at the twelfth annual national NFA convention held at Southern University in Louisiana. To qualify for the national music contest, Davis won first place in vocal solo at the TXNFA state competition and the regional music contest at the Almot (Arkansas, Louisiana, Mississippi, Oklahoma, and Texas) regional NFA meeting. The accomplishments of Davis were part of a Randolph NFA dynasty that shaped the Collins era of the chapter.[29]

One year after the amazing accomplishments of Randolph NFA member Milbrew Davis, the Collins era of the chapter abruptly ended, in October 1947. Due to several internal conflicts at the school and district levels, Principal Collins was dismissed from the school by the La Grange school board due to undisclosed reasons that have not been corroborated. Nonetheless, he went on to obtain a doctorate degree in education from Cornell University and became a university professor and administrator. But his impact on the Randolph NFA chapter was solidified, and remnants of his work were seen through his successor, Mr. James C. Jackson Jr., who was locally known as J. C. Jackson. Four months after Principal Collins left Randolph High School, the roles of principal and vocational agriculture were separated, and Jackson was hired as the school's vocational agriculture teacher. In this role, as expected, he served as the advisor of the Randolph NFA chapter, ushering in the Jackson era of the chapter.[30]

The Jackson Era

At the annual Randolph NFA Father-Son Banquet in the school gymnasium on the evening of Saturday, May 5, 1951, J. C. Jackson delivered the keynote address. As attendees enjoyed a delicious locally sourced menu of barbecued farm-raised chicken, homemade potato salad, fresh string beans, and dinner rolls, Jackson stood before the crowd to speak. He chose the theme of "champions" for his address, alluding to the Randolph NFA chapter's reputation as the top producer of prize-winning livestock in NFA Area 3, among numerous other accolades in the region and the state. His speech included a discussion of the chapter's "recipe" for raising such livestock. First, you have to select a good animal, Jackson declared. "Second, have a good feeding program, and third, use good management. With all of these, will come out a good animal." Transposing this logic to producing Black farm boys who were proven winners, he continued: "First, get a good boy; second, feed him the nutrients required for sound judgment." Then he looked directly at the boys in attendance: "Third, it is your responsibility to manage yourself properly by using the knowledge you get in school, and you will be a champion in your own right." Jackson's address was followed by the reading of the chapter's 1950–51 accomplishments, which included two historic moments when five Randolph NFA members earned the NFA improved farmer degree, the first time in the history of the chapter, and the chapter's recognition as the best chapter of Area 3.[31]

Jackson's address, as well as the unprecedented successes of the Randolph NFA chapter during the 1950–51 academic year, provides the necessary entry point for understanding who he was as an agriculture teacher and his era as advisor to the chapter. Born in 1920 in the Matagorda County, Texas, city and seat of Bay City, Jackson was a World War II veteran and two-time graduate of PVAMU's School of Agriculture, earning a bachelor of science degree in agriculture in 1948 and a master of science degree in agricultural education, with a minor in agricultural economics, in 1954 from the university. His era as advisor of the Randolph NFA chapter began when he launched his career at the school on February 1, 1948, just one day after he received his undergraduate degree. For eleven years, Mr. Jackson worked with Black farm boys in the Randolph NFA chapter to realize their full potential through agriculture, making him the longest-serving NFA advisor in the history of the local chapter. He was also deeply embedded in Black farming communities in the La Grange area, providing adult education classes for Black farmers to discuss agricultural topics

James C. Jackson (*fourth from left*) and Randolph NFA members holding NFA contest winning banners, 1958. From *A School with a Mission: Randolph High School* (La Grange Randolph Alumni Association, 2018). Courtesy of the Fayette Heritage Museum and Archives, Fayette Public Library, La Grange, TX.

and exchange knowledge on best practices on the farm. Jackson's master's thesis research, which he conducted while advising the Randolph NFA, emerged out of these experiences and focused on the marketing practices of Black farmers in La Grange and surrounding rural Black communities in Fayette County.[32]

The formative years of Jackson's tenure as advisor of the Randolph NFA chapter were shaped by various efforts surrounding the TXNFA basketball league, father-son banquets, co-programming with the Randolph New Homemakers of America chapter, multimedia learning opportunities, and active involvement in contests at all levels within and beyond the NFA. Through these efforts, especially the contests, the Randolph NFA chapter maintained a statewide reputation as a force to be reckoned with in the TXNFA, in that it always took home a prize. In fact, a number of judges who witnessed the Randolph NFA chapter under Jackson's direction agreed with a judge from PVAMU who saw the chapter at an Area 3 competition and commented that in "all the years of my directing the contest, I have never seen such a smooth operating chapter." To be sure, the posture and cadence of Randolph NFA members were inextricably linked to Jackson's discipline, serious demeanor, and competitive agricultural spirit. As one of his former students in the Randolph NFA put it: "Mr. Jackson was strict and serious about his teaching, and he was straightforward."

Jackson's straightforwardness challenged the Randolph NFA chapter to perform at optimal capacity when engaging in competition.[33]

For instance, Jackson placed an emphasis on contests focusing on the production of high-quality animals that would be entered into livestock shows and fairs. Every semester, Randolph NFA members would participate in these activities as a central part of their practical training in agricultural education. Jackson taught them how to raise and manage animals, providing the proper care for them to grow and then be put on display at contests and shows. In his study on the educative nature of livestock shows and fairs, Hoover Carden, the first administrator of the PVAMU Cooperative Extension Program, argued that these activities should be viewed as educational and social "institutions" that would enhance the creative ability of students and community participants. As educational institutions, Carden wrote that livestock shows and fairs "provide a concentrated survey of agriculture activity . . . setting forth a vast number of visual educational stimuli." Such stimuli exposed attendees to inspirational content needed to engage in the process of "learning by observation," which allowed them to make connections between various farm experiences that could help improve agricultural competency and methods. As social institutions, livestock shows and fairs were configured as spaces for education, entertainment, and interpersonal interactions that would benefit all.[34]

In many respects, Carden's ideas about livestock shows and fairs reverberated through Jackson's vision for the Randolph NFA chapter. In addition to participating in such activities, Black farm boys who made up the chapter also organized them as part of the Randolph NFA's community scene, offering educational content for Black agriculture students and a vital social space for community members to support and participate in. Between 1948 and 1959, local newspapers in La Grange and regional media outlets provided substantial coverage of the chapter's participation in livestock shows and fairs, recording the Randolph NFA's noteworthy prizes obtained at these events. While it is impossible to document this vast record in this section, at least three achievements in 1955 alone illustrate the high honors that the Randolph NFA chapter received at competitions with the support of Jackson and the members' communities. First, the Randolph NFA participated in the annual PVAMU Livestock Exposition, where members took home two first-place and three second-place prizes. Second, with the aid of La Grange State Bank, the chapter was able to enter several projects in the coveted swine exhibits at the state fair, taking home second, third, and ninth places in one category, along with ninth place in another. Third, freshman Randolph NFA member Charles

Randolph represented the chapter at the invitational Charles Pfizer and Company, Inc. National Livestock and Poultry Judging Contest, where he won third place, receiving a cash award, a congratulatory letter, and a certificate of excellence.[35]

In looking back at the Randolph NFA chapter's record of achievements at livestock shows and fairs, 1955 was an exemplary moment for the group, but the climax of its Jackson era occurred in 1958 and 1959 at the San Antonio Livestock Show, one of the largest shows in Texas. The show was segregated at the time, and the Randolph NFA participated only in the Negro Boys Division, which showcased the work of Black farm boys across the state. At the 1958 show, sophomore Manor Thomas made history by being the first Randolph NFA member to produce the Grand Champion hog, the highest placing livestock entry of the show. Thomas's hog was bought for $1,000 by San Antonio's Pearl Brewing Company and catapulted the chapter into a new dimension of accomplishments. One year later, in the 1959 show, the Randolph NFA exceeded its previous record. With financial assistance from La Grange State Bank and First National Bank, sophomore Lester Ray Moore's hog was awarded Grand Champion, which sold at $1,100, and sophomore Billy Ray East took home the Reserve Grand Champion award, the second-highest placing entry, which was sold at $500. Other members of the chapter took home prizes as well, and collectively the Randolph NFA profited $2,258.24 at the 1959 show.[36]

On February 20, 1959, the local newspaper the *Fayette County Record* ran a front-page story on the Randolph NFA under the headline "Randolph Scores High: Lad Takes Big S.A. Prize." In the article, the reporter highlighted the chapter's impressive victories at the San Antonio Livestock Show and argued that the Randolph NFA's two-year winning streak of Grand Champion honors at the show was "unusual" in that the chapter was setting a precedent. This unusual occurrence was due, in part, to the work of Jackson and the community scene of the Randolph NFA. "Under the advice of the Ag. Instructor J. C. Jackson Jr.," the reporter wrote, "the big winners selected, fed, and managed" the livestock toward these "big wins." The article concluded with a special thanks to key actors in the Randolph NFA's community scene: "The Randolph NFA chapter is grateful to the parents for the support given [to] . . . the Ag boys, making their achievements possible." Indeed, Black farm boys in the Randolph NFA chapter were an extension of their families; their parents made up a close-knit network of support embedded within the chapter's community scene, and Mr. Jackson was the nucleus.[37]

Less than two months after making the front page of the *Fayette County Record*, the Randolph NFA staged its 1959 Father-Son Banquet to commemorate its tremendous accomplishments during the 1958–59 academic year. While guests enjoyed the festivities and celebrated the Black farm boys for all their hard work, none of them were aware that this would be Jackson's final banquet with the Randolph NFA. A few weeks later, Jackson's contract was not renewed due to several disagreements between him and Randolph High School's leadership surrounding the direction of the Randolph vocational agriculture department, and in the fall of 1959, he began working as the agriculture teacher at Ralph J. Bunche High School in Brookshire, about one hour east of La Grange. Jackson's departure was likely met with mixed feelings by the Black farm boys who would be returning to the chapter in the fall and were looking forward to being under his guidance. For eleven years, Jackson devoted his life to building the Randolph NFA chapter and was a vital part of its community scene. His reputation in vocational agriculture spoke for itself, and it would take a special person to replace him. That person would end up being Mr. Lorenza Crosby Jr., a recent college graduate who was also a fellow alumnus of the PVAMU School of Agriculture. While Crosby knew that he would have big shoes to fill, he was ready for the challenge, ushering in a new era and outlook for the Randolph NFA.[38]

The Crosby Era

The Randolph NFA chapter suffered a great loss with J. C. Jackson's departure from the school. But the decision to recruit Lorenza Crosby Jr. as his replacement breathed new life into the Black farm boys at the school. Under the guidance of W. M. Collins and J. C. Jackson, the Randolph NFA had focused mostly on producing the next generation of Black farmers through agricultural activities such as livestock shows and fairs. Crosby saw the value of this approach but was also mindful of how the agricultural economy and industry of the nation in the late 1950s were rapidly becoming mechanized, which would require the use of farm machinery and related technology. The 1960s agri-tech boom, which replaced physical labor in agriculture with machinery and chemicals, was brought about by this change in the US agricultural industry. This transformation was a crucial part of what historian Valerie Grim has described as the first phase of "Black farmers' quest for agribusiness participation" from 1945 to 1970. Grim writes that this phase "considers how African American farmers responded to the changing structure of agriculture and the growth of agribusiness. During this time . . . tractors, machines, and other equipment replaced farm labor, and pesticides, hybrid seeds, and other processed inputs greatly increased yields and tied farmers to industrial agriculture." Recognizing this, Crosby extended the Randolph NFA's program of work to include a strong focus on farm mechanics, illuminating a new pathway for Black farm boys surrounding the economic and technological dimensions of agricultural production in rural Black communities.[39]

Born in 1934 in the rural East Texas town of Harleton, located about fifteen miles northwest of Marshall in Harrison County, Lorenza Crosby was raised on his family farm where he first became interested in agricultural mechanics. His grandfather John Crosby, whom he described as "Mr. Magnificent," was a prominent figure in their community and established several successful agribusinesses through an agriculture shop that provided technical assistance to Black farmers. As Crosby put it, "My granddad, John Crosby, was a special fellow. I don't know where he got his know-how, but he could run a cotton gin or a sawmill. He had a shop with an old forge where he could bend metal and weld things together by heating and beating the pieces. He had a truck, cattle, and a tractor." John Crosby's shop was ahead of its time in that he had several agricultural machines that would gin cotton, grind corn, and cut lumber for Black farming communities. It was at this shop that Crosby was first exposed to farm mechanics, which set him on a path toward the PVAMU School of Agriculture, where he was awarded the prestigious Jesse Jones Agricultural Scholarship and participated in the university's Army Reserve Officers' Training Corps program. While his mother, Bertha Crosby, was an educator who instilled in him at an early age the importance of education, his interest in becoming an agriculture teacher was solidified through his participation in the collegiate NFA chapter at PVAMU, which served as a pipeline for Black agriculture teachers.[40]

After graduating from PVAMU in 1956, Crosby served three years in the US military to fulfill his Army ROTC obligation and then began his career in 1959 at Randolph High School. His first year as the advisor of the Randolph NFA was difficult, as most of his senior students wanted to focus only on raising livestock for shows and fairs. Crosby was willing to work with them on these projects, but he wanted to diversify their agricultural portfolio to include the development of skills in farm mechanics that would allow them to repair tractors, fix engines, install electricity, and build farm infrastructure, among other things. "I was more mechanical, and so I went with small engines and carpentry, electricity, and that kind of thing, which was of more value to the kids . . . and their whole families," Crosby remarked when discussing his first year. He wanted to create what he called a "lifetime program" for the Randolph NFA, where "we could build screen doors, steps, furniture." To build out this lifetime program, Crosby worked with Texas Education Agency specialists in ag mechanics through adult education to become an expert in the area and enhance his classes, making him better prepared to train the students. By the end of the 1959–60 academic year, Crosby's lifetime program was embraced by Randolph NFA members as they saw the benefits of such skills in their communities.[41]

In Crosby's eyes, his lifetime program for the Randolph NFA would empower Black farm boys to lead their communities as the agricultural economy of the nation changed, and he believed there would be a need for competent professionals in farm mechanics who would service new

Group picture of Randolph NFA with Lorenza Crosby (*third from left*) beside Principal S. L. Hatch (*in suit*). Courtesy of the Lorenza and Myrtle Crosby Collection, La Grange, TX.

Lorenza Crosby (*center*) and two Randolph NFA members working on farm machinery. Courtesy of the Lorenza and Myrtle Crosby Collection, La Grange, TX.

agricultural machines. Such service would require various forms of training in skills such as welding, equipment maintenance, mechanical troubleshooting, farm power, agricultural engineering, and related topics. Through these topics, Crosby transformed the school's agriculture shop and, later, vocational agriculture building into an active laboratory for Black farm boys to learn how to safely operate farm machinery, know how to perform diagnostic tests on the machinery and equipment, study operator service manuals, understand what machinery and equipment were needed based on farm type and field condition, and keep meticulous maintenance records regarding repairs of equipment, among many other things. A survey of projects conducted under the advisement of Crosby included the challenging tractor project that required Randolph NFA members to take a tractor engine apart and rebuild it. Another project required the members to construct quality feeders for livestock using recycled marine plywood. These feeders would then be delivered to Black farms around the area for use; the students also used them to feed their own animals.[42]

Beyond the farm gate, Black farm boys in the Randolph NFA were able to use the skills learned in farm mechanics to complete community-based projects that were unrelated to agricultural production. One of the most important community-based projects they completed was in collaboration with a local Black church. As the "greatest social institution" in Black life, borrowing the words of sociologist W. E. B. Du Bois, the Black church played a major role in rural Black communities across the South and especially in the vitality of the Randolph NFA, since Crosby and many of the members were religious. The Randolph NFA's local Black church project

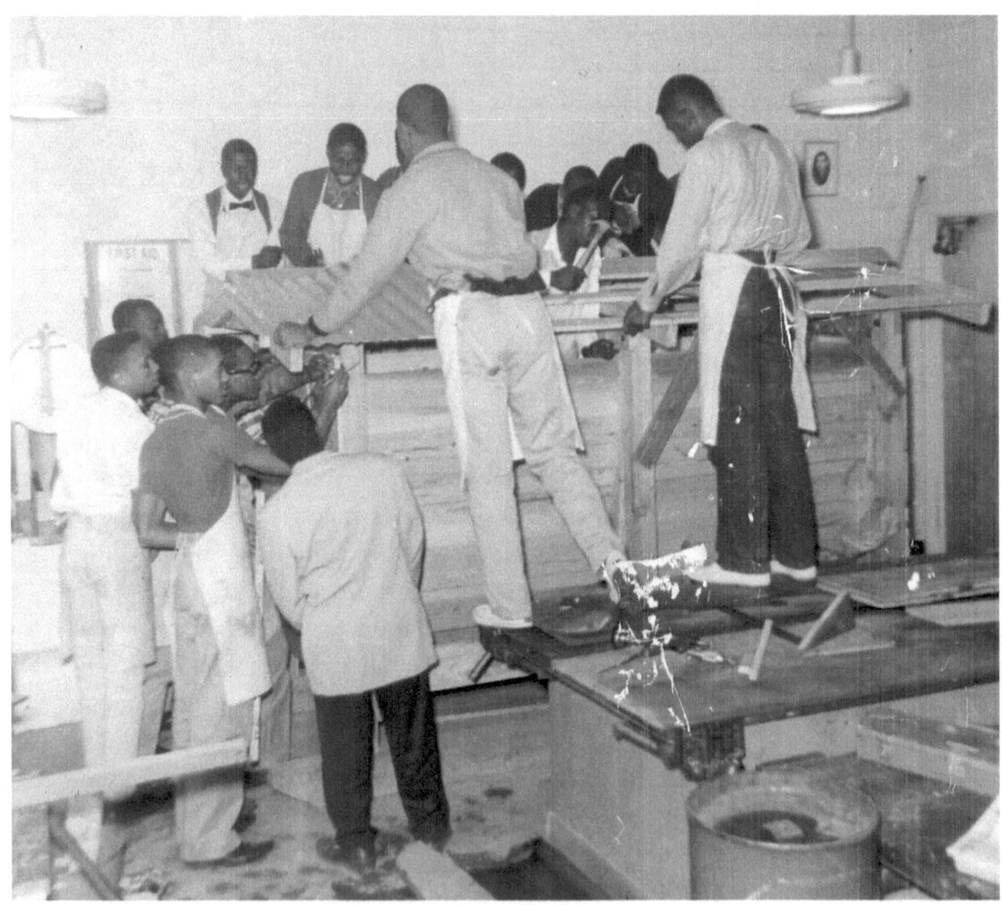

Randolph NFA members building an animal feeder. Courtesy of the Lorenza and Myrtle Crosby Collection, La Grange, TX.

was designed to address issues with the external and internal physical infrastructure of the building. Externally, the church was in dire need of steps for its members to safely enter the building, so the Randolph NFA constructed a new set of concrete steps for the church. Internally, the church needed new pews for members to comfortably worship on, so the Randolph NFA built new pews for the congregation. Such upgrades to the church enabled it to fulfill its role as a critical social institution for its rural Black membership.[43]

Traditional aspects of the Randolph NFA were also essential to Crosby's lifetime program. For example, the chapter's music program was a major component of the community scene. Previous eras included music, but Crosby repositioned it at the forefront. His wife, Myrtle, led the program that produced the award-winning Randolph NFA quartet that participated in contests. According to the 1963 edition of the *Guide for New Farmers of America*, the stated purpose of NFA quartet groups was "to develop a greater appreciation for good music, including the Negro spirituals. It should stimulate NFA members to sing and develop desirable musical talent among farm boys." The NFA talent contests were "designed to encourage the use of desirable entertainment and develop musical ability in NFA members." For Myrtle Crosby, who was a teacher in the Randolph Junior High School music program, the opportunity to work with the Randolph NFA quartet was a delight. While she always traveled as co-chaperone with her husband on NFA trips, she took center stage when it came to the Randolph NFA quartet. "It was first tenor, second tenor, baritone, and bass, four-part harmony," Mrs. Crosby remembered as she discussed the NFA quartet, "and they would be useful for other programs around the school," especially at the annual father-son banquets. Mrs. Crosby's work with the Randolph NFA quartet garnered the group multiple prizes, including first place in the TXNFA's southern district in 1962 and 1963, third place in the same area in 1960 and 1961, and fourth place in the state in 1962.[44]

Another traditional aspect of Mr. Crosby's Randolph NFA program was the annual Randolph NFA Livestock and Poultry Show and Sale at the Fayette County Fairgrounds. This event was a huge success and served as a major social activity in the lives of rural Black people in Fayette County and the surrounding areas. Each year, hundreds of folks would come out to enjoy locally grown or raised food, such as barbecued chicken, and purchase quality livestock raised by the Randolph NFA in support of the community and the competitions. Crosby invited a panel of judges from PVAMU to oversee the competition, including the renowned Black veterinarian and professor of animal science Dr. Alfred N. Poindexter Jr. After the livestock and poultry were judged, they would be auctioned off and purchased by local meat markets, farmers, and community members. In addition to the Randolph NFA Livestock and Poultry Show and Sale, the chapter worked with Crosby to sponsor a short course on various topics and issues that were directly related to local farmers in the area. During the 1964–65 academic year, this adult education course consisted of four evening classes over one week and was held in the Randolph High School vocational agriculture building. Instructors were representatives from the vocational agriculture division of the Texas Education Agency, and upon successful completion of the course, farmers would be given certificates.[45]

Looking back on the Crosby era of the Randolph NFA, La Grange resident and former Crosby student Jeff Kelly recalled, "Mr. Crosby was straight up, he didn't mess around, he was the real deal, and my parents knew him so they trusted him, all the Black people in my neighborhood trusted him, and saw him as being a good role model." While under the guidance of Crosby, Kelly continued, "I learned a few things that I still use in my home today, how to repair some stuff, work with electricity . . . wiring, carpentry, welding . . . how to work together, we learned some things that stay with you forever." Kelly's words capture the essence of Crosby's efforts during his time as the advisor of the Randolph NFA. As each year passed, Crosby worked diligently to refine the Randolph NFA program and improve the lives of Black farm boys, providing them with the skills to enhance their communities. He had inherited a Randolph NFA chapter that was mostly focused on livestock shows and fairs—activities designed to build a generation of farm boys who would become farmers—but recognized the shift in the agricultural economy of the nation in the 1960s and decided to lead the Randolph NFA in a different direction. While he worked with the boys to keep their tradition of livestock and fairs alive, Crosby also challenged them to think differently about agriculture as it related to careers through the lens of agricultural mechanics.[46]

What Lorenza Crosby didn't know when he started at Randolph High School in 1959, however, was that he would be the last agriculture teacher and NFA advisor in the histories of the school and the national NFA. But when he traveled to the annual Black agriculture teachers' meeting at PVAMU in the summer of 1964, he knew that the end was near. That summer, President Lyndon B. Johnson signed the landmark Civil Rights Act, prohibiting segregation and discrimination based on race in public facilities, including schools. While the *Brown v. Board of Education* ruling

Group picture (Lorenza Crosby, first row on steps, third from left) from the 1964 Texas state meeting of Black vocational agriculture teachers, Prairie View A&M University. Courtesy of the Lorenza and Myrtle Crosby Collection, La Grange, TX.

in 1954 had outlawed segregation in public schools, the Civil Rights Act produced a federal mandate that legally enforced the integration of public schools, further prohibiting the extension of federal funds to segregated public school systems and school-related activities based on race. Such consequences pressured school districts, particularly in the South, to integrate.[47]

This sociopolitical context was the backdrop of the summer 1964 meeting at PVAMU. Crosby vividly remembered being in a large room on the campus, talking with other teachers about integration, when Dr. Ernest M. Norris, national NFA executive secretary and head of the Department of Agricultural Education, stood to address the teachers. As he started his discussion about the coming 1964–65 school year for Black agriculture teachers, Dr. Norris began to cry. As Crosby put it, in retrospect, "We were at what would be one of our last Black agriculture teachers meeting, and Dr. E. M. Norris stood to address the meeting, and he cried— openly wept. That moment was a signal, in his wisdom, coming from him, of troubled times ahead, very difficult times. And he was right. . . . He was trying to prepare us for it." Dr. Norris explained to the teachers the implications of the federal mandate on both the Black public high schools and, by extension, the national NFA. Integration would lead to the closing of all segregated Black public high schools, with the students being required to attend the previously all-white high schools. The national NFA, due to its status under the US Office of Education, would have to cease to exist at all levels and merge with the Future Farmers of America organization. While the NFA in New Jersey had already disbanded, and six state associations had already merged with their state FFA associations, Texas and the remaining ten states had not.[48]

As Dr. Norris's address ended, the room fell silent, and the tone of the meeting dramatically shifted. One year later, everything that Dr. Norris mentioned in his 1964 address was beginning to be made real in the lives of Black agriculture teachers in Texas. In May 1965, Crosby was notified that Randolph High School would close after graduation that year and would be converted into La Grange Junior High School. This also meant that the Crosby era of the Randolph NFA was over and the twenty-four-year existence of the chapter had come to a close. In recounting his feelings during that moment of his life, Crosby remarked, "To see the NFA destroyed still kind of hurts." The remaining Randolph High School students would attend La Grange High School that fall, and Randolph NFA members would now be members of the La Grange Future Farmers of America. While most of the Black agriculture teachers lost their jobs to white teachers, as the vocational agriculture division of public school districts could not accommodate two agriculture teachers, Crosby was fortunate to be hired as the assistant agriculture teacher at La Grange High School, working under the longtime white agriculture teacher there. In a few short years, he would become the head agriculture teacher at the school and make history in its FFA.[49]

The Visionary Thinking of Black Agriculture Teachers

This chapter canvassed the community scene of the Randolph NFA through the lens of three eras of Black agriculture teachers: William M. Collins, James C. Jackson Jr., and Lorenza Crosby Jr. The chapter focused on the dynamic ways these men used agricultural education as a foundation to support the dreams and aspirations of Black farm boys who participated in the NFA. Each era of the Randolph NFA emerged out of the needs of Black farm boys and the visionary thinking of the advisor at the time, weaving together agricultural training and community development. By examining the three eras of the Randolph NFA, we gain a deeper understanding of the inner workings of the NFA at the local level. With over one thousand chapters nationwide, each with its own unique community scene, it is clear that Black agriculture teachers were crucial in bridging the gaps between Black farm boys, agricultural education, and their communities. These men dedicated their lives to empowering Black youth in agriculture and are the unsung heroes of the NFA. But their devotion to the NFA was lost, as were their voices, when the NFA was acquired by the FFA in 1965.

As the story of the Randolph NFA goes, the NFA's acquisition by the FFA was instigated by national integration efforts that trickled down to La Grange, offering us a glimpse into how this crucial moment in the history of the NFA played out in a single NFA chapter. Integration also contributed to the closing of Randolph High School, which also paved the way for the eventual disappearance of the NFA from the grassroots level. While Lorenza Crosby's position as one of the few Black agriculture teachers survived the disappearance, many of his peers's jobs—in Texas and beyond—did not survive integration, and they were forced to abandon their commitment to training Black farm boys and establish new careers. Roughly five months after the closing of Randolph High School and the disbandment of its NFA chapter, the national NFA disappeared in October 1965. As Crosby settled into his new role as assistant agriculture teacher at La Grange High School, the NFA was now a distant memory and source of grief. In a matter of months, as integration reached every local NFA chapter across the rural South, the NFA's community scenes ceased to exist.

In keeping with this kind of thinking, this chapter serves as a prelude to the disappearance of the NFA. From the view of community scenes, integration was the main culprit in this part of the NFA's story. But when zooming out from the scenes, integration was just the tipping point that sealed the fate of the NFA. For years leading up to that moment, national representatives of the NFA were well aware that officials in the US Office of Education wanted the NFA to surrender its identity and join forces with the FFA, yet they strived to uphold the legacy and values of the organization. The next chapter shifts back to the national story of the NFA and jumps into the narratives surrounding the end of the NFA's history. This shift brings into focus the myriad variables that were used to put a line through the decades of blood, sweat, and tears that Black farm boys, Black agriculture teachers, and national representatives put into the development of the NFA. The end of the NFA's story was not one of an organization's downfall or some failure on the part of the NFA; it was the result of a set of racialized performances and power struggles that manufactured particular conditions and complexities that redesigned the NFA, making it susceptible to being erased from the American memory.

1965

The Mysterious Disappearance of the NFA

Please be reminded that the spirit of the New Farmers of America does not die here today. Rather, we awake into the dawn of a new day. Together we walk into dawn as Future Farmers and toward a fuller realization of our educational aim and purposes. . . . May this occasion prove to be an additional stone to be used in building a stronger foundation in agriculture for the future of our great country—America the Beautiful.

—**Adolphus D. Pinson,** 1964–65 national NFA president

Thirty years of service; thirty years of developing agricultural leadership, cooperation, citizenship, and patriotism among young men in the New Farmers of America Organization was now history. The organization truly strengthened the confidence of young men in themselves and their work. . . . The New Farmers of America Organization left a great legacy to be forever remembered by all those who were affiliated.

—**Cecil Strickland Sr.,** 1955–56 national NFA president

On the evening of Wednesday, October 13, 1965, the New Farmers of America disappeared without a trace. By then, the NFA was the largest organized Black youth farm organization in the world, boasting an active membership of over fifty-five thousand Black farm boys. Around fifty of those boys attended the October 1965 national convention of the majority-white Future Farmers of America—known today as the National FFA Organization—in Kansas City, Missouri. At the convention, a ceremony took place to confirm the July 1, 1965, decision to merge the NFA and FFA due to federal regulations around public education in the Civil Rights Act of 1964. The ceremony required Adolphus Pinson of Texas, the NFA's last president, to surrender NFA artifacts and financial records to FFA President Kenneth Kennedy.[1]

As the lights went up, President Pinson appeared on stage in his black and old gold NFA jacket. This jacket—made up of durable twelve-ounce water-repellent vat-dyed black corduroy, with Swiss-embroidered NFA

National NFA President Adolphus Pinson speaking at the NFA-FFA merger ceremony, 1965. Courtesy of the National FFA Organization Records, 1916–2008 (Mss 035), RLSCA.

Pinson (*right*) giving NFA documents to National FFA President Kenneth Kennedy at the NFA-FFA merger ceremony, 1965. Courtesy of the New Farmers of America Records, 1929–1965 (Mss 059), RLSCA.

emblems in full color, on the front and back, including state and chapter unit designations and the NFA member's name—had served as the visual representation of the organization's unifying identity. For decades, NFA members proudly wore this jacket at school, community events, judging contests, conventions, and related events to publicly acknowledge and declare to the world their unabashed devotion to the organization. Therefore, as Pinson stood on that stage, he was still sending this message to the world as he began his remarks: "To me this occasion is momentous. . . . In this merging of the New Farmers of America with the FFA, we are pleased to bring into the folds of the Future Farmers more than 50,000 students of vocational agriculture." President Pinson concluded: "Please be reminded that the spirit of the New Farmers of America does not die here today. Rather, we awake into the dawn of a new day." With these words, moving off-stage, President Pinson gave the NFA national charter and the permanent record of NFA officers to FFA President Kennedy, signaling the next part of the ceremony.[2]

In many respects, the ceremony was deeply ritualistic and represented the final scene of the NFA. Pinson returned to center stage following a number of statements and the transfer of other NFA relics. He then removed his NFA jacket and handed it to Kennedy, stating, "You asked that my NFA jacket be presented along with the other NFA symbols. I've worn this jacket proudly, and I'm pleased to present it to you for the FFA archives." In return, Kennedy approached Pinson and presented him with a blue and gold FFA jacket. As he helped Pinson put on the jacket, he commented on the NFA garment: "Adolphus, this jacket, along with the other NFA symbols, so nicely presented, will occupy a prominent place in the FFA Archives. . . . The exchanging of this NFA jacket for the FFA jacket by you, the last NFA President, symbolizes the joining together [of] all students of vocational agriculture into one great organization." Kennedy concluded: "We must all work together to develop occupational competency, agricultural leadership, cooperation, and citizenship." After making this last declaration, Kennedy and Pinson shook hands at the edge of the stage, the FFA band started playing, and the NFA vanished into thin air.[3]

Pinson (*right*) giving his NFA jacket to Kennedy at NFA-FFA merger ceremony, 1965. Courtesy of the National FFA Organization Records, 1916–2008 (Mss 035), RLSCA.

For the last sixty years, the "pageantry of the merger," borrowing the words of Cecil Strickland of Texas, the 1955–56 national NFA president and professor, has been played on a loop. This loop reinforces the idea that the acquisition of the NFA by the FFA was a "merger," severely mischaracterizing the dramatic conditions and complexities that led to the grand performance at the 1965 FFA convention. This mischaracterization distorts the end of the NFA's story and has been used to support a narrative of progress in relation to the struggle for civil rights and the full desegregation of the FFA. This narrative suggests that the symbolic moment of the NFA's absorption by the FFA was an event that represented the climax of a three-year conversation between the organizations that led to the restructuring of the racial makeup of the FFA. This narrative is encountered every time a person learns of the history of the NFA or the FFA, even in passing, marking the end of the NFA's historical timeline and a watershed moment in the history of the FFA. Such encounters erase the process that led to the final years of the NFA, producing "a particular bundle of silences," as anthropologist Michel-Rolph Trouillot would say, surrounding the terminal phase of the NFA. The silences in this part of the story of the NFA perpetuate the idea that the "merger" was an isolated event rather than a dynamic process. Consequently, "the operation required to deconstruct these silences will vary accordingly," as Trouillot put it.[4]

Building on Trouillot's logic, this chapter rejects the idea of a "merger" between the NFA and the FFA. It attempts to decipher and retrace the dynamic process that led to what I call the mysterious disappearance of the NFA. By definition, a mysterious disappearance is the loss of something under unknown or puzzling circumstances that are difficult to explain or understand. Indeed, it is hard to explain the end of the NFA's story as there are so many unanswered questions, and those who would be able to tell this part of the story are no longer with us. Put differently, the case of the NFA's final moment has gone cold. What is clear, though, is that the NFA's disappearance was instigated by a head-on collision between conflicting notions of power as conceptualized by the NFA and the FFA. For the NFA, power in the pursuit of agricultural education was a form of Black power. In their book *Black Power*, activist Kwame Ture (formerly known as Stokely Carmichael) and Charles V. Hamilton define Black power as the ability of Black people to define themselves in society, even if it means that society will need to be completely transformed or reconstructed in order for these terms to be accepted. The primary objective of Black power, historian Ashley Farmer writes, is "to overturn existing structures and cultures and replace them with black-centered ones," emphasizing Black self-reliance and self-determination.[5]

In contrast, the FFA—in relation to the Agricultural Education Service of the US Office of Education—envisioned agricultural education through the prism of paternalistic power in the hands of white men. Here, public policy researcher Alison Conrad's definition of paternalism is helpful. Conrad writes that "paternalism involves interfering in an individual's or community's ability or opportunity to choose and make decisions. It has the objective of improving the welfare of individuals or communities and involves making decisions without the consent of the individuals or communities concerned." As this chapter will show, the paternalistic power of the FFA undermined the Black power of the NFA, making it susceptible to being acquired. Such susceptibility was shaped by what bell hooks calls the "politics of domination": a complex system of power struggles that produces and upholds racial hierarchies and institutions based on the beliefs that white people are superior to Black people.[6]

Rather than be exhaustive in detailing every element that led to the NFA's mysterious disappearance, this chapter jumps right into the action surrounding the onset of intense power struggles between the NFA and FFA. Questions of race, organizational leadership, governance, and legal compliance are woven into the fabric of these struggles. Moving chronologically, the chapter maps these questions along the contours of the historical timeline of the NFA between 1941 and 1965, revealing a montage of episodes that, when viewed together, clarify the perplexing circumstances surrounding the last days of the NFA.

1941

In the early months of 1941, the national NFA leadership began planning the seventh annual NFA convention to be held August 17–20 at Florida A&M University. The theme of the convention was "Promoting Greater Defense Through Health" and focused on the NFA's efforts in World War II. While NFA leaders planned to welcome over five hundred Black farm boys to the convention, who represented over one thousand chapters, they also worried about the organization's future. Since its founding in 1935, the NFA had successfully operated outside the AES-USOE. As chapter 1 hinted at, the only stipulations were that the NFA would be considered FFA's counterpart and would be required to work with Dr. H. O. Sargent, the white federal agent for Negroes and Special Groups in the

AES-USOE, to administer programs and access limited federal funds for travel expenses related to NFA activities. Upon Dr. Sargent's death in 1936, the AES-USOE appointed another white man, W. N. Elam of Texas, as his successor. This decision angered NFA leaders, as they had strongly petitioned for Sargent's replacement to be a Black man who understood the Black experience in agriculture. Nonetheless, the NFA's location outside the AES-USOE allowed it to remain independent of government oversight and controlled by Black agricultural leaders at 1890 land grant institutions. By 1941, however, considerable rumors circulated around "legalizing" the NFA as part of the AES-USOE. Put differently, the white male leaders of the AES-USOE wanted to reposition the NFA under their administrative control, undermining the NFA's all-Black leadership.[7]

What is analytically fascinating about the discussions around "legalizing" the NFA is that the national advisor of the FFA was also legally designated as the head of the AES-USOE. This agreement was brought into law in 1930 when the US Federal Board of Vocational Education—which was created by the Smith-Hughes Act of 1917—made a ruling that the AES-USOE would assume administrative control and leadership of the national FFA. The ruling, among other things, specified that the national FFA advisor would serve as the chief of the AES-USOE, the FFA's national executive secretary would be a member of his staff, and the FFA headquarters would be in Washington. For twenty years, this arrangement continued until it was formalized in 1950 under Public Law 81-740, which granted the FFA a public charter. Such administrative power, exerted by the FFA under the auspices of the AES-USOE, was met with resistance from NFA leaders. They understood how this relationship could impact them, creating the perfect storm for the FFA and AES-USOE to possibly make a move to establish a legal foundation to subsume the NFA under their authority.[8]

This perfect storm of administrative power blew the NFA's way on the night of August 16, 1941, when NFA leaders were summoned to a special meeting with AES-USOE officials, less than twelve hours before the opening of the seventh annual national NFA convention. National FFA advisor Dr. William T. Spanton, who was the chief of the AES-USOE at the time, and W. N. Elam called the meeting to issue the NFA a strict ultimatum: Agree to being under the authority of the AES-USOE, comparable to the FFA, or no longer have access to federal funds for NFA-related travel. Dr. Spanton's ultimatum was initially met with resistance from NFA leaders as they considered this proposed arrangement demoralizing and designed to strip them of their autonomy. They also knew that the ultimatum was loaded in that the need to "legalize" the NFA within the AES-USOE meant that the NFA had been operating illegally. The announcement of the ultimatum shifted the atmosphere of the meeting and amplified the racial undertones of the plan to "legalize" the NFA. For the white leadership of the AES-USOE, the ultimatum was a "necessary legal umbrella," commented Dr. Ernest M. Norris, one of the NFA leaders in attendance at the meeting. For NFA leaders, the ultimatum was "an unnecessary 'white father's' imposition." These conflicting views were made clear at the meeting, but NFA leaders knew that they had been backed into a corner.[9]

Consequently, NFA leaders acquiesced to the AES-USOE's terms and agreed to be legally recognized by the federal government. They quickly discovered, however, that the terms had less to do with the threat of no access to federal funds. In fact, the terms were designed to completely reorganize the NFA's national governance structure in several ways. First, the NFA would relocate its national headquarters from North Carolina A&T State University to the AES-USOE. Second, the dual NFA position of executive secretary-treasurer would be separated into two separate positions: executive secretary and executive treasurer. Third, and most drastic, the governance structure of the national NFA would be expanded to include two new national positions: administrative advisor and administrative executive secretary. These two would also serve on what the AES-USOE organized as the NFA National Advisory Council, made up of the executive secretary, the executive treasurer, the southern regional agent for agricultural education, and three sectional advisors (one representative from each NFA section). The plan to operationalize these changes required the NFA leaders to amend the organization's constitution to reflect its "legal" status. This new status, as indicated in article VI, section A of the revised constitution, designated the chief of the AES-USOE as the administrative advisor and gave him the full power to appoint a member of his staff as the administrative executive secretary. While the other national adult officer positions of advisor, executive secretary, and executive treasurer would be elected each year at the national NFA convention, the administrative advisor and the administrative executive secretary were decided at the discretion of the AES-USOE. Therefore, Dr. Spanton—in addition to his capacity as national FFA advisor—controlled the national affairs of the NFA. In other words, the FFA had acquired quasi-power to control the NFA.[10]

From this point on, the meeting was dedicated to brainstorming how to proceed and execute these terms. Dr. Spanton assured the group that by accepting these new arrangements, the NFA would have access to federal funds comparable to the financial allocations devoted to the FFA. Even with this information, NFA leaders still expressed their apprehension about being under the authority of the chief of the AES-USOE and how that would impact their ability to determine the direction of the organization and its program of work. To remedy this particular problem, they asked Dr. Spanton in good faith to increase Black representation in the AES-USOE by hiring a Black person to his staff who could then be designated as the administrative executive secretary of the NFA. This would overcome the racialized paternalistic undertones of the new governance structure so that the NFA could have real power—beyond the elected positions—to shape the organization. Dr. Spanton promised the NFA leaders that he would make every effort to hire a Black person in his office who would then be eligible to be appointed as administrative executive secretary.

The meeting ended with the NFA leaders feeling defeated and full of despair. They considered what would be lost in this new legal relationship with the AES-USOE. For them, this relationship was a form of what legal scholar Dean Spade has defined as "administrative violence"—a term that captures the use of legal functions and methods to perpetuate social inequalities and coercive control. Such administrative violence drove NFA leaders to silence as a way to process all that took place in the meeting. Soon, rumors began to circulate at the convention about the changes in the organization that night, which left a bad taste in the mouths of NFA leaders and members. At the first general session of the seventh annual convention the next morning, the president of Florida A&M University, John Robert Edward Lee, delivered his welcome address to the attendees and made a strong public plea to the AES-USOE to hire a Black person who would represent the agricultural livelihoods of Black people and serve as the administrative executive secretary of the NFA. This plea broke the silence of the NFA leaders and placed questions of race and Black representation at the center of the AES-USOE and put Dr. Spanton on notice regarding his promise of Black representation in his federal office. President Lee's welcome was met with several rounds of applause and a standing ovation. His speech became known among NFA members as the "Lee Welcome," and it served as the convention's keynote, reshaping the context of the seventh annual convention. The Lee Welcome encouraged the adult NFA officers and other leaders to continue to fight for the hiring of Black men in the AES-USOE.[11]

Three months after the seventh annual NFA convention in Florida, the issue of the NFA and its struggle for Black representation in the AES-USOE

was a central topic at the final meeting of the nineteenth annual conference of the Presidents of Negro Land Grant Colleges in Chicago. The
theme of the conference was "Cooperation with Federal Agencies with
Particular Reference to Agricultural Extension Service and the National
Defense Program." W. N. Elam was asked to attend the final meeting to
provide an oral report on the progress of securing Black employees in the
AES-USOE. Of course, he reported the AES-USOE had failed to make
real the demands of the NFA, which sparked a discussion about the future
of the NFA. Initiated by John Warren Davis, president of West Virginia
State University and chair of the conference's Committee on Agricultural
Extension Among Negroes, the discussion raised questions about the
legalization of the NFA under the authority of the AES-USOE. According to the conference proceedings, "Mr. Elam explained legal difficulties
in connection with the government furnishing material and visiting [the]
N.F.A. unless the organization was under government control." To be sure,
Elam's explanation was unsatisfactory in that it failed to provide concrete
reasons why the NFA needed to be under the control of the AES-USOE.
His explanation also failed to address what NFA leaders wanted the most:
Black representation in the AES-USOE.[12]

The private and public discussions held at the seventh annual NFA convention and the nineteenth annual conference of the Presidents of Negro
Land Grant Colleges about the NFA and its relationship to the AES-USOE
represent a small part of the conversations that NFA leaders had about this
relationship. Many of these conversations are not documented, but what
we do know is that they raised more questions than they answered at the
time. How would this new relationship between the NFA and the AES-
USOE work? When would a Black man be hired by the AES-USOE and be
appointed as the administrative executive secretary? What would be the
duties of the administrative advisor and the administrative executive secretary? After the seventh annual convention, the NFA's new governance
structure was in place. The "official" leadership of the NFA, as agricultural
education scholar Gary Moore writes, "was the Administrative Advisor
and Administrative Executive Secretary in the US Office of Education
(white folks). However, the real work of operating the NFA resided in the
hands of the National Advisor, Executive Secretary, and Executive Treasurer, who were black teacher trainers. If you needed to charter an NFA
chapter, you didn't contact Washington, you contacted Dr. Norris at Prairie View A&M." Essentially, the administrative advisor and the administrative executive secretary were mere figureheads, and the national advisor,

executive secretary, and executive treasurer were the real adult leaders of the NFA who handled all the operations of the organization.[13]

In a larger sense, the dynamic of white leadership and subservient Black labor in relation to the AES-USOE was the taproot of tensions between the NFA and the FFA, which instigated the NFA's eventual disappearance. The years following the seventh annual NFA convention were filled with several disappointments. For example, at the eighth annual convention in South Carolina, Dr. Spanton informed NFA leaders that he was unable to meet their demands and "asked" whether the national executive secretary of the FFA might also serve—in a temporary capacity—as the administrative executive secretary. The NFA leaders agreed to these terms, hoping that this would give Dr. Spanton enough time to hire a Black person in the AES-USOE. Two years later, Dr. A. Webster Tenney, who was the national executive secretary of the FFA at the time, was appointed the first administrative executive secretary of the NFA and remained in the position on a temporary basis until 1947. That year, Dr. Spanton skipped the NFA's annual convention and appointed W. N. Elam as the NFA's administrative executive secretary without consulting NFA leaders. This decision angered NFA leaders as it reminded them of the circumstances surrounding Elam's initial appointment as federal agent over Negroes and Special Groups in the AES-USOE.[14]

In the decade following Spanton's decision to designate Elam as the permanent administrative executive secretary, NFA leaders received the silent treatment from Spanton. Repeatedly, he ignored their demands, refusing to appear at NFA conventions. Such issues unknowingly prepared the NFA as an organization for the next episode of its existence as it faced the impact of the *Brown v. Board of Education* decision on some of the NFA state associations. In many ways, the *Brown* decision ushered in a new era of the organization that would push it closer to disappearing. A tapestry of disappointments, empty promises, and unrealized dreams shaped this era of the NFA. Despite this tapestry, which provides a backdrop to the final years of the NFA, the organization still produced a number of scenes and continued to grow tremendously, including the creation of the Missouri NFA in 1949.[15]

1954

By 1954, NFA leaders were at odds with Dr. Spanton's unwillingness to cede to their one demand: Hire a Black person in the AES-USOE. What angered NFA leaders was that Spanton continued to overlook the fact that there were many qualified Black men with advanced degrees in agricultural education who could work in the AES-USOE. Meanwhile, the national NFA reorganized itself as it welcomed the Missouri NFA and suffered the unexpected loss of the New Jersey Association of the NFA. This loss occurred sometime between 1945 and 1955, when the NJNFA ceased operation and Black farm boys from the Garden State were no longer a part of the organization. During this time period, the Manual Training and Industrial School for Colored Youth in Bordentown, New Jersey, which was the headquarters of the NJNFA and the site of the fifth annual national NFA convention, omitted agricultural education from its curriculum. Consequently, the NJNFA no longer had an institutional base that could be recognized by the AES-USOE. This change was reflected in the organization's national guide as the NJNFA appears in only the first three editions of the guidebook, published between 1938 and 1944. Beginning in 1946, the NJNFA was erased from the guide with no explanation. Years later, the MTIS closed in May 1955 in response to the US Supreme Court's May 17, 1954, historic ruling in *Brown v. Board of Education*, reinforcing New Jersey's integration efforts.[16]

But before the ink could fully dry on the *Brown v. Board of Education* ruling, NFA leaders received a direct order from the AES-USOE to eliminate any reference to race, including the word "Negro," from all its organizational materials and records. The purpose of this directive was to adhere to the *Brown* decision, which overturned the monumental *Plessy v. Ferguson* doctrine of "separate but equal" in public education, rendering illegal the practice of racial segregation in public school systems. While the *Brown* decision was a monumental moment in the American civil rights movement that produced full-scale school integration efforts across the nation, the consequences of the decision decimated the educational infrastructure that sustained Black public schools. "The message transmitted by the *Brown* decision, and by the desegregation strategies implemented to carry out its mandates," Mildred J. Hudson and Barbara J. Holmes write, "implied that the White education system was intrinsically better than the Black education system." This kind of thinking, according to Irving Joyner, "intentionally ignored the reality that African-American communities were doing an excellent job in providing high-quality education to their children." In the case of the system of agricultural education in the South, *Brown* indicted the social order of segregation that shaped the region and created a world where Black farm boys were banned from joining the FFA.

The idea that school integration was the answer to this issue forced the AES-USOE to address the burning question: How can Black students be integrated into a desegregated agricultural education system?[17]

For Dr. Spanton and his office, the answer to this question was to strip the NFA of its racial identity and promote a false sense of equality in relation to the FFA. For the NFA, as its leaders continued to make clear, the answer was to hire a Black person in the AES-USOE to work on such issues so that the Black experience of agriculture would be taken seriously. Regardless, NFA leaders heeded the AES-USOE's directive and removed all mentions of race in its national guide, constitution, and bylaws. For instance, NFA guides printed through 1954 stated that the NFA was a "national organization of *Negro* farm boys studying vocational agriculture in the public schools throughout the United States." Beginning in 1956, all guides read that the NFA was a "national organization of farm boys studying vocational agriculture in the public schools in the United States." On the surface, the removal of race in NFA guides and related governing documents represented a sign of progress as the nation moved toward equality in education. But in reality, this move increased the organization's vulnerability, and NFA leaders saw this move—albeit legal—as another way for the AES-USOE to exert its power over the organization. NFA leaders knew that now there was no way to technically distinguish the NFA from the FFA. To put it bluntly, at least at the federal level, the NFA was now the FFA in blackface.[18]

What must be added to the conversations surrounding the AES-USOE's directive to the NFA regarding race is that the collective actions of Dr. Spanton—whether intentionally or unintentionally—set the opening stage for the integration of the NFA into the FFA at the state level. To be clear, his actions were in harmony with integration efforts in some Southern states that led to the closing of Black public high schools, mandating Black children attend previously segregated white schools. Blannie E. Bowen observed that once the federal mandates were enforced, they "triggered the rapid disappearance of African American teachers . . . [and] their strong community leadership roles were not sustained by white teachers." As Black high schools closed, many Black teachers were jobless and no longer worked to improve the lives of their students in the school setting. Given these circumstances, Black farm boys were forced to abandon their communities and attend white high schools where their agriculture teacher would be a white man who was likely unconcerned with their lives beyond their legal obligation—from the AES-USOE—to let them join the FFA. Between 1954 and 1964, an additional six state NFA associations—Delaware, Kentucky, Maryland, Missouri, Oklahoma, and West Virginia—integrated into their respective FFA state associations, providing a blueprint to merge the national NFA out of existence. Yet despite the NFA's decrease in state associations, which impacted the lives of Black farm boys, their agriculture teachers, and their communities in those states, the organization's membership continued to grow.[19]

In a larger sense, the detrimental consequences of the *Brown* decision, including the vanishing of Black agriculture teachers and the state-level micromergers of the NFA and the FFA, constituted a backdrop to several behind-the-scenes maneuverings in the AES-USOE that further estranged the NFA from the AES-USOE. First was the brief appearance of Dr. Spanton at the twenty-fifth annual national NFA convention in 1959 that commemorated the silver anniversary of the organization. By attending the convention, at the request of NFA leaders, Dr. Spanton broke his silence toward the organization but was present at only one session, infuriating NFA leaders. As NFA leader Dr. Norris put it, in his observation of Spanton at the convention, "It was apparent that he was too busy to otherwise devote official time to NFA." Furthermore, Spanton's actions during the twenty-fifth convention were exacerbated by the fact that he had not attended a convention in fourteen years, ignoring the organization and his role as the NFA's national administrative advisor.[20]

Second, a few weeks following the twenty-fifth annual national NFA convention, W. N. Elam retired from the AES-USOE, and NFA leaders saw this as the perfect opportunity to reengage with the AES-USOE and allow Dr. Spanton to finally fulfill his promise to hire a Black person. While Elam had served the NFA through many rough organizational transitions as its national administrative executive secretary, NFA leaders were always skeptical of him because of how he was hired by the AES-USOE and because Dr. Spanton had imposed him upon the organization. But with his retirement at hand, NFA leaders were hopeful that a Black person would replace him. This hope quickly faded as the AES-USOE terminated the staff position that Elam held and reconfigured the office. The role of national administrative advisor of the NFA was attached to the position, and NFA leaders saw this as a declaration of war against the organization. For at least two decades, they had pushed for Black representation in the AES-USOE, and every time NFA leaders got closer to this becoming a reality, they were severely disappointed. By the end of 1959, Dr. Spanton appointed another white man, AES-USOE Assistant Director R. Edward

Naugher of South Carolina, to the temporary post of national administrative executive secretary of the NFA. The position was supposedly temporary, as Spanton continued to make more empty promises about hiring a Black person in his office.[21]

Third, in 1961, Dr. Spanton retired after twenty years as chief of the AES-USOE. He was promptly replaced by Dr. Tenney, former FFA national executive secretary and the NFA's first national administrative executive secretary, who was a program analyst in the USOE's Division of Vocational Education at the time. For NFA leaders, the appointment of Tenney as AES-USOE chief, and by extension FFA's national advisor and the national NFA's administrative advisor, was met with mixed feelings of distrust and hope. The feelings of distrust were triggered by past numerous disappointments at the hands of Spanton. The feelings of hope were attached to working with Tenney, as they anticipated a fresh perspective on Black representation in the AES-USOE. NFA leaders thought that Tenney would recognize the value of the organization and effectively address their administrative needs. A glimpse of this hope appeared when the assistant commissioner of vocational education sent letters out to NFA leaders and their affiliates encouraging them to apply to the AES-USOE. NFA leaders mobilized a considerable number of qualified applicants who submitted applications. Such mobilization efforts, however, were in vain. The applications were met with silence from Tenney and the AES-USOE. NFA leaders well understood what the silence meant, but this time it hurt more as they had been offered false hope. The next time NFA leaders would hear from Tenney would be a year later in 1962, when he approached them about merging with the FFA, initiating a hostile takeover of the NFA.[22]

1962

The NFA's attempts to resist the FFA's hostile takeover of the organization shaped the three years leading up to its mysterious disappearance. Set in motion by the AES-USOE, this takeover ensured that the NFA would be "swallowed up" by the FFA, as Dr. Norris put it. Norris was the national NFA's executive secretary at the time, witnessing firsthand how the NFA was lured into surrendering its full autonomy to the FFA. According to Norris, the years 1962–65 revealed that the NFA would not be around much longer. As Norris argued in his executive secretary's report at the thirtieth annual NFA convention in 1964, this time period was occupied by two questions: "At this time, I choose to speak to the point of a line of thinking in answer to a question uppermost in most of our minds—'How much longer NFA?' This question arises out of curiosity by some, apprehension by others, and out of genuine interest and real concerns by others still. What should be the attitude and working reaction of an organization that knows its days are numbered?" These questions were raised in the wake of critical discussions about the Civil Rights Act of 1964 and its impact on the AES-USOE's role in the administration of the NFA and FFA. Such discussions were the culmination of a sequence of actions that coerced the NFA into an unequal agreement with the FFA. The script of this sequence goes as follows.[23]

In 1962, the AES-USOE's subtle acts to legally undermine the NFA's autonomy became hostile as the office's leadership initiated the discussion stage of a potential national merger between the NFA and FFA. While in previous years, as micromergers occurred in some states and the AES-USOE imposed changes on the NFA without asking the organization to surrender its full identity, this year, the rules of the game changed. The discussions of 1962 came to a head at an exploratory meeting between the national officers of the NFA and FFA. At first, the plan was to develop a smooth transition surrounding the merger. This strategy was built on a seemingly democratic process in that both organizations would have to agree on how to approach a merger. The plan included the possibility of creating a new name that would represent both organizations, codeveloping a clear path toward the merger, minimizing membership attrition in response to the merger, and building a super organization that would honor the strengths of the NFA and FFA. NFA leaders agreed to this proposal in good faith but remained apprehensive given the many years of disappointments and neglect, recognizing that their powers had been limited by the AES-USOE since 1941, when the national NFA had been restructured.[24]

Over the next two years, in the shadow of the passage of the Vocational Education Act of 1963—which ushered in an expansive agricultural education program beyond farming—and the Civil Rights Act of 1964, the tone of the conversations surrounding the NFA-FFA merger became serious. Yet, NFA leaders were not included in *all* conversations. The conversations they were included in were on a strict need-to-know basis as decided by FFA officials in the AES-USOE. NFA leaders understood what such exclusion meant, recognizing that the merger was inevitable and that they would more than likely be on the losing end of the conversation. Within a matter of months, it became clear that FFA officials would be taking the lead in operationalizing the merger and that NFA leaders would be forced to agree. While available records suggest the NFA and FFA ami-cably agreed on the merger, NFA leaders were always concerned about working with the FFA officials in the AES-USOE. Dr. Norris made this clear, writing that during the discussion stages of the merger, "it became more and more apparent that one party and one only would be the conces-sionaire. NFA would be giving up all—name, charter, constitution, bylaws, special prizes, awards, insignia, emblem, jacket, creed, flag, banner, colors, adult leadership for guidance, consultation, and advice. FFA would give up nothing—not even alter its constitution to provide for one board mem-bership from the NFA." This power dynamic between the NFA and FFA created a rocky road toward the merger as it became a reality.[25]

On October 11–12, 1964, just three months after President Lyndon B. Johnson signed the Civil Rights Act of 1964 and three days after the thirti-eth national NFA convention, the FFA's national board of directors held its annual meeting before the national FFA convention in Kansas City, Missouri. According to the minutes of the board meeting, three NFA leaders were present: national advisor George W. Conoly of Florida A&M University, national executive secretary Ernest M. Norris of Prairie View A&M Univer-sity, and national executive treasurer Walter T. Johnson of North Carolina A&T State University. They had been asked by AES-USOE chief and FFA national advisor Dr. Tenney to "sit in on the meeting to review some of the latest developments, on the National level, with respect to the forthcoming merger of the FFA and NFA"; he added that "their counsel would be quite valuable in helping to solve some of the problems which may be encoun-tered." It is important to note here that the NFA was invited to essentially sit on the sidelines of a merger discussion that was led by the FFA.[26]

As the meeting progressed, Dr. Tenney updated everyone on official conversations about legal compliance in the context of the NFA-FFA merger that he was having with Francis Keppel, who was the US com-missioner of education, and the Civil Rights Commission. Then, Norris was asked to make a report about the thirtieth national NFA convention, which he thought was the "most successful convention, with very good attendance and participation," the board minutes read. While the con-vention was a success, the last day of the gathering had sent shockwaves through the NFA as rumors about the merger permeated every aspect of the convention. Norris explained that at the closing of the convention, Dr. Malcolm C. Gaar, federal agent of the AES-USOE and administrative exec-utive secretary of the NFA, announced that the 1964 convention would be the last one of the NFA. Norris, Conoly, and Johnson expressed their dismay about this statement and asked Dr. Tenney to ask Commissioner Keppel to allow them to hold a final convention so that they could officially end the NFA and prepare for termination. The minutes state that Tenney agreed to send a letter on behalf of the NFA to Keppel, and the meeting transitioned to a brainstorming session about the merger with the hopes of establishing "concrete recommendations for accomplishing the merger of the two organizations." The session included a conversation about the Civil Rights Act of 1964 and how it would impact both the NFA and FFA, allowing both parties to suggest items and placing them on a blackboard for consideration.[27]

After deliberations that took several hours, due to this being the first time that all leaders of the two organizations had gathered to map out a clear course for the proposed merger, they decided on five initial recommendations:

1. Each state that had both NFA and FFA state associations would set up a joint committee between the NFA and FFA to develop a plan for merging.

2. Black educators would serve as merger consultants at national FFA board meetings.

3. Effective July 1, 1965, the merger would be complete and all NFA members who met all membership qualifications as outlined in the FFA constitution would immediately become members of the FFA.

4. The NFA would hold its final national convention no later than October 1965 to rectify and terminate all official business, including the presentation of final awards and preparation for the merger.

5. Preselected NFA members and officers would attend the 1965 national FFA convention to participate in special activities regarding the merger.

Subsequently, the meeting proceeded, and Dr. Tenney informed everyone that he would have to submit the recommendations to all state FFA advisors at the convention and then to Commissioner Keppel for final approval. The meeting adjourned shortly after Tenney's statement and concluding remarks regarding FFA business. Three weeks later, on November 2, 1964,

Tenney sent a letter that outlined the merger recommendations to Commissioner Keppel, and the merger was one approval away from becoming reality.[28]

1965

The months of 1965 that preceded the NFA's mysterious disappearance on the evening of Wednesday, October 13, 1965, were fraught with further unfulfilled promises and uncertainty. In retrospect, it was evident that the NFA had everything to lose and the FFA had everything to gain. Merger discussions resumed on January 27, 1965, when Commissioner Keppel sent a response to Dr. Tenney's November 1964 letter that included a proposal for the merger. The delay in response time was due to President Johnson issuing the regulations and procedures in the Civil Rights Act for state and local educational agencies in relation to racial segregation. Commissioner Keppel connected the regulations and procedures to vocational education and the NFA-FFA merger, laying out three required modifications to Tenney's proposal and approving the final NFA convention. The first modification was to include the NFA board of directors in all merger discussions and to expand the pool of potential merger consultants beyond educators, regardless of race. The second modification suggested eliminating the FFA's constitutional prohibition on chapter administration and membership in order to make all NFA chapters and members instant members of the FFA upon the completion of the merger. Concerning the 1965 FFA convention and the proposal that only particular NFA members would be permitted to attend, the third modification made all NFA members eligible to attend the convention. Keppel concluded his letter by requesting that Tenney revise his proposal and send it back by March 4, 1965, for final approval.[29]

Less than one week later, after discussing Keppel's modifications with the FFA board of student officers and board of directors, Tenney resubmitted a revised proposal on February 4, 1965. "After considerable study, the [FFA] Board of Student Officers and the Board of Directors approved the following recommendations":

1. States concerned should set up state committees to study and work on the problem of merging the NFA with the FFA.

2. The merger would be developed jointly by members of the boards of directors of the FFA and the NFA.

3. NFA members would become FFA members July 1, 1965.

4. A convention would be held in Atlanta, Georgia, in October 1965 for the final presentation of NFA awards.

5. Since NFA members would become FFA members July 1, 1965, they would be eligible to attend the 1965 national FFA convention.

Given these revised recommendations, Tenney informed Keppel that there would be no need to change the FFA's constitution to initiate and complete the merger. If a problem were to occur, Tenney assured Keppel that the FFA constitution would be changed. Within a matter of days, Keppel approved Tenney's new proposal for the NFA-FFA merger, and the process began immediately.[30]

What must be inserted into this part of the story is that available records regarding the merger following its final approval are sparse, and only limited official documentation surrounding the merger process is available. Detailed information about the meetings that occurred between official business matters that are referenced in correspondences is not accessible. What is clear is that the FFA took the lead in the merger conversation and that the NFA would be acquired by the organization, erasing the NFA from existence. Dr. Tenney, as the chief of the AES-USOE, FFA national advisor, and national administrative advisor of the NFA, wielded complete authority over the merger process, serving as the single point of contact between the commissioner and the two organizations. As the first step, Tenney required the NFA's national advisory board to vote for the merger. Dr. Norris sent out a mail-in ballot to members of the board in early February to vote on the process for the merger of the NFA and FFA into one organization. According to the ballot, while the merger would be effective July 1, 1965, all legal matters regarding the separate governing board entities of the two organizations would be reconciled by October 1965 and actualized at the national FFA convention.[31]

To be sure, the NFA's advisory board vote was performative and resulted in a unanimous decision to merge with the FFA. By this point, the board knew that the NFA would be acquired by the FFA and that the two associations would organize under the banner of the FFA. The NFA's advisory board vote signaled to the FFA and the AES-USOE that the NFA rendered itself obsolete. Between February and August 1965, the merger process accelerated, and many decisions were made without question at the state, regional, and national levels. At the state and regional levels, NFA leaders held final meetings in preparation for the national merger. At the national level, NFA leaders organized the final national NFA convention and planned to attend a joint NFA-FFA meeting of adult and student leaders in late July to discuss final steps in the merger. Each level required different actors, operating in and out of sync, attempting to wrap up the NFA before it would be erased from the AES-USOE. This erasure came into focus when the decision was made to dispose of all NFA materials, except for one sample of major NFA items to be deposited in the FFA archives. Essentially, after the merger, the NFA would be viewed as an illegal organization since it was founded for Black farm boys, and race could no longer be a factor in the context of the organization. Said differently, the NFA's existence illuminated the segregationist past of the FFA in the South, and that was now unconstitutional due to the Civil Rights Act of 1964.[32]

Consequently, on July 1, 1965, the FFA at the state and local levels was opened to all public high school students in vocational agriculture regardless of race, color, or national origin. That same day, the NFA faded into the dustbins of American memory in general and Black American consciousness in particular. But NFA leaders did not see July 1 as the last day of the NFA. They were looking forward to meeting with FFA leaders in late July to discuss legal processes surrounding the merger. This meeting took place on July 29–30 in Washington, DC. While Dr. Tenney and other FFA leaders entered the meeting ready to discuss the unveiling of the merger at the 1965 national FFA convention, NFA leaders had a different agenda in mind. At the center of this agenda were grievances and questions of equitable representation of the NFA in the process. NFA leaders presented a document of resolutions to the FFA that read like a manifesto. In this moment, NFA leaders realized that they had nothing else to lose and situated the resolutions within the context of the last twenty-four years of disappointments. They recalled the events and broken promises of the August 1941 meeting on the night before the seventh annual NFA convention in Florida, when the NFA's governance structure was reorganized and the NFA was brought under the authority of the AES-USOE and, by extension, the FFA.[33]

Twenty-four years later, as NFA leaders sat in the July 1965 meetings with FFA leadership, it became apparent that they were tired of being lied to by the AES-USOE. In their resolutions, NFA leaders requested that (1) the FFA's constitution be revised to reflect the merger with the NFA, (2) the AES-USOE chief finally appoint a Black person (preferably a former

NFA member) to a permanent civil service post in his office who would also serve on the FFA board of directors—ensuring that the NFA would have equitable representation on the board, and (3) former NFA chapters would be permitted to use funds from the state NFA accounts to assist members in purchasing FFA paraphernalia. NFA leaders also requested that, since the merger was a "wholesome product of the Civil Rights Act . . . the US Department of Justice be asked for a legal review of the resolutions." After the presentation of these resolutions, the tone of the meeting dramatically shifted. As Dr. Norris put it, the meeting went from "an amicable atmosphere into one of consternation, suspicion, and 'off-side' whispers." From that point on, the AES-USOE took over the meeting, carefully facilitating an open but "limited and guarded discussion" about the requests of the NFA leaders. The discussion ended with NFA leaders being pulled aside into a brief meeting by Dr. Tenney, who "emphasized the hazards to intra-branch progress in solving the problem if these

Joint NFA-FFA board meeting with national student and adult officers, Washington, DC, July 29, 1965. Courtesy of the National FFA Organization Records, 1916–2008 (Mss 035), RLSCA.

resolutions were implemented at this time." Norris recalled that Tenney "further pledged diligence in effort toward resolution of the matter by the beginning of the next calendar year." Tenney referred the resolutions to the FFA governing board for consideration, and the meeting ended with a lack of closure, except for the decision that former NFA chapters would receive funds to purchase FFA paraphernalia.[34]

Between August and October 1965, the national NFA and FFA separately planned their conventions, communicating only about the merger. NFA leaders focused on the organization's final convention that would allow them to close out the organization and disband on their own terms. At the same time, FFA leaders were preparing to publicly recognize their acquisition of the NFA on the evening of October 13, 1965, the last day the NFA existed in real time. As the "pageantry of the merger," returning to the words of Cecil Strickland Sr., faded into the background of the FFA's memory, NFA leaders were soon reminded of their long-term tumultuous relationship with the FFA and the AES-USOE. One month after the NFA's erasure at the 1965 FFA convention, NFA leaders were angered by the minutes of the November 30 meeting of the FFA board of directors. The minutes included a discussion about the NFA's resolution regarding the hiring of a former NFA member by the AES-USOE who would also serve on the FFA board. It was reported that the efforts to create a new position for a former NFA member in the AES-USOE by Mr. H. Neville Hunsicker, who succeeded Dr. Tenney as AES-USOE chief and national FFA advisor after the merger, were not approved by the USOE, but efforts would continue.[35]

Compounded by the fact that the FFA refused to alter its constitution to reflect the merger, the unsuccessful hire infuriated NFA leaders, and they mobilized to appeal this situation "to whatever level and branch in the federal government from which redress might come," Norris later told Hunsicker. What angered NFA leaders even more was that they had to find out about the unsuccessful efforts of Hunsicker and the AES-USOE through the November 1965 meeting minutes of the FFA's board of directors. But they also knew that since the merger was over, the AES-USOE had no obligation to inform them, as the NFA no longer existed and former NFA leaders were not part of the FFA board of directors. Yet, NFA leaders— led by Norris—continued to petition Hunsicker and the AES-USOE. For eighteen months, Norris and other leaders sent several letters to the AES-USOE and met with the commissioner of education and the USOE's legal counsel to secure employment for a Black person in the AES-USOE who was a former NFA member. These efforts yielded positive results as they paved the way for Mr. James W. Warren, a state-level supervisor of agricultural education in North Carolina and the 1940–41 NFA national president, to be appointed to a position that included responsibilities in the AES-USOE in 1967. While Warren had been considered for the position in previous conversations between NFA leaders and the AES-USOE, pressure from Norris and others made Warren's appointment a reality. This position made him the first Black person to work in the AES-USOE and be qualified to serve as a member of the FFA board of directors. Ironically, his appointment to that board was effective on April 5, 1967, which was the NFA's designated date for the annual NFA Day.[36]

Questions and Answers

This chapter began at the scene of the NFA's mysterious disappearance. Through a series of episodes between 1941 and 1965, the chapter retraced the actions and steps of NFA leaders, members, and affiliates that led up to this final scene in the existence of the NFA. Parts of this chapter are necessarily hazy because the final days of the NFA's existence are still unclear, which raises the question: When exactly did the NFA go missing? Was it at the 1941 meeting in Florida, when the national NFA was "legalized" and restructured under the authority of the AES-USOE? Or was it in the wake of the 1954 *Brown* decision, when the AES-USOE legally stripped the NFA of its Black identity in all formal documents? Maybe it was in 1962, as some state associations of the NFA were merging into the FFA, and the AES-USOE initiated a hostile takeover of the national body of the NFA via the FFA? Or was it in 1965, when the NFA became the FFA that July and publicly disbanded later in October? In reading these questions against the conditions and circumstances surrounding the NFA's disappearance that were outlined in this chapter, the words of anthropologist and Black writer Zora Neale Hurston come to mind: "There are years that ask questions and years that answer."[37]

Between the years of 1941 and 1965, NFA leaders asked numerous questions about the fate and future of the only educational organization designed for and by Black farm boys in the rural South. As the AES-USOE used legal compliance to dismantle the NFA with surgical precision, NFA leaders understood that the machinations of the AES-USOE and FFA were designed to erase the NFA from the story of American agriculture. Such erasure was engineered by white paternalistic power—via administrative

Dr. Ernest M. Norris (*standing in center*), George W. Conoly (*sitting far left*), and Walter T. Johnson (*sitting far right*) with the 1963–64 national NFA student and adult officers at a meeting with Dr. Walter Arnold (*center, seated*), assistant US commissioner of vocational and technical education, 1964. Courtesy of the New Farmers of America Records, 1929–1965 (Mss 059), RLSCA.

violence—that sought to undermine the NFA's ability to exercise Black power in agricultural education. At the same time, NFA leaders reckoned with the deaths of several key figures who had paved the way for the NFA—C. S. Woodward of Arkansas, Church H. Banks of Texas, S. B. Simmons of North Carolina, George W. Owens of Virginia, J. R. Thomas of Virginia, D. C. Jones of Oklahoma, Arthur Floyd of Alabama, J. P. Burgess of South Carolina, Alva Tabor of Georgia, W. A. Flowers of Tennessee, and A. D. Fobbs of Mississippi, to name a few. These men, along with countless Black agriculture teachers in each of those states, devoted their lives to the NFA. Those who were left behind after 1965 included Dr. Ernest M. Norris of Texas, George W. Conoly of Florida, and Walter T. Johnson of North Carolina, who represented the last national NFA adult leadership team and carried the spirit of the NFA with them as they continued their efforts in ensuring Black representation in the FFA after the merger.[38]

To return to the wake of the merger, Norris, Conoly, and Johnson understood that the fight for the dreams of Black farm boys could not die with the erasure of the NFA. Against the backdrop of struggles to secure a position for a Black person in the AES-USOE and the FFA board, which resulted in the successful appointment of James Warren, these men continued to meet and correspond with officials in the AES-USOE and FFA leaders. The purpose of these strategies was to push for Black farm boys to have equity in the FFA and ascend to national leadership positions in the FFA. In fact, in 1969, Johnson sent a four-page letter about the merger to President Richard Nixon on behalf of Norris, Conoly, and other NFA stakeholders. In his letter, he expressed his disdain with the aftermath of the NFA-FFA merger and petitioned President Nixon to appoint a committee to investigate how Black farm boys were being included in the affairs of the FFA. While they were denied the opportunity to be in positions of power in the national administrative body of the FFA and never received adequate answers to the questions they raised to the AES-USOE and FFA, Norris, Conoly, and Johnson refused to allow decades of unfilled promises to deter them. Even in the face of hopelessness, humiliation, and exhaustion, the men fought to ensure that the NFA's work would not be in vain. And to be sure, their work was not in vain, as the three decades that followed the merger revealed.[39]

In the 1970s, Frederick McClure of San Augustine, Texas, became the first Black person to be a national officer in the FFA, serving as the 1973–74 national FFA secretary. A year prior to that, McClure also made history as the first Black president of the Texas FFA. In the 1980s, Dave Weatherspoon, a Black college student at Michigan State University, worked with his advisor, Dr. Eunice Foster, to create the Minority Agriculture and Natural Resources Association in 1982. In the spirit of the NFA collegiate chapters, this association was designed to combat the lack of support for Black students and other marginalized populations in college-level agricultural programs. In 1985, representatives from the group traveled to the Pennsylvania State University to help minority students there form the Minorities in Agriculture organization. One year later, the Minority Agriculture and Natural Resources Association and Minorities in Agriculture jointly organized "The First Annual Conference of Minority Students in Agriculture and Natural Resources" at Michigan State. In 1988, this conference gave birth to the National Society for Minorities in Agriculture, Natural Resources, and Related Sciences (MANRRS). The mission of MANRRS is to "empower individuals of underrepresented and diverse backgrounds in agriculture, natural resources, continuing education, peer and professional mentor networks and advocacy leading to access to rewarding economic avenues, accomplishment and advancement." In the 1990s, MANRRS expanded its purview and initiated the Junior MANRRS program for minority middle school and high school students in 1994. That same year, Corey Flournoy of Chicago was elected the first Black president of the FFA, serving the 1994–95 school year.[40]

To be sure, Fredrick McClure's position as the first Black person to be a national officer in the FFA, Dave Weatherspoon's desire to create an organization that would become MANRRS, and Corey Flournoy's rise to becoming the first Black president of the FFA represent more than just significant moments in the story of American agriculture and the context of those organizations. These moments represent the dreams of Norris, Conoly, Johnson, and thousands of other Black leaders and teachers in the NFA. Sadly, Norris, Conoly, and Johnson got to collectively see and celebrate only Frederick McClure's success in the FFA. In 1980, Conoly passed away in Florida at the age of seventy-eight. In 1986, Johnson passed away in North Carolina at the age of seventy-nine, just two years before the founding of MANRRS. In 1993, Dr. Norris passed away at the age of ninety, one year before Corey Flournoy assumed the highest position in the FFA. The significant losses that these men and their contemporaries endured in the NFA are difficult to comprehend, but even more perplexing is the fact that they are hardly ever acknowledged for paving the way for Black farm boys to be national leaders in the FFA and providing a template for the creation of MANRRS. Regardless, their dreams, aspirations, wins, and losses provided a solid foundation for the self-actualization of Black farm boys from the 1920s to the 1960s, laying brick by brick the base block for Black youth and other underrepresented groups to be part of the story of American agriculture from 1965 to today. In this way, the NFA's work cannot be overstated. Generations of Black farm boys and related youth, as well as those who will come in the future, will always be part of the NFA's enduring legacy.[41]

WRITING THE NFA BACK INTO HISTORY

The New Farmers of America was the most successful student organization for Black male youth in the history of the states where the organization was located. . . . Responsibility, the work ethic, self-esteem, belongingness, cooperation, scholarship, management, home and family life, and patriotism are common threads for the NFA.

—James A. Franklin Sr., Mims NFA chapter,
McCormick, South Carolina

I am writing these final words of *Black Farm Boys* in the summer of 2025.

This year marks significant anniversaries for the NFA. It is the ninetieth anniversary of the organization's founding and the sixtieth anniversary of its disappearance. It is the 150th birthday of George Washington Owens, the architect of the New Farmers of Virginia, who paved the way for the NFA. But as I sit here writing, I can't help but think about how these anniversaries will likely go unnoticed and that there will be no major events to commemorate them. Former NFA members who are still living will not be invited to the nation's capital to be recognized for the difference they made through agriculture in the lives of those who lived in their neighborhoods and communities. Those who were part of the opening scene of the NFA will not be posthumously honored for understanding the transformative power of agricultural education in the lives of Black people. The thousands of Black men and boys who made up the convention, camp, and community scenes produced by the NFA will not be celebrated for their abilities to redesign the agricultural realities of Black people while making sense of a complex and ever-changing world that didn't even consider their lives or humanity worthy of attention. It is as though the NFA never existed.

But not here. This book is evidence that the NFA was here. It bears witness to the beautiful lives of Black farm boys in the NFA who dared to not abandon agriculture in the face of their complicated historical relationship to land and the farm gate. It memorializes the Black men who remained in their communities to be agriculture teachers, mentors, and professors, guiding Black farm boys to the light of a new day where they could use agriculture to change their lives. As I look back at the scenes of this book, rereading each page, each quote, taking careful notes about each character and each moment, I still feel like so much of the NFA's untold story is missing. Every time I travel back in time via the scenes, I learn something new about the NFA. While I know it is impossible to capture the entire story of the NFA in one book, the scenes in this volume provide a front-row seat to the work of the NFA, revealing more than we knew before.

For far too long, the NFA has been ignored and deemed insignificant. What we do know about the NFA has been reduced to two points on the historical timeline of the Future Farmers of America organization—one point that recognizes its founding in 1935, and the other its merging with the FFA in 1965. This placement of the NFA in relation to the FFA is not accidental. The larger story about American agricultural education—a narrative manufactured by white male leaders in the now defunct Agricultural Education Service of the US Office of Education who are viewed as the fathers of the field—argues that the NFA should be considered only as an offshoot of the FFA. But the NFA was not that. The NFA entered American history as part of what I have observed as the Black youth farm movement—which was both a movement and a framework—and was built on generations of Black leaders and visionaries who developed colleges, schools, and community spaces to practice new visions of agriculture in rural Black communities.

Such new visions of Black agriculture, and the historical context by which they emerged, have long been relegated to the sidelines of Black studies and the discourses surrounding the multidiscipline. To be clear, this statement is not an indictment of Black studies. Rather, it is a call to action for scholars who write in the tradition of Black studies to think seriously about how we have overlooked such an important facet of Black life in America and then to shift our focus to what historian Valerie Grim has called "next directions" in the study of Black life. Undoubtedly, one of those next directions in Black studies must involve an in-depth treatment of agriculture and rurality in Black life, for there is much we don't know about the agrarian lives of Black people, and it is our duty to bring this to the forefront of scholarly and public discourses. Might I propose that the NFA and the BYFM be used as starting points for carving out a pathway for the next directions in Black studies which could influence new research in rural sociology and agricultural education?[1]

I recognize that I am raising this question at a peculiar moment in American history. The nation's current administration is working overtime to dismantle institutions and programs that preserve knowledge of the contributions and lives of marginalized groups, especially Black people. These narratives seek to tell a more complete story of America that does not fit prefigured narratives upheld by those in positions of authority who seek to distort the past. To be sure, these ongoing threats in relation to the Black studies enterprise are not new. But this current moment we are witnessing is conjuring up a painful past, as if salt is being poured into wounds that never fully healed. As historian Michael Gomez, the director of the Center for the Study of Africa and the African Diaspora at New York University, wrote in his letter to Black studies scholars in response to the current political climate in the United States, "Our stories have never been accurately told, our experiences long hidden and ignored, and now their traces, once again, undergo caricature and erasure. . . . We have entered a realm in which reality is undergoing yet another round of revisionism, a world of inversion." As we think about next directions in Black studies, we must contend with this reality. As Gomez insisted, "We can only press forward now, drawing upon our faith and integrity, upon the rectitude of our cause, upon the lessons of the past."[2]

Indeed, the untold story of the NFA offers us lessons and insights into how oppressive forms of power operate through erasure and how Black folks—with little to no resources—have continuously fought back, (re)building institutions and dreaming new futures through self-determination. It also illuminates a pathway to understand the future of Black people's connection to agriculture, therefore creating a Black agricultural blueprint for the nation and the world—a pathway that would otherwise remain hidden and unknown, unless we choose to see it. Gomez concluded with a call to action: "Let us go to work, to ensure that what we are passing through now will never again come this way." This book represents my response—an intentional refusal to let the story of the NFA remain a relic of a forgotten yet pivotal moment in the history of Black life in America.[3]

That refusal began with a question. Throughout my research on the NFA and the process of writing *Black Farm Boys*, I kept asking people—prominent scholars, activists, community members, friends, and even family members—whether they had ever heard of the NFA. The answer was always the same: a resounding no. Yet, each time I heard no, I was inspired to dig deeper into the story of the NFA. At some point, I was able to locate a few former NFA members, and I remember one response that stuck out to me when I inquired about the group: "I haven't talked or heard about the NFA in over fifty years; what do you know about the NFA? It made a difference in the lives of so many Black boys and their communities." I even contacted two of my former professors and mentors at my alma mater, Prairie View A&M University—Dr. Alfred L. Parks and Dr. Freddie L. Richards, whose voices open chapters 1 and 2, respectively—to inquire about their knowledge of the NFA. I was surprised to learn that they were both former members of the organization. In our many conversations, both told me that the NFA is the reason they decided to pursue a career in agriculture through the prism of teaching, research, and service in higher education. They also made clear to me that the NFA is one of the reasons they wanted to train the next generation of Black boys like me who majored in agriculture and were interested in pursuing a career related to agriculture and food systems research.

Learning about my own connection to the NFA—realizing how it made a difference in the lives of my former professors and, through them, helped shaped the scholar I am today—completely transformed how I thought about writing this book. This moment reconfigured my adventure through the shadows of Black agricultural history. While this adventure has been full of twists and turns, many of which I could never have anticipated, I came to realize in that moment that I was uniquely poised and positioned to tell this part of the NFA's story. I have learned that the NFA offered Black farm boys a clear pathway to use agriculture as a site for Black self-determination, community uplift, economic vitality, educational achievement, career training, and many other things that are not necessarily articulated in narratives about the organization. It was also a pipeline for Black boys who wanted to study agriculture at the college level at HBCUs, and these institutions provided administrative space for the organization. This pipeline produced generations of Black farmers, college professors, college presidents, federal USDA agents, congressmen, cooperative extension personnel, and state agriculture officials, to name a few roles that NFA members assumed over the years.

To be honest, as I write this final paragraph of *Black Farm Boys*, this book feels unfinished. I started it in the shadows of Black agricultural history, and I am ending it there as well. And maybe that's the point of my writing a postscript reflection instead of a traditional conclusion. There is no way to end the untold story of the NFA just yet. The story remains unfinished—left incomplete. Said differently, the NFA's story does not end with these pages and continues to unfold. And there remains so much more work to do. The NFA operated through at least 1,000 local chapters across eighteen states, and each element of the organization deserves its own study. There are more voices, more stories, more moments, more ideas to recover and uncover surrounding the NFA that will expand our understandings of the organization and Black people's historical relationship to agriculture. At present, across the nation, there appears to be a renewed interest in the story of agriculture in Black life in relation to the precarious plight of Black farmers and the future of this demographic. Whether this interest continues or not, those of us who are committed to enhancing the lives of Black people through agricultural systems should reclaim the work of the NFA. Such reclamation efforts of lost and overlooked parts of Black people's historical interactions with agriculture could yield a new approach by which we can ensure brighter Black agrarian futures. *Black Farm Boys* represents one example of these efforts.

Acknowledgments

Writing *Black Farm Boys* felt like home. Each time I sat to put words on these pages, it was a deeply personal, emotional, and spiritual exercise in faith, perseverance, discipline, and—above all—love. In many ways, it was indescribable. I am thankful to God for bringing the untold story of the New Farmers of America into my life and placing it on my heart to attempt to tell part of it. Every step along this unexpected journey was divine, and I felt the Spirit urging me to write this story. And just like God, the right people showed up at the right time to help me get through this process, and for the next few paragraphs, I want to sincerely thank them.

I couldn't imagine a world without my family: my mother, Cheryl Smith; my father, Bobby Smith Sr.; my sister, Sherry Smith; my niece, Kyleigh Smith; and my nephews, Josiah Smith and Treysen Peterson. Thank you for always being in my corner. I love you.

My editor at the University of North Carolina Press, Lucas Church, has been supportive of this project since the first moment I told him about it, and it was truly a pleasure to work with him again to bring *Black Farm Boys* into the world. Thomas Bedenbaugh, assistant editor, helped with book logistics. I also want to express my sincere appreciation to the two anonymous manuscript and proposal reviewers selected by UNC Press. Both reviewers offered words of encouragement and generative feedback.

My brilliant colleagues and students in the Department of African American Studies at the University of Illinois at Urbana-Champaign (UIUC) have created a thriving environment for intellectual pursuits, which has tremendously helped me in my research and writing. Among them, I especially want to thank my colleagues Ronald Bailey, Merle Bowen, and Erik McDuffie for their mentorship and many conversations surrounding my progress on this book. I also sincerely thank Shaniya Brown and Sharetta Hall, the department's office staff, for their patience and tremendous logistical help in supporting the final production stages of this book. Outside the Department of African American Studies, I could not have completed research for this project without the Multiracial Democracy Scholarship Award from the UIUC Campus Research Board and the Helen Corley Petit Scholar Award from the UIUC College of Liberal Arts & Sciences. Views, findings, conclusions, or recommendations expressed in this book do not necessarily reflect those of the Campus Research Board or LAS.

A special shout-out goes to the UIUC Office of Research Advising and Project Development team: Maria Gillombardo, Kevin Hamilton, Kelley Frazier, Carol Symes, Shelley E. Weinberg, and Andrew Greenlee. These colleagues, along with Chris Prom, were so very generous with their time in the early stages of this book process, and I am thankful to them all for supporting me in the development of *Black Farm Boys.*

Archival research methods and access to historical materials were central to the creation of *Black Farm Boys*, and I must express my utmost admiration and appreciation to the staff and stakeholders at the following libraries and repositories: the Fayette Heritage Museum and Archives in La Grange, Texas (Rox Ann Johnson and Maria Rocha); Bordentown Historical Society in Bordentown, New Jersey (John Medley, Bonnie Goldman, Steven Lederman, and Doug Kiovsky); the blog *Friday Footnote Archive: Focusing on the History of Agricultural Education and Rural America* (Gary Moore); Sheppard Memorial Library in Greenville, North Carolina (Kim Averette); Kansas City Public Library in Kansas City, Missouri (Stephanie McClinton); Special Collections/Archives Department, John B. Coleman Library at Prairie View A&M University in Prairie View, Texas (Phyllis Earles and Frank Jackson); Ruth Lilly Special Collections and Archives, University Library, Indiana University Indianapolis (Denise Rayman, Angela White, and Molly LaPorte); USDA National Agricultural Library in Beltsville, Maryland (Paul Wester, Scott Hanscom, Kirstin Nelson, Triza Crittle, Sara Lee, Amy Morgan, Kay Derr, Manuel Jusino, Pamela Veal, and Timothy Schoepke); Interlibrary Borrowing Office at the UIUC Library in Urbana, Illinois (Alissa Marcum); and Archives and Special Collections, F. D. Bluford Library at North Carolina A&T State University in Greensboro (James Stewart, Edward Love, and Netta Cox).

A special word of thanks is due Kimberly Gay, the head of Reference and Information Services at the John B. Coleman Library at Prairie View A&M University, for her encouragement, patience, and unwavering support over the course of this entire project and more. As it relates to the production process of this book, I want to sincerely thank Matthew Somoroff (UNC

Press project editor) for shepherding this book through the production process; Julie Bush (copyeditor) for her care in copyediting this book; Jessica Ryan for her critical proofreading services; and Eric Anderson and Arc Indexing Inc. for their crucial work on the index.

To Mr. Lorenza Crosby and the late Mrs. Myrtle Crosby: I am overwhelmed with gratefulness that God brought me into your lives via *Black Farm Boys*. You opened your home and personal archival collections to me, and I will always be grateful. Chapter 4 of this book would not exist without you both, along with Jeff Kelly and Jan Dockery.

I am forever indebted to the NFA members I spoke with over the course of this project, including Alfred Parks, Freddie Richards, E. W. Wesley, Donald Reese, Alvin Larke Jr., and Horace Drisdale, among others. Parks and Richards, along with Wash Jones, who has written about the NFA, mentored me while I was a student at Prairie View A&M University, and their guidance throughout my writing of *Black Farm Boys* is immeasurable.

Writing a book is hard, but with the love and encouragement of extended family, friends, and mentors—too many to name here—the writing doesn't feel so daunting. Among this group of folks in my life, I want to shout-out Sherry Zhang, Scott Peters, Lori Leonard, Cheryl Jones and family, Carrell Johnson, John Briscoe, Pia Hunter, Desirée McMillion, Denise Poindexter, Andre (Smiley) Collins, Devon Worth, Paige Cormier, Keith Fraley, Rafael Aponte, Jamila Simon, Nelicia Loftis, Francis Loftis, Mia Hardy, Royce Brooks, Letitia Anderson, Roshawn Anderson, Arlene Anderson, Ida Pearl Blount, Teresa Mathews Smith and family, and so many more. I want to especially highlight my dear friend and personal editor, Leah Jordan, for her patience, compassion, and energy in helping me work through the final months of revising this book. She always encouraged me to "say what you know." And that's exactly what I did. Honestly, there are not enough pages to capture all the love I received as I wrote this book, so I want to again thank everyone who is in my corner.

Lastly, I want to thank E. M. Norris and Cecil Strickland Sr., who are part of the great cloud of witnesses that can testify to the story of the NFA. Because of your decisions to devote your lives to the preservation and documentation of the story of the NFA, I was able to pick up where you both left off and continue to let the world know that the NFA did exist and it did matter. My sister's discovery of your widely unknown books on the NFA in our mother's garage changed my life, and I hope that I have made you proud in uplifting and remembering Black farm boys—past, present, and future.

Forever onward.

Behind the Scenes of Black Farm Boys

A BRIEF NOTE ON METHODS

The creative interpretive research design used to construct *Black Farm Boys* emerged from the Black studies tradition and took the shape of an instrumental collective case study approach. Each scene was carefully curated and constructed using different forms of qualitative data and then situated within the socio-physical world in which the New Farmers of America existed. To construct this world, I tracked one hundred years of agricultural mobilizations of rural Black youth in the South and recast these efforts as what I defined in this book as the Black youth farm movement. Drawing on theories of social movements and rural development paradigms in Black life, the BYFM represents the historical movement space that the NFA existed within, where rural Black youth were empowered to reimagine their agrarian futures in the face of a shifting agricultural economy that perpetuated inhumane and inequitable conditions for their families and communities. By locating the NFA within this movement space, each scene was an element of its own particular context that was located along the contours of the movement. As *Black Farm Boys* moved from scene to scene and context to context, the book brought into focus how the NFA redefined Black people's historical relationship to agriculture, initiating a forgotten critical inflection point in the history of African American life and the development of American agriculture.

What must be added to this line of thinking is that Black people's historical relationship to agriculture can be mapped along the multiple contours of what historian and archivist Debra Newman Ham describes as the "rich mosaic of African-American life that depicts scorn and admiration, defeat and triumph, tears and laughter." Probing the agricultural outlines of the mosaic of African American life—from slavery through today—reveals that we have more to learn about Black people's historical relationship to agriculture and how they used it to simultaneously advance America's competitive edge in scientific agriculture and transform agriculture into a site for the expansion and development of rural Black communities in the American South. By locating the NFA within the mosaic of African American life, the scenes of *Black Farm Boys* displace the pervasive presence of the Future Farmers of America in the untold story of the NFA that relegates the organization to the periphery of the story of American agricultural education. To do this, I actively repositioned the FFA to the backstage of the NFA's story—resurrecting the NFA's agency and autonomy in its own story. This placement of the FFA foregrounds the NFA's role in advancing Black agricultural practices and challenging dominant narratives about who could access agricultural education.[1]

Throughout the process of writing and researching material to build the scenes of *Black Farm Boys*, I also had to actively work with sources that were not easily accessible to shed light on a frequently overlooked corner of Black history. I had to retrieve the untold story of the NFA from marginal subparts of primary and secondary sources—creating my own archive—that required a specific reading and analytical device to decipher. Specifically, the analytical device I used was prominent Black novelist and editor Toni Morrison's method of "literary archaeology." In her essay "The Site of Memory," Morrison writes about her own process of constructing Black worlds in her work, specifically those of enslaved Black people, which provides a window into the interior lives of those Black people who didn't necessarily write about their own lives. Morrison asserts that those who study Black life must engage in a "literary archaeology" that enables us to uncover "what remains were left behind and to reconstruct the world that these remains imply." When engaging in this archaeological technique, Morrison argues that the remains can be read as text and subtext and that researchers arrive at such texts "in thousands of ways, learning each time they begin anew how to recognize a valuable idea and how to render the texture that accompanies, reveals or displays it to its best advantage." Such recognition brings to life the remains—documents, images, reports, notes, correspondences, letters—offering a site of memory.[2]

Said differently, Morrison's method of literary archaeology is a creative research process that works with the remains of Black history, weaving them together to tell a dynamic and constantly evolving story of Black life through the artistic interplay of care, memory, imagination, and evidence. This creative research process is foundational in what a new generation of scholars in Black studies is calling "Black archival practice." In her article

"Notes on Black Archival Practice," sociologist Amaka Okechukwu writes that "Black Archival Practice is a relationship to evidence that recognizes Black humanity and complexity, it is concerned with history, memory, and community vitality. In this way, Black Archival Practice could be considered a subset of memory work, a broad range of practices that preserve, resurrect, frame, and contest the past." Reading Morrison's method of literary archaeology as part of the lineage of Black archival practice, I took the remains—including organizational documents and records, personal letters, memoirs, photographs, oral histories, interviews, government records, and cultural artifact—left behind by participants, leaders, and affiliates of the NFA to write *Black Farm Boys*. These remains were context-dependent and read at an "angle," borrowing the words of historian Philippa Levine, that positions agriculture as a site of Black freedom: a perspective that shaped how I interpreted the data and used that data to generate the scenes, which each represent a separate case study of some aspect of the NFA.[3]

When viewed in sync, the scenes of *Black Farm Boys* represent a collective site of memory—as an instrument of research and function of recovery—composed of remains that illuminate the world of the NFA interfaced with the BYFM to reshape Black people's historical relationship to agriculture. This collective site of memory was converted into an instrumental collective case study model as outlined by social scientist Robert Stake. This model is characterized by a set of cases examined to provide insights into a specific issue or phenomenon, and not necessarily into the cases themselves. Here, the cases provide a supportive role in facilitating the understanding of a broader experience or social occurrence. In *Black Farm Boys*, the scenes are used collectively to assemble the untold story of the NFA as a space to explore and learn about the organization's existence, significance, and legacy.[4]

To wrap up this brief note on methods, I operationalized a creative interpretive research design to transform remains of the past into vibrant scenes that honor the thousands of Black farm boys in the NFA. These boys are often erased from our American memory of Black people's historical relationship to agriculture, and their remains are discarded into the dustbins of Black history. These remains, when read collectively, represent a robust archive that is a living site of memory. The idea of a living archive comes from the mind of sociologist Stuart Hall, who argued that a living archive is "present, on-going, continuing, unfinished, open-ended." This type of thinking posits that "it is impossible to describe an archive in its totality. . . . As work is produced, one is, as it were, contributing to and extending the limits of that to which one is contributing. It cannot be complete because . . . our new interpretations inflect it differently. An archive may be largely about 'the past' but it is always 're-read' in the light of the present and the future." Thinking with Hall in the present while looking to the future of Black life, *Black Farm Boys* reads the archive of scenes produced by the NFA as unfinished—an animated, interactive space that invites new questions and creates something meaningful from the remains left behind by Black people who envisioned a brighter future with agriculture at the center.[5]

Notes

Abbreviations Used in the Notes

BAE-US Black Agricultural Experience in the United States, Special Collections, National Agricultural Library, United States Department of Agriculture, Beltsville, MD (https://archive.org/details/usda-black agriculturalexperience)

KCPL Special Collections, Kansas City Public Library—Central Library, Kansas City, MO

NCATCOE North Carolina A&T State University Cooperative Extension Service Archives Collection (ncatcoe), Archives and Special Collections, F. D. Bluford Library, North Carolina A&T State University, Greensboro, NC

NCATNFA New Farmers of America Collection (ncatnfa), Archives and Special Collections, F. D. Bluford Library, North Carolina A&T State University, Greensboro, NC

NCATSBS S. B. Simmons Collection (ncatsbs), Archives and Special Collections, F. D. Bluford Library, North Carolina A&T State University, Greensboro, NC

RLSCA Ruth Lilly Special Collections and Archives, University Library, Indiana University Indianapolis, Indianapolis, IN

UNTPTH University of North Texas Libraries, The Portal to Texas History, Denton, TX.1.

Introduction

1. Norris, *Forty Long Years*; Strickland, *New Farmers of America in Retrospect*; Alston et al., *Legacy of the New Farmers of America*.

2. B. Smith, "In Search of the New Farmers of America."

3. Alston et al., *Legacy of the New Farmers of America*; Norris, *Forty Long Years*; Strickland, *New Farmers of America in Retrospect*.

4. To date, the only article published in a Black studies journal that includes a treatment of the NFA is Simmons, "Negro Youth and the US Junior Employment Service." As it relates to dissertation research, Wakefield, "Impact of the New Farmers

of America," and Gilman, "Examining the Merger of the NFA and FFA," are very useful for understanding the NFA. For additional scholarship that argues that the study of Black people's historical relationship to agriculture has focused mostly on inequality and oppression, see G. Grant et al., "Black Farmers United"; Gilbert et al., "Loss and Persistence"; Gilbert et al., "Who Owns the Land?"; Grim, "African American Landlords"; Grim, "African American Rural Culture"; Hinson and Robinson, "'We Didn't Get Nothing'"; Hunte, "African American Experience in Agriculture"; H. Jones, "Federal Agricultural Policies"; White, *Freedom Farmers*; and Wood and Gilbert, "Returning African American Farmers to the Land." For scholarship that examines Black people's historical relationship to agriculture beyond its oppressive dynamics, see Grim, "Impact of Mechanized Farming"; Grim, "Politics of Inclusion"; Grim, "1890 Land-Grant Colleges' Work"; White, "'Pig and a Garden'"; White, "Collective Agency"; Jones-Branch, "African Americans in Twentieth-Century Agriculture"; Brown et al., "Structural Changes in U.S. Agriculture"; Mclean-Meyinsse and Brown, "Survival Strategies of Successful Farmers"; King et al., "Black Agrarianism"; and Zabawa et al., "Decline of Black Farmers."

5. Carrillo et al., "Race, Ethnicity"; Julie Zimmerman, personal communication, August 1, 2025.

6. Connors, "Historical Analysis of the Role of Music"; Connors et al., "Recounting the Legacy"; S. Jones et al., "Role of NFA Camps"; W. Jones et al., "Voices of African American Agriculture Teachers"; Wakefield and Talbert, "Historical Narrative."

7. Diani, "Concept of Social Movement"; Kelley, *Freedom Dreams*.

8. Haunss and Leach, "Social Movement Scenes," 73.

9. Walcott, *Long Emancipation*, 2.

10. Zella Patterson, comp., "History of Oklahoma Association New Homemakers of America, 1945–1965," 1965, The Gateway to Oklahoma History, crediting Oklahoma Historical Society, https://gateway.okhistory.org/ark:/67531/metadc2024891/.

11. The creative interpretive research design used in this book centers the experiences and perspectives surrounding the leaders, members, and affiliates of the NFA. This research approach blends methodological insights from Hall, "Constituting an Archive"; Ham, *African-American Mosaic*; Levine, "Discipline and Pleasure"; Morrison, "Site of Memory"; Okechukwu, "Notes on Black Archival Practice"; Stake, *Art of Case Study Research*; and Stake, "Case Studies."

12. S. Franklin, *After the Rebellion*; S. Franklin, "Black Youth Activism"; Bynum, *NAACP Youth*.

13. C. Johnson, *Growing Up in the Black Belt*.

Chapter 1

1. Du Bois, "Last Word in Caste," 70; Du Bois, *Souls of Black Folk*. In the rural sociological intellectual tradition, the broader agrarian question focuses on the interaction between farmers, labor relations, rurality, and the structure of agricultural systems (see Constance, "Emancipatory Question"; and Constance, "2008 AFHVS Presidential Address").

2. Hightower, "Hard Tomatoes"; Hightower and Agribusiness Accountability Project Task Force on the Land Grant College Complex, *Hard Tomatoes*; Beardall, "Settler Simultaneity"; Hill, "Environmental Thought and Activism"; Lee and Keys,

"Land-Grant but Unequal"; Allen and Esters, "Historically Black Land Grant Universities"; J. Grant et al., "Overview of the History, Role, and Struggles."

3. Parks and Robbins, "Human Capital Needs"; Jones and Parks, "1890 Institutions"; Neyland, *Historically Black Land-Grant Institutions*; Schor, *Agriculture in the Black Land-Grant College System to 1930*; Schor, "Anachronisms or Rising Stars"; Schor, "Black Presence"; Christy and Williamson, *Century of Service*; Mayberry, *Century of Agriculture*; National Association of State Universities and Land-Grant Colleges, *Leadership and Learning*; Williams, *Unique Resources of the 1890 Land-Grant Institutions*.

4. Alston et al., *Legacy of the New Farmers of America*; Association of Public and Land-Grant Universities, *Land-Grant Tradition*, 13; US Congress, "Second Morrill Act"; Neyland, *Historically Black Land-Grant Institutions*, 21.

5. Anderson, *Education of Blacks in the South*.

6. Anderson, *Education of Blacks in the South*, 102; Washington, *Working with the Hands*, 135.

7. I. Reid, "Negro Movements and Messiahs," 364.

8. Seals, "Formation of Agricultural and Rural Development Policy"; Neyland, *Historically Black Land-Grant Institutions*; Kremer, *George Washington Carver*.

9. Carver, *Nature Study and Children's Gardens*; Carver, *Nature Study and Gardening*, 3.

10. Martin, *Decade of Negro Extension Work*; Harris, "States' Rights"; Thompson, "'Give Us a Status Above That of a Submarginal People'"; Crosby, "Struggle for Existence"; Crosby, "Roots of Black Agricultural Extension Work"; A. Jones, "South's First Black Farm Agents"; A. Jones, "Improving Rural Life for Blacks"; Brown, "1890 Institutions' Extension Program"; Harris, "'Extension Service Is Not an Integration Agency.'"

11. L. W. Jones, "South's Negro Farm Agent"; Martin, *Decade of Negro Extension Work*.

12. Purvis M. Carter, "The Philosophy of Robert Lloyd Smith—A Precursor for the Present?," *Texas Standard* 38, no. 2 (1964): 4–5, retrieved from https://digitalcommons.pvamu.edu/texas-standard/45; Carter, "Robert Lloyd Smith"; Pitre, "Robert Lloyd Smith"; Sturdevant, "FIS School"; Reid, *Reaping a Greater Harvest*.

13. Simmons, "Negro Youth and the US Junior Employment Service"; Martin, *Decade of Negro Extension Work*; *Extension Work Among Negroes in the South, 1944–1945* (US Department of Agriculture Extension Service, 1945), BAE-US; *Report of Regional Negro Workshop on Extension Supervision for Alabama, Arkansas, Georgia, Kentucky, Louisiana, Maryland, Mississippi, N. Carolina, Oklahoma, S. Carolina, Tennessee, Texas, Virginia, West Virginia* (Southern University, Scotlandville, LA, USDA Extension Service, 1946), BAE-US.

14. Strickland, *New Farmers of America in Retrospect*, 71; Stimson and Lothrop, *History of Agricultural Education*, 642.

15. Stimson and Lothrop, *History of Agricultural Education*, 461; Elam, "New Farmers of America."

16. Elam, "New Farmers of America"; Owens, "New Farmers of Virginia"; Fields, *New Farmers of America*; Crawford, *Autobiography of George Washington Owens*.

17. Crawford, *Autobiography of George Washington Owens*, 11.

18. Crawford, *Autobiography of George Washington Owens*.

19. Crawford, *Autobiography of George Washington Owens*; New Farmers of America, *N.F.A. Guide for New Farmers of America* (2nd ed.); Strickland, *New Farmers of America in Retrospect*, 72; "'Ag' Instructors Stage Conference," *Pittsburgh Courier*, July 25, 1931, www.proquest.com/historical-newspapers/ag -instructors-stage-conference-2/docview/201932539/se-2; "Farmers Form Aid Society in Virginia: To Invest in Statewide Farming System," *Chicago Defender*, July 16, 1927, www.proquest.com/historical-newspapers/farmers-form-aid-society-virginia /docview/492154955/se-2.

20. Elam, "New Farmers of America"; New Farmers of America, *Guide for New Farmers of America* (12th ed.).

21. "James City Co. Farm Student Wins Honors," *New Journal and Guide* (Norfolk, VA), July 23, 1927, www.proquest.com/historical-newspapers/james-city-co -farm-student-wins-honors/docview/567017653/se-2; "New Farmers of Virginia," *New Journal and Guide*, July 30, 1927, www.proquest.com/historical-newspapers /new-farmers-virginia/docview/567020142/se-2; Charles A. Wright, "Virginia State College," *Afro-American* (Baltimore, MD), May 3, 1930, www.proquest.com/historical -newspapers/virginia-state-college/docview/530818349/se-2; "Farmers Form Aid Society in Virginia: To Invest in Statewide Farming System," *Chicago Defender*, July 16, 1927, www.proquest.com/historical-newspapers/farmers-form-aid-society -virginia/docview/492154955/se-2.

22. Elam, "New Farmers of America"; Strickland, *New Farmers of America in Retrospect*; Norris, *Forty Long Years*.

23. Strickland, *New Farmers of America in Retrospect*. In some research, S. B. Simmons's middle name is spelled "Britten."

24. Strickland, *New Farmers of America in Retrospect*; New Farmers of America, *Proceedings First National Meeting of the New Farmers of America: Held at Tuskegee Institute, Alabama, August 4, 5, 6, and 7, 1935*, BAE-US.

25. Woodson, *Rural Negro*; New Farmers of America, *N.F.A. Guide for New Farmers of America* (1st ed.); Alston et al., *Legacy of the New Farmers of America*, 87.

26. Strickland, *New Farmers of America in Retrospect*, 1; New Farmers of America, *N.F.A. Guide for New Farmers of America* (1st ed.).

27. "New Farmers Have 11-Point Program," *New Journal and Guide*, October 7, 1939, www.proquest.com/historical-newspapers/new-farmers-have-11-point -program/docview/567346268/se-2; New Farmers of America, *Proceedings of the Fifth National Convention of New Farmers of America and Results of National Contests for Negro Students of Vocational Agriculture*, 33–34, RAMOS PF Q 630.717 N53P 1939, KCPL.

28. Simmons, "Negro Youth and the US Junior Employment Service," 412; Strickland, *New Farmers of America in Retrospect*, 101.

Chapter 2

1. New Farmers of America, *Proceedings of the Fifth National Convention of New Farmers of America and Results of National Contests for Negro Students of Vocational Agriculture*, 45, RAMOS PF Q 630.717 N53P 1939, KCPL (Barnett quote, emphasis mine); Hargraves, "Fifth National FFA Convention."

2. "Claude A. Barnett Dies at 77; Founder of Negro News Agency; Service Added Journals in New African Countries as They Emerged," *New York Times*, August 3, 1967, www.nytimes.com/1967/08/03/archives/claude-a-barnett-dies-at-77-founder -of-negro-news-agency-service.html; Petty, "I'll Take My Farm"; Horne, *Rise and Fall of the Associated Negro Press*; Pattillo, "Black Advantage Vision."

3. Juris, "Spaces of Intentionality," 55, 50.

4. New Farmers of America, *Proceedings of the Fifth National Convention*, KCPL.

5. Du Bois, "Last Word in Caste"; Strickland, *New Farmers of America in Retrospect*.

6. New Farmers of America, *Proceedings First National Meeting of the New Farmers of America: Held at Tuskegee Institute, Alabama, August 4, 5, 6, and 7, 1935*, BAE-US; Strickland, *New Farmers of America in Retrospect*.

7. New Farmers of America, *Proceedings First National Meeting*, BAE-US; Strickland, *New Farmers of America in Retrospect*.

8. Fields, *New Farmers of America*; Strickland, *New Farmers of America in Retrospect*.

9. Wright, *Education of Negroes in New Jersey*, 178; Hunter et al., "Black Placemaking," 31.

10. Manual Training and Industrial School for Colored Youth, *State of New Jersey Manual Training School Pictorial Bulletin* (New Jersey Manual Training School, 1940), Reports by and about the Manual Training and Industrial School for Colored Youth at Bordentown, New Jersey State Library, Trenton; Goddard, "The Bordentown School as Institution and Idea"; Washington, *Working with the Hands*, 135.

11. Goddard, "Bordentown"; A. Jones, "Improving Rural Life for Blacks"; Washington quoted in E. Adams, "Role and Function," 123.

12. E. Adams, "Role and Function," 71, 15; Goddard, "Bordentown," 54; Interracial Committee of the New Jersey Conference of Social Work, *Negro in New Jersey*, 3; Manual Training and Industrial School for Colored Youth, *Bulletin of Information* (State of New Jersey, Manual Training School for Colored Youth, 1943), Reports by and about the Manual Training and Industrial School for Colored Youth at Bordentown, New Jersey State Library, Trenton.

13. "Bordentown School Holds Farmers Meeting: Starts Agricultural Activities Modeled After Tuskegee and Hampton," *Philadelphia Tribune*, April 20, 1918, www .proquest.com/historical-newspapers/bordentown-school-holds-farmers-meeting /docview/530784008/se-2; "Jersey Prepares for Conference with Farmers," *New Journal and Guide*, January 20, 1934, www.proquest.com/historical-newspapers /jersey-prepares-conference-with-farmers/docview/567311174/se-2; "Farmers' Conference Huge Success," *Ironsides Echo*, March 1938, https://dspace.njstatelib.org /items/97cee759-4dfd-4aa1-84d7-967e501d7c91.

14. "Farmers Meet Here March 2; Record Crowd Expected," *Ironsides Echo*, February 1939, https://dspace.njstatelib.org/items/efe1e18e-7cbb-4a5b-89b5 -779811735388; "New Jersey Farm Conference Reaches Attendance Peak," *New Journal and Guide*, March 15, 1941, www.proquest.com/historical-newspapers /new-jersey-farm-conference-reaches-attendance/docview/567453914/se-2; Lu Ann Jones, "In Search of Jennie Booth Moton"; "Bordentown Now a Second Tuskegee," *Chicago Defender*, January 3, 1931, www.proquest.com/historical-newspapers /bordentown-now-second-tuskegee/docview/492281150/se-2; Neyland, *Historically Black Land-Grant Institutions*, 92.

15. E. Adams, "Role and Function," 58, 60–66; Floyd J. Calvin, "Bordentown Industrial School Urges Youth Toward Farm Life," *Pittsburgh Courier*, August 4, 1928, www .proquest.com/historical-newspapers/industrial-school-youth-toward-farm-life /docview/201883422/se-2; "Bordentown Takes Lead in Pure Breeding of Cows, Hogs, Horses: Many Champions Are Produced by Experts Courses Are Popular with Students in Training," *New York Amsterdam News*, February 20, 1937, www.proquest .com/historical-newspapers/bordentown-takes-lead-pure-breeding-cows-hogs /docview/226117662/se-2.

16. Goddard, "Bordentown," 54; Stimson and Lothrop, *History of Agricultural Education*, 305.

17. New Farmers of America, *Proceedings of the Fifth National Convention*, 40–41, KCPL; Frederick A. Williams, "Problem of Negro Marginal Farmer Still to Be Solved: Too Often Neglected in Government and Individual Programs for Alleviating Conditions, and Improving Rural Life," *New Journal and Guide*, September 30, 1939, www .proquest.com/historical-newspapers/problem-negro-marginal-farmer-still-be -solved/docview/567438339/se-2.

18. New Farmers of America, *Proceedings of the Fifth National Convention*, 40–41, KCPL.

19. "Bordentown, N.J., Senior at National Farm Meet," *Afro-American*, August 24, 1935, www.proquest.com/historical-newspapers/bordentown-n-j-senior-at -national-farm-meet/docview/531120145/se-2; Strickland, *New Farmers of America in Retrospect*, 101–2; "Gets N.F.A. Key," *Ironsides Echo*, April 1938, https://dspace .njstatelib.org/items/61bdccac-f699-4665-b82c-c87d61aaa931; "Mr. Urquhart to Get N.F.A. Key," *Ironsides Echo*, April 1939, https://dspace.njstatelib.org/items /efd20455-2832-4d01-8b14-434d8e177213.

20. "Clubs Organize and Elect Officers," *Ironsides Echo*, October 1937, https:// dspace.njstatelib.org/items/8eefbdde-8177-4859-8d54-73373377c2a7; "Jersey Prepares for Farmers Conference," *New Journal and Guide*, January 20, 1934; "Bordentown Takes Lead in Pure Breeding of Cows, Hogs, Horses."

21. "Clubs Organize and Elect Officers"; "Jersey Prepares for Farmers Conference"; "Bordentown Takes Lead in Pure Breeding of Cows, Hogs, Horses"; Edward Livingston, "News from N.F.A.," *Ironsides Echo*, December 1936, https://dspace.njstatelib .org/items/bb1ace98-030a-4394-b0fa-05c0c79c4379.

22. "Ag Experts Visit School," *Ironsides Echo*, January 1939, https://dspace .njstatelib.org/items/8afb67f7-7e8a-4d9a-9ef9-d7dfb9205d8c; "N.F.A. Will Convene Here August 6–8," *Ironsides Echo*, May–June 1939, https://dspace.njstatelib.org /items/664b0d67-8d9a-4139-8586-70b1fbf82405; "Bordentown Summer Host; 600 N.F.A.'s Assemble," *Ironsides Echo*, October 1939, https://dspace.njstatelib.org/items /a302b5ff-84fa-4a7e-b644-b7849fa2c9bd; New Farmers of America, *Proceedings of the Fifth National Convention*, 13, KCPL.

23. Ms. Murphy's name is misspelled as "Francis" in New Farmers of America, *Proceedings of the Fifth National Convention*, 9–11, KCPL; Simmons, "N.F.A. in Annual Convention"; J. Archie Hargraves, "Texas Youth Named Ranking 'Superior Farmer' of America," *New Journal and Guide*, August 19, 1939, www.proquest.com /historical-newspapers/texas-youth-named-ranking-superior-farmer-america /docview/567452414/se-2.

24. New Farmers of America, *Proceedings of the Fifth National Convention*, 41–44, KCPL; White, *Freedom Farmers*; Hunt, *Dreaming the Present*; Nembhard, *Collective Courage*.

25. New Farmers of America, *Proceedings of the Fifth National Convention*, 54–55, KCPL; Simmons, "N.F.A. in Annual Convention."

26. New Farmers of America, *Proceedings of the Fifth National Convention*, 52, KCPL; New Farmers of America, *N.F.A. Guide for New Farmers of America* (4th ed.), 40; Simmons, "N.F.A. in Annual Convention"; Strickland, *New Farmers of America in Retrospect*, 19.

27. New Farmers of America, *Proceedings of the Fifth National Convention*, 9–13, KCPL; "'Wings Over Jordan' Big Radio Feature," *Chicago Defender*, April 15, 1939, www.proquest.com/historical-newspapers/wings-over-jordan-big-radio-feature /docview/492520383/se-2.

28. "Bordentown Summer Host; 600 N.F.A.'s Assemble"; S. Smith, "Remembering the Walker-Gordon Dairy"; New Farmers of America, *Proceedings of the Fifth National Convention*, 9–17, KCPL.

29. "Preliminary Announcement. Seventh World's Poultry Congress and Exposition," *Seventh World's Poultry Congress and Exposition*; New York World's Fair, *Official Guide Book*; Madera, "Early Black Worldmaking," 483.

30. Te Hennepe, "Seventh World's Poultry Congress and Exposition"; "Preliminary Announcement. Seventh World's Poultry Congress and Exposition," 13; "Exhibit at World's Poultry Congress by Negro Youths Hits Sharecroppers' Plight," *Cleveland Call and Post*, August 3, 1939, www.proquest.com/historical-newspapers /exhibit-at-worlds-poultry-congress-negro-youths/docview/184058178/se-2.

31. "Exhibit at World's Poultry Congress by Negro Youths Hits Sharecroppers' Plight."

32. Arthur, "Vocational Summary," 23; "Exhibit at World's Poultry Congress by Negro Youths Hits Sharecroppers' Plight."

33. New York World's Fair, *Official Guide Book*, 40–41.

34. New Farmers of America, *Proceedings of the Fifth National Convention*, 11, KCPL; Simmons, "N.F.A. in Annual Convention"; Hargraves, "Texas Youth Named Ranking 'Superior Farmer' of America."

35. New Farmers of America, *Proceedings of the Fifth National Convention*, 60–65 (Spaulding's quote, 65), KCPL.

36. New Farmers of America, *Proceedings of the Fifth National Convention*, 60–65, KCPL; Hargraves, "Texas Youth Named Ranking 'Superior Farmer' of America."

37. "Bordentown Summer Host; 600 N.F.A.'s Assemble."

38. "New Farmers Have 11-Point Program," *New Journal and Guide*, October 7, 1939, www.proquest.com/historical-newspapers/new-farmers-have-11-point -program/docview/567346268/se-2; New Farmers of America, *Proceedings of the Fifth National Convention*, 33–34, KCPL; New Farmers of America, *Proceedings of the Fourth National Convention of the New Farmers of America*, 39, BAE-US.

Chapter 3

1. "NFA Day TV Program over Station WFMY-TV," April 6, 1956, ncnfa-010-003-001, NCATNFA.

2. "Dedication Program: The S. B. Simmons Camp," June 20, 1958, ncatcoe-001-011-002, NCATCOE; "$100,000 NFA Camp Is Dedicated in North Carolina: New Site Honors S. Simmons," *New Journal and Guide*, July 5, 1958, 14, www.proquest.com/historical-newspapers/100-000-nfa-camp-is-dedicated-north-carolina/docview/568523650/se-2; "Late S. B. Simmons Honored as NFA Camp Is Dedicated," *Atlanta Daily World*, June 26, 1958, www.proquest.com/historical-newspapers/late-s-b-simmons-honored-as-nfa-camp-is-dedicated/docview/491144359/se-2.

3. Glave, *Rooted in the Earth*, 6.

4. Ginwright, *Black Youth Rising*, 147.

5. Turner, foreword to *A Place for Us*, 5–6; Cromley, "Transforming the Food Axis," 9.

6. W. Johnson, "Camping Experiences Develop Leadership," 248; Chatelain, *South Side Girls*, 130–31.

7. Young, *Camping Grounds*, 182–88; "Camp Atwater," May 24, 1955, ncatsbs11003, NCATSBS; "History," Camp Atwater, retrieved from www.campatwater.org/history on July 19, 2024; Watson, "Camp Atwater (1921–)"; Van Slyck, *Manufactured Wilderness*, xxvi.

8. J. Johnson, "History and Development of the Oklahoma Association," 37–40.

9. J. Johnson, "History and Development of the Oklahoma Association," 37–40 (Johnson's quote, 37–38).

10. J. Johnson, "History and Development of the Oklahoma Association," 37–40 (Johnson's quote, 39–40).

11. S. Jones et al., "Role of NFA Camps"; "New Farmers' Camp"; J. Franklin, *Golden Nuggets*; Tabor, "Camp John Hope"; "Plans Are Big for Texas Association of New Farmers," *Prairie View Standard* 44, no. 6 (February 1954): 4, retrieved from https://digitalcommons.pvamu.edu/pv-newspapers/183/; Lee, "Some Aspects of Activity Programs"; "New Farmers of America Camp for Mississippi Boys"; P. Adams, "Time Remembered"; P. Adams, *Place for Us*.

12. Guy Minger, "Negro Farm Youths Launch Recreation Season This Week," *Greensboro (NC) Daily News*, June 12, 1955, ncatsbs11052, NCATSBS; *Mosquito Express* 3, no. 2, NFA Camp, Hammocks Beach—Swansboro, NC, June 18–22, 1956, ncnfa-009-002-001, NCATNFA.

13. Arthur Bell, C. E. Dean, Walter T. Johnson, and Lee Alan Yates, *Biographical Sketch of Simmons*, 1958–1959, ncatsbs11001, NCATSBS; for biographical information on Rev. Robert H. Simmons, a presiding elder, and Julia A. Simmons, see Find a Grave, database and images, memorial page for Julia A. Covington Simmons (September 9, 1865–October 19, 1966), Second Baptist Cemetery, Fayetteville, Cumberland County, NC, retrieved from www.findagrave.com/memorial/149415509/julia_a-simmons; "S. B. Simmons Is Given Testimonial," *New Journal and Guide*, November 27, 1954, www.proquest.com/historical-newspapers/s-b-simmons-is-given-testimonial/docview/568213518/se-2; *Testimonial Dinner Honoring S. B. Simmons*, July 12, 1954, ncnfa-002-003-001, NCATNFA.

14. Bell et al., *Biographical Sketch of Simmons*, NCATSBS; Elam, "New Farmers of America," 553; Manor and Pronovost, "4-H and Home Demonstration."

15. Bell et al., *Biographical Sketch of Simmons*, NCATSBS; "Grimesland," *New Journal and Guide*, October 29, 1927, www.proquest.com/historical-newspapers/grimesland/docview/566976136/se-2; Pitt County Historical Society, "Short History

of Pitt County Education"; "Advance in Negro Education"; Minger, "Negro Farm Youths Launch Recreation Season This Week," NCATSBS.

16. "First Vocational Camp Starts Thursday," *Afro-American*, September 6, 1930, www.proquest.com/historical-newspapers/first-vocational-camp-starts-thursday/docview/530823712/se-2; "Three Hundred New Farmers of America Hold Camp," *New Journal and Guide*, August 13, 1932, www.proquest.com/historical-newspapers/three-hundred-new-farmers-america-hold-camp/docview/567164866/se-2; "Dedication Program: The S. B. Simmons Camp," NCATCOE.

17. S. Jones et al., "Role of NFA Camps"; Bell et al., *Biographical Sketch of Simmons*, NCATSBS.

18. "Dedication Program: The S. B. Simmons Camp," NCATCOE; S. Jones et al., "Role of NFA Camps"; "History of the N.F.A. Camp Idea in North Carolina," *Mosquito Express* 3, no. 2, NCATNFA; Bell et al., *Biographical Sketch of Simmons*, NCATSBS; Rehder and Cohen, "Eccentric Neurosurgical Virtuoso"; Sharpe, *Brain Surgeon*, 202–4; Sanders, "Blue Water."

19. A. M. Rivera Jr., "Instructors Enjoy Gift of 4,000-Acre Beach in Tarheelia," *Courier* (Pittsburgh) July 5, 1952, www.proquest.com/historical-newspapers/instructors-enjoy-gift-4–000-acre-beach-tarheelia/docview/202284066/se-2; "North Carolina Teachers Get 4,000-Acre Land Grant: Property to Be Used for Recreation," *New Journal and Guide*, September 23, 1950, www.proquest.com/historical-newspapers/north-carolina-teachers-get-4-000-acre-land-grant/docview/567919064/se-2; Sharpe, *Brain Surgeon*, 216; Sanders, "Blue Water."

20. Rivera, "Instructors Enjoy Gift of 4,000-Acre Beach in Tarheelia"; Sanders, "Blue Water."

21. Minger, "Negro Farm Youths Launch Recreation Season This Week," NCATSBS; Noakes, "New York F.F.A. Camping Program."

22. "Dedication Program: The S. B. Simmons Camp," NCATCOE; *Mosquito Express* 3, no. 2, NCATNFA; Noakes, "New York F.F.A. Camping Program"; Minger, "Negro Farm Youths Launch Recreation Season This Week," NCATSBS; Alston et al., *Legacy of the New Farmers of America*.

23. *Mosquito Express* 3, no. 2, NCATNFA; "Dedication Program: The S. B. Simmons Camp," NCATCOE.

24. *New Farmers of America Needs You! Help to Complete N.F.A. Camp* (brochure), July 1, 1955, ncnfa-003-012-001, NCATNFA; *Confidential Report on Fundraising Campaign*, April 26, 1954, ncatsbs11069, NCATSBS.

25. Minger, "Negro Farm Youths Launch Recreation Season This Week," NCATSBS; *Confidential Report on Fundraising Campaign*, NCATSBS; "$100,000 NFA Camp Is Dedicated in North Carolina: New Site Honors S. Simmons"; *New Farmers of America Needs You! Help to Complete N.F.A. Camp* (brochure), NCATNFA; "Dedication Program: The S. B. Simmons Camp," NCATCOE; *Mosquito Express* 3, no. 2, NCATNFA.

26. *New Farmers of America Fifth Annual Encampment Hammocks Beach Near Swansboro, North Carolina*, June 9–August 8, 1958, ncnfa-003-012-004, NCATNFA; "Vocational Agriculture Leader Simmons Passes," *Atlanta Daily World*, August 2, 1957, www.proquest.com/historical-newspapers/vocational-agriculture-leader-simmons-passes/docview/491123017/se-2; Warmoth T. Gibbs and D. C. Jones quoted in "Dedication Program: The S. B. Simmons Camp," NCATCOE; J. Johnson, "History and Development of the Oklahoma Association."

27. Simmons, "Negro Youth and the US Junior Employment Service," 413;
W. Johnson, "Camping Experiences Develop Leadership," 248; *New Farmers of
America's Annual Encampment Hammocks Beach Near Swansboro, North Carolina,
June 6–29, 1956*, ncnfa-003-012-002, NCATNFA; *New Farmers of America Fifth
Annual Encampment*, NCATNFA; S. Jones et al., "Role of NFA Camps," 284.

28. Minger, "Negro Farm Youths Launch Recreation Season This Week,"
NCATSBS; *New Farmers of America Fifth Annual Encampment*, NCATNFA.

29. *Mosquito Express* 3, no. 2, NCATNFA; camper quoted in Walter T. Johnson,
"For Training Carolina Youth: There's No Better Place Than Simmons NFA Camp,"
New Journal and Guide, June 17, 1961, www.proquest.com/historical-newspapers
/training-carolina-youth/docview/568759204/se-2; Minger, "Negro Farm Youths
Launch Recreation Season This Week," NCATSBS.

30. Simmons, "Negro Youth and the US Junior Employment Service," 413; for-
mer camp chief quoted in *Mosquito Express* 3, no. 2, NCATNFA; *New Farmers of
America's Annual Encampment*, NCATNFA; *New Farmers of America Fifth Annual
Encampment*, NCATNFA.

31. Alston et al., *Legacy of the New Farmers of America*, 105; Glave, *Rooted in the
Earth*, 93–103.

32. W. Johnson, "For Training Carolina Youth: There's No Better Place Than Simmons NFA Camp"; W. Johnson, "Camping Experiences Develop Leadership," 249;
New Farmers Boys Camp, n.d., ncnfa-002-003-014, NCATNFA.

33. Minger, "Negro Farm Youths Launch Recreation Season This Week,"
NCATSBS; *Mosquito Express* 3, no. 2, NCATNFA.

34. *Proceedings of the 33rd Annual Convention North Carolina Association New
Farmers of America*, June 5–8, 1961, NCATNFA; James Eaton quoted in Minger,
"Negro Farm Youths Launch Recreation Season This Week," NCATSBS.

35. W. Johnson, "Camping Experiences Develop Leadership"; *NFA Camp Booklet*,
n.d., ncatsbs11055, NCATSBS; Alston et al., *Legacy of the New Farmers of America*;
Simmons, "Negro Youth and the US Junior Employment Service," 413.

36. Sanders, "Blue Water."

37. *Mosquito Express* 3, no. 2, NCATNFA.

38. "A Trip to the Dandy Beach by Boat," *Mosquito Express* 3, no. 2, NCATNFA.

39. Ginwright, *Black Youth Rising*, 57.

40. N. L. Dillard quoted in "Comments by a Principal," *Mosquito Express* 3, no. 2,
NCATNFA.

41. *Proceedings of the 33rd Annual Convention*, NCATNFA; Alexander Dawson
quoted in W. Johnson, "For Training Carolina Youth: There's No Better Place Than
Simmons NFA Camp."

42. North Carolina FFA Association, "History of the NC FFA Center"; S. Jones
et al., "Role of NFA Camps."

Chapter 4

1. Elaine Thomas, "Stories I've Been Told: A Close Harmony," *Fayette County
Record* (La Grange, TX), May 30, 2014, A1, A11.

2. For information about Lorenza and Myrtle Crosby's graduation credentials, see Prairie View Agricultural and Mechanical College, "Convocation Exercises—May 1956," Commencement and Convocation Exercises, Academic Affairs Collections, University Archives, Prairie View A&M University, 1956, retrieved from https://digitalcommons.pvamu.edu/academic-affairs/29.

3. Grim, "African American Rural Culture," 122–28.

4. G. Johnson, *All Boys Aren't Blue*, 163; Beauford, "Revitalizing Rural America"; W. Jones, "Factors Influencing Career Choice."

5. Beauford, "Revitalizing Rural America," 7; Donald Reese, personal communication, September 2, 2022.

6. Floyd, "Teaching and Learning as Applied to Vocational Agriculture."

7. Hickson, "Needs of Farm Families"; J. Franklin, *Golden Nuggets*, 114.

8. Kersey, "My Hopes for a Greater Development." For more coverage of Holloway High School's NFA activities, see the October 1938, November 1938, and December 1938 editions of *American Farm Youth*.

9. "Mississippi Association of N.F.A. Stresses Home Improvement Program"; "Monthly Meetings of District Association on NFA Programs of Work."

10. Alston et al., *Legacy of the New Farmers of America*, 42; Hicks, "New Farmers of America and National Defense"; Strickland, *New Farmers of America in Retrospect*, 21–23.

11. Conoly, "Some Benefits from N.F.A. Banquets"; Conoly, "Program of Education."

12. George Moore, "North Carolina Convention."

13. Strickland, *New Farmers of America in Retrospect*, 1.

14. L. E. Moore, "Lest We Forget: History of the La Grange Negro High School—1934," *La Grange (TX) Journal*, September 25, 1941, UNTPTH, https://texashistory.unt.edu/ark:/67531/metapth998611/; "Negro Principal Here 31 Years Claimed by Death," *La Grange Journal*, November 8, 1945, FREYTAG RAM_RIV 1994.81.278, folder: Randolph High School, Fayette Heritage Museum and Archives, Fayette Public Library, La Grange, Texas; Prairie View State Normal and Industrial College, *Annual Catalog—The School Year 1905–1906*, PV Annual Catalog Collection, University Archives, Prairie View A&M University, 1905, retrieved from https://digitalcommons.pvamu.edu/pv-annual-catalog/97; Rox Ann Johnson, personal communication, May 15, 2024.

15. Carver, *Nature Study and Children's Gardens*; Carver, *Nature Study and Gardening*, 3.

16. "Colored County Agent," *La Grange Journal*, July 6, 1933, UNTPTH, https://texashistory.unt.edu/ark:/67531/metapth999059/; "Negro 4-H Club Boys Install Sub-Irrigation System," *La Grange Journal*, October 17, 1935, UNTPTH, https://texashistory.unt.edu/ark:/67531/metapth998854/; "Outstanding Negro Community in Texas Is Named La Grange," *La Grange Journal*, June 13, 1940, UNTPTH, https://texashistory.unt.edu/ark:/67531/metapth998813/; L. Moore, "Lest We Forget," UNTPTH.

17. L. Moore, "Lest We Forget," UNTPTH.

18. Collins, "Health Conditions of One Hundred Negro Households."

19. Collins, "Health Conditions of One Hundred Negro Households."

20. Stimson and Lothrop, *History of Agricultural Education*, 438; Luter, "Historical and Educational Analysis"; Prairie View State Normal and Industrial College, *Catalog Edition—The School Year 1933–1934*, 25, no. 3, PV Annual Catalog Collection, University Archives, Prairie View A&M University, 1934, retrieved from https://digitalcommons.pvamu.edu/pv-annual-catalog/6; Prairie View State Normal and Industrial College, *Annual Catalog—The School Year 1942–1943*, 34, no. 4, PV Annual Catalog Collection, University Archives, Prairie View A&M University, 1943, retrieved from https://digitalcommons.pvamu.edu/pv-annual-catalog/50; Strickland, *New Farmers of America in Retrospect*, 51.

21. "Annual Progressive Farmer Contests Held April 16," *Prairie View Standard* 17, no. 7 (April 1930): 2, retrieved from https://digitalcommons.pvamu.edu/pv-newspapers/19; Strickland, *New Farmers of America in Retrospect*, 51; Elam, "New Farmers of America," 554.

22. Collins, "Health Conditions of One Hundred Negro Households"; "Schulenburg Colored School Wins Banner at Prairie View," *Schulenburg Sticker*, April 1, 1938, COM 1994.6.1, folder: Schulenburg Tx./Pioneers of Yesteryear and Today, Fayette Heritage Museum and Archives, Fayette Public Library, La Grange, Texas.

23. "Negro Group Asks Nurse and Health Center in Fight Against Disease," *Fayette County Record*, April 5, 1946, 1, UNTPTH, https://texashistory.unt.edu/ark:/67531/metapth1254427/; "Colored High School Improvements in Two Years, Three Months," *La Grange Journal*, November 4, 1943, 8, UNTPTH, https://texashistory.unt.edu/ark:/67531/metapth1004405/; "Homemaking Department," *La Grange Journal*, November 4, 1943, 8, UNTPTH, https://texashistory.unt.edu/ark:/67531/metapth1004405/.

24. Walter Green, "Some Historical Events of the La Grange Chapter of New Farmers of America," *La Grange (TX) High School N.F.A. News*, May 1, 1946, 1, UNTPTH, https://texashistory.unt.edu/ark:/67531/metapth1126035/; Dorothy Bernice Sims, "The Subject I Like Best," *La Grange High School N.F.A. News*, May 1, 1946, 4, UNTPTH, https://texashistory.unt.edu/ark:/67531/metapth1126035/; Jesse Williams Jr., "My First Year in Home-Making," *La Grange High School N.F.A. News*, May 1, 1946, 4, UNTPTH, https://texashistory.unt.edu/ark:/67531/metapth1126035/; "Practice Teachers Get Training Here," *Fayette County Record*, August 8, 1947, 4, UNTPTH, https://texashistory.unt.edu/ark:/67531/metapth1195775/.

25. Green, "Some Historical Events of the La Grange Chapter of New Farmers of America," UNTPTH.

26. Green, "Some Historical Events of the La Grange Chapter of New Farmers of America," UNTPTH; "N.F.A. Boys Success at State Judging Contest," *La Grange Journal*, February 25, 1943, 2, UNTPTH, https://texashistory.unt.edu/ark:/67531/metapth997873/.

27. "N.F.A. Boys Success at State Judging Contest," UNTPTH.

28. "Live Stock and Poultry Show, Dec. 18," *La Grange Journal*, November 23, 1944, 1, UNTPTH, https://texashistory.unt.edu/ark:/67531/metapth1004305/.

29. "NFA Boys Receive Awards at Fair," *Prairie View Standard*, 37, no. 3 (November 1946): 3, retrieved from https://digitalcommons.pvamu.edu/pv

-newspapers/155; Bullock Texas State History Museum, "NAACP Youth Council Picket Line"; "Negro Boy Wins in National Contest," *Fayette County Record*, November 29, 1946, 4, UNTPTH, https://texashistory.unt.edu/ark:/67531/metapth1254463/; "La Grange Negro Boys Score High in Contest," *Fayette County Record*, February 19, 1946, 2, UNTPTH, https://texashistory.unt.edu/ark:/67531/metapth1254647/.

30. "Negro Principal Fired Following Pupils' Walk-Out," *Fayette County Record*, October 31, 1947, 1, UNTPTH, https://texashistory.unt.edu/ark:/67531/metapth1196751/; Jackson, "Some Aspects of Farming"; Rox Ann Johnson, personal communication, May 15, 2024.

31. "NFA Hold Annual Father-Son 'Feed,'" *La Grange Journal*, May 17, 1951, 8, UNTPTH, https://texashistory.unt.edu/ark:/67531/metapth1349112/; "Five Randolph Boys Get NFA Degrees," *La Grange Journal*, December 14, 1950, 8, UNTPTH, https://texashistory.unt.edu/ark:/67531/metapth1349090/; "Randolph N.F.A. Wins Five Places in Area III Meet," *La Grange Journal*, March 8, 1951, 7, UNTPTH, https://texashistory.unt.edu/ark:/67531/metapth1349102/; New Farmers of America, *N.F.A. Guide for New Farmers of America* (7th ed.).

32. Jackson, "Some Aspects of Farming"; Prairie View University, "Commencement Exercises—May 1948," Commencement and Convocation Exercises, Academic Affairs Collections, University Archives, Prairie View A&M University, 1948, retrieved from https://digitalcommons.pvamu.edu/academic-affairs/113; "Randolph High Will Conduct Evening Agriculture Classes," *La Grange Journal*, January 17, 1952, 3, UNTPTH, https://texashistory.unt.edu/ark:/67531/metapth1254759/; "Negro Classes for Adults Announced," *La Grange Journal*, October 2, 1952, 3, UNTPTH, https://texashistory.unt.edu/ark:/67531/metapth1254303/.

33. "District NFA Cage Tourney Is Jan. 26," *La Grange Journal*, January 19, 1950, 3, UNTPTH, https://texashistory.unt.edu/ark:/67531/metapth1349043/; "NFA Hold Annual Father-Son 'Feed,'" UNTPTH; "Randolph NFA and NHA at Conference," *La Grange Journal*, April 19, 1951, 5, UNTPTH, https://texashistory.unt.edu/ark:/67531/metapth1349108/; "150 Attend Randolph Banquet and Tour," *La Grange Journal*, May 25, 1950, 3, UNTPTH, https://texashistory.unt.edu/ark:/67531/metapth1349061/; "NFA Students See Ag Movie Wednesday," *La Grange Journal*, January 19, 1950, 2, UNTPTH, https://texashistory.unt.edu/ark:/67531/metapth1349043/; "Randolph NFA Group Places High in Meet," *La Grange Journal*, March 30, 1950, 5, UNTPTH, https://texashistory.unt.edu/ark:/67531/metapth1349053/; "Randolph NFA Receives Invitation to National Contest," *La Grange Journal*, March 15, 1956, 5, UNTPTH, https://texashistory.unt.edu/ark:/67531/metapth1255517/; "Randolph N.F.A. Wins Five Places in Area III Meet," *La Grange Journal*, March 8, 1951, 7, UNTPTH, https://texashistory.unt.edu/ark:/67531/metapth1349102/; Horace Drisdale, personal communication, June 12, 2023.

34. Horace Drisdale, personal communication, June 12, 2023; Gloria Mosby, "Former Cooperative Extension Head Hoover Carden Expires," *Faculty and Staff News* (Prairie View A&M University), 3, no. 2 (November 1998): 2, Faculty and Staff News, Academic Affairs Collections, University Archives, Prairie View A&M University, retrieved from https://digitalcommons.pvamu.edu/faculty-and-staff-news/49; Carden, "Educational Value of Livestock Shows and Fairs," 24–25.

35. "Randolph NFA Place High at Live Stock Exposition," *La Grange Journal*, March 24, 1955, 6, UNTPTH, https://texashistory.unt.edu/ark:/67531 /metapth1254643/; "NFA Boys Place at Dallas Fair," *La Grange Journal*, November 3, 1955, 5, UNTPTH, https://texashistory.unt.edu/ark:/67531/metapth1254344/; "Randolph NFA Receives Invitation to National Contest," UNTPTH.

36. "Randolph N.F.A. Cops Big Prize at San Antonio Show," *La Grange Journal*, February 13, 1958, 3, UNTPTH, https://texashistory.unt.edu/ark:/67531 /metapth997693/; "Randolph NFA Lad Shows Grand Champ at San Antonio Show," *Fayette County Record*, February 11, 1958, 5, UNTPTH, https://texashistory.unt.edu /ark:/67531/metapth988820/; "Randolph Scores High: Lad Takes Big S.A. Prize," *Fayette County Record*, February 20, 1959, 1–2, UNTPTH, https://texashistory.unt.edu /ark:/67531/metapth990009/; "Randolph NFA Cops Two High Prizes at San Antonio Show," *La Grange Journal*, March 12, 1959, 4, UNTPTH, https://texashistory.unt.edu /ark:/67531/metapth998909/; "Randolph NFA Lads Sell SA Champ Hogs for $1600 Total," *Fayette County Record*, February 24, 1959, 1, UNTPTH, https://texashistory .unt.edu/ark:/67531/metapth989026/.

37. "Randolph Scores High: Lad Takes Big S.A. Prize," UNTPTH.

38. "Randolph NFA's Banquet a Success," *Fayette County Record*, April 7, 1959, 5, UNTPTH, https://texashistory.unt.edu/ark:/67531/metapth987977/; "NFA of Former Ag Teacher Place in San Antonio Show," *La Grange Journal*, March 3, 1960, 7, UNTPTH, https://texashistory.unt.edu/ark:/67531/metapth1254128/.

39. Grim, "Politics of Inclusion," 257–58.

40. Thomas, "Stories I've Been Told: A Close Harmony," A1, A11; Lorenza Crosby personal communication, June 23, 2022, and August 14, 2024; "Students Awarded Scholarships," *Prairie View Standard* 45, no. 1 (September 1945): 2, retrieved from https://digitalcommons.pvamu.edu/pv-newspapers/178.

41. Thomas, "Stories I've Been Told: A Close Harmony," A1, A11; Lorenza Crosby personal communication, June 23, 2022.

42. Lorenza Crosby personal communication, June 23, 2022; "Ag Shop Plans for Randolph Are Announced," *Fayette County Record*, April 21, 1964, 1, UNTPTH, https://texashistory.unt.edu/ark:/67531/metapth988742/.

43. Lorenza Crosby personal communication, June 23, 2022; Du Bois, "Talented Tenth," 54.

44. Prairie View Agricultural and Mechanical College, "Convocation Exercises— May 1956," University Archives; Myrtle Crosby, personal communication, June 23, 2024; New Farmers of America, *Guide for New Farmers of America* (12th ed.), 38; Connors, "Historical Analysis of the Role of Music."

45. For more information on the Randolph NFA Livestock and Poultry Show and Sale, see "NFA Show's Champ Barrow Nets 41¼¢; Event Is Success," *Fayette County Record*, April 3, 1962, 1, UNTPTH, https://texashistory.unt.edu/ark:/67531 /metapth986762/; "NFA Livestock Show Thursday," *La Grange Journal*, April 23, 1964, 10, UNTPTH, https://texashistory.unt.edu/ark:/67531/metapth1254506/; "Randolph NFA Show and Sale April 22," *Fayette County Record*, April 13, 1965, 4, UNTPTH, https://texashistory.unt.edu/ark:/67531/metapth988550/; "Randolph NFA Show Calf Champ Brings 41¢ Lb.; Barrow 50¢," *Fayette County Record*, April 30, 1965, 1–2, UNTPTH, https://texashistory.unt.edu/ark:/67531/metapth988955/; "Randolph

Slates Short Course on Insects Oct. 5–8," *Fayette County Record*, September 8, 1964, 1, UNTPTH, https://texashistory.unt.edu/ark:/67531/metapth989071/.

46. Jeff Kelly, personal communication, September 1, 2022.

47. Lorenza Crosby, personal communication, June 23, 2022; Flatt, "Recapturing a Lost Culture."

48. Lorenza Crosby, personal communication, June 23, 2022; Flatt, "Recapturing a Lost Culture."

49. Lorenza Crosby, personal communication, June 23, 2022; Rox Ann Johnson, personal communication, May 15, 2024; Flatt, "Recapturing a Lost Culture."

Chapter 5

1. Alston et al., *Legacy of the New Farmers of America*, 17; Strickland, *New Farmers of America in Retrospect*, 43.

2. Strickland, *New Farmers of America in Retrospect*, 100.

3. Strickland, *New Farmers of America in Retrospect*, 46.

4. Strickland, *New Farmers of America in Retrospect*, 43; Trouillot, *Silencing the Past*, 27.

5. Ture and Hamilton, *Black Power*; Farmer, *Remaking Black Power*, 4.

6. Conrad, *Research Brief*, 3; hooks, *Talking Back*, 175–76.

7. Norris, *Forty Long Years*; Strickland, *New Farmers of America in Retrospect*.

8. For detailed information on the legal process that formed the relationship between the AES-USOE and the FFA, see Tenney, *FFA at 50*, 78–84.

9. Norris, *Forty Long Years*, 50; Strickland, *New Farmers of America in Retrospect*.

10. To view the revised NFA constitution, see appendix B in Strickland, *New Farmers of America in Retrospect*.

11. Spade, *Normal Life*; Norris, *Forty Long Years*, 51; Strickland, *New Farmers of America in Retrospect*, 15.

12. *Proceedings of the Nineteenth Annual Conference of the Presidents of Negro Land Grant Colleges, November 11, 12, 13, 1941*, Chicago, 9, Office of the President Collections, University Archives, Prairie View A&M University, https://digitalcommons.pvamu.edu/negro-land-grant-colleges/1.

13. Gary Moore, "New Farmers of America (2/8/2019)."

14. Norris, *Forty Long Years*.

15. Norris, *Forty Long Years*; "Missouri Holds First NFA Meet," *Pittsburgh Courier*, April 16, 1949, www.proquest.com/historical-newspapers/missouri-holds-first-nfa-meet/docview/202227373/se-2; "Missouri Farmers Attend First of Educational Conferences," *New Journal and Guide*, April 16, 1949, www.proquest.com/historical-newspapers/missouri-farmers-attend-first-educational/docview/567857859/se-2.

16. Norris, *Forty Long Years*; E. Adams, "Role and Function," 54; New Farmers of America, *N.F.A. Guide for New Farmers of America* (1st ed.); New Farmers of America, *N.F.A. Guide for New Farmers of America* (2nd ed.); New Farmers of America, *N.F.A. Guide for New Farmers of America* (3rd ed.).

17. Hudson and Holmes, "Missing Teachers," 389; Joyner, "Pimping *Brown v. Board of Education*," 161.

18. Norris, *Forty Long Years*; New Farmers of America, *N.F.A. Guide for New Farmers of America* (7th ed.), 11; New Farmers of America, *Guide for New Farmers of America* (12th ed.), 7.

19. Bowen, "Reflections on the Need for Diversity," 7; Strickland, *New Farmers of America in Retrospect*, 26–34.

20. Norris, *Forty Long Years*, 22.

21. Norris, *Forty Long Years*, 23; Gary Moore, "Identifying the First Generation Leaders"; US Department of Health, Education, and Welfare, *Education Directory 1960–1961*, 9.

22. Norris, *Forty Long Years*, 22–24; US Department of Health, Education, and Welfare, *Education Directory 1960–1961*, 9; Strickland, *New Farmers of America in Retrospect*; Tenney, *FFA at 50*.

23. Norris, *Forty Long Years*, 23; Strickland, *New Farmers of America in Retrospect*, 30.

24. Norris, *Forty Long Years*, 15; Strickland, *New Farmers of America in Retrospect*, 35; Gary Moore, "'Merger' of the FFA and NFA."

25. Norris, *Forty Long Years*, 23.

26. "Excerpts from FFA Board Minutes (October 11–12, 1964)," in Selected Documents Related to the Merger of the FFA and NFA, curated by Gary Moore, 8–9, *The Friday Footnote: Focusing on the History of Agricultural Education and Rural America*, 2019, https://footnote.wordpress.ncsu.edu/files/2019/02/Documents-FFANFA-MERGER.pdf.

27. Francis Keppel to A. W. Tenney dated September 22, 1964, box 1, folder 7: Merger with FFA, 1962–1967, 1972, New Farmers of America Records, 1929–1965 (Mss 059), RLSCA; "Excerpts from FFA Board Minutes (October 11–12, 1964)," 8–9; US Department of Health, Education, and Welfare, *Education Directory 1960–1961*, 9.

28. "Excerpts from FFA Board Minutes (October 11–12, 1964)," 8–9; A. W. Tenney to Francis Keppel dated November 2, 1964, box 1, folder 7: Merger with FFA, 1962–1967, 1972, New Farmers of America Records, 1929–1965 (Mss 059), RLSCA.

29. Francis Keppel to A. W. Tenney dated January 27, 1965, box 1, folder 7: Merger with FFA, 1962–1967, 1972, New Farmers of America Records, 1929–1965 (Mss 059), RLSCA.

30. "Letter from A. W. Tenney to Commissioner Keppel (February 4, 1965)," in Selected Documents Related to the Merger of the FFA and NFA, curated by Gary Moore, 10–11, *The Friday Footnote: Focusing on the History of Agricultural Education and Rural America*, 2019, https://footnote.wordpress.ncsu.edu/files/2019/02/Documents-FFANFA-MERGER.pdf.

31. Ballot letter from E. M. Norris to Members of National Advisory Council, NFA (n.d.), box 42, folder 35: FFA History Subject NFA/FFA Merger, 1964–1969, National FFA Organization Records, 1916–2008 (Mss 035), RLSCA.

32. Norris, *Forty Long Years*, 23; E. M. Norris to Sectional and State Advisors of the NFA dated May 19, 1965, box 42, folder 35: FFA History Subject NFA/FFA Merger, 1964–1969, National FFA Organization Records, 1916–2008 (Mss 035), RLSCA; Strickland, *New Farmers of America in Retrospect*, 37.

33. Norris, *Forty Long Years*, 15–18.

34. Norris, *Forty Long Years*, 17–18; E. M. Norris to H. N. Hunsicker, dated February 3, 1966, box 1, folder 7: Merger with FFA, 1962–1967, 1972, New Farmers of America Records, 1929–1965 (Mss 059), RLSCA.

35. Norris, *Forty Long Years*, 17–18; Strickland, *New Farmers of America in Retrospect*, 43; US Department of Health, Education, and Welfare, *Education Directory 1960–1961*, 9; E. M. Norris to H. N. Hunsicker, dated February 3, 1966, RLSCA.

36. E. M. Norris to H. N. Hunsicker, dated February 3, 1966, RLSCA; Sherrill D. McMillen to Dr. John R. Ludington, January 25, 1966, box 1, folder 7: Merger with FFA, 1962–1967, 1972, New Farmers of America Records, 1929–1965 (Mss 059), RLSCA; H. N. Hunsicker to John Beaumont and Edwin Rumpf, dated November 8, 1965, box 42, folder 35: FFA History Subject NFA/FFA Merger, 1964–1969, National FFA Organization Records, 1916–2008 (Mss 035), RLSCA; E. M. Norris to Harold Howe, Commissioner of Education, April 21, 1966, box 42, folder 35: FFA History Subject NFA/FFA Merger, 1964–1969, National FFA Organization Records, 1916–2008 (Mss 035), RLSCA; A. W. Tenney to H. N. Hunsicker, dated March 31, 1966, box 42, folder 35: FFA History Subject NFA/FFA Merger, 1964–1969, National FFA Organization Records, 1916–2008 (Mss 035), RLSCA; H. N. Hunsicker to Grant Venn, dated April 4, 1967, box 1, folder 7: Merger with FFA, 1962–1967, 1972, New Farmers of America Records, 1929–1965 (Mss 059), RLSCA; Gary Moore, "'Merger' of the FFA and NFA."

37. Hurston, *Their Eyes Were Watching God*, 53.

38. E. M. Norris to H. N. Hunsicker, dated February 3, 1966, RLSCA.

39. E. M. Norris to H. N. Hunsicker, dated February 3, 1966, RLSCA; W. T. Johnson to President M. Nixon, dated May 15, 1969, box 42, folder 35: FFA History Subject NFA/FFA Merger, 1964–1969, National FFA Organization Records, 1916–2008 (Mss 035), RLSCA. For an in-depth examination of the communication between the NFA, FFA, and federal officials in the US Office of Education, see box 1, folder 7: Merger with FFA, 1962–1967, 1972, New Farmers of America Records, 1929–1965 (Mss 059), and box 42, folder 35: FFA History Subject NFA/FFA Merger, 1964–1969, National FFA Organization Records, 1916–2008 (Mss 035), RLSCA.

40. Frederick McClure interview, September 20, 2001, George H. W. Bush Oral History Project, Presidential Oral Histories, Miller Center, University of Virginia, Charlottesville, https://millercenter.org/the-presidency/presidential-oral-histories /frederick-mcclure-oral-history; Clark, "He Made History as Student in the '70s"; "FFA Moment: 1973"; Minorities in Agriculture, Natural Resources, and Related Sciences, *MANRRS Annual Report 2016–2017*; Minorities in Agriculture, Natural Resources, and Related Sciences, *MANRRS 2020 Annual Report*; Minorities in Agriculture, Natural Resources, and Related Sciences, "History of MANRRS"; Scott Spilky, "Leading with the Heart," *Illinois Quarterly* 9, no. 6 (1997): 32, box 41, folder 9: FFA History People Corey Flournoy, 1994–1997, National FFA Organization Records, 1916–2008 (Mss 035), RLSCA; Gabriel Rosenberg, "Urban Frontiersman," *Issue Magazine* 1, no. 5 (1995): 6–7, box 41, folder 9: FFA History People Corey Flournoy, 1994–1997, National FFA Organization Records, 1916–2008 (Mss 035), RLSCA.

41. George W. Conoly, August 1, 1978, Tallahassee Civil Rights Oral History Collection, Florida State University Libraries Digital Repository, https://repository.lib .fsu.edu/islandora/object/fsu%3A911944; "Agriculture Leader Walter T. Johnson Dies at Age of 79," *Greensboro (NC) News & Record*, August 6, 1986, retrieved from https:// digital.library.ncat.edu/documents/61; "Norris, Former PV Ag Professor, Dies," *The Panther* (Prairie View, TX), 70, no. 2 (1993): 3, retrieved from https://digitalcommons .pvamu.edu/pv-panther-newspapers/445.

Postscript: Writing the NFA Back into History

1. Valerie Grim, personal communication, September 26, 2024.
2. Gomez, "From the Director: Descent into Deceit."
3. Gomez, "From the Director: Descent into Deceit."

Behind the Scenes of *Black Farm Boys*: A Brief Note on Methods

1. Ham, *African-American Mosaic*, ix.
2. Morrison, "Site of Memory," 92–98.
3. Okechukwu, "Notes on Black Archival Practice," 27; Levine, "Discipline and Pleasure," 322.
4. Stake, *Art of Case Study Research*; Stake, "Case Studies."
5. Hall, "Constituting an Archive," 89, 91–92.

Bibliography

Primary Sources

MANUSCRIPT AND ARCHIVE COLLECTIONS

Ann Arbor, Michigan
    ProQuest Historical Papers: Black Newspapers
Austin, Texas
    Bullock Texas State History Museum
Beltsville, Maryland
    National Agricultural Library, United States Department of Agriculture
        Special Collections
            Black Agricultural Experience in the United States
Charlottesville, Virginia
    Presidential Oral Histories, Miller Center, University of Virginia
        George H. W. Bush Oral History Project
Denton, Texas
    University of North Texas Libraries
        The Portal to Texas History
Greensboro, North Carolina
    North Carolina A&T State University
        Archives and Special Collections, F. D. Bluford Library
            New Farmers of America Collection (ncatnfa)
            North Carolina A&T State University Cooperative Extension Service
                Archives Collection (ncatcoe)
            S. B. Simmons Collection (ncatsbs)
Greenville, North Carolina
    Sheppard Memorial Library
        Pitt County Historical Society
            Chronicles of Pitt County North Carolina (Volume 1)
Indianapolis, Indiana
    Indiana University Indianapolis
        Ruth Lilly Special Collections and Archives, University Library
            National FFA Organization Records, 1916–2008 (Mss 035)
            New Farmers of America Records, 1929–1965 (Mss 059)

Kansas City, Missouri
   Kansas City Public Library—Central Library
      Special Collections
La Grange, Texas
   Fayette Public Library
      Fayette Heritage Museum and Archives
      Lorenza and Myrtle Crosby Collection
Oklahoma City, Oklahoma
   Oklahoma Historical Society
      The Gateway to Oklahoma History
Prairie View, Texas
   John B. Coleman Library, Prairie View A&M University
      Digital Commons@PVAMU: A Repository of Archives, Research &
         Scholarship
      University Archives
         Academic Affairs Collections
         Office of the President Collections
         PVAMU-Theses
         PV Annual Catalog Collection
         PV Standard Newspapers
         *Texas Standard: Official Publication of the Teachers State Association of
            Texas* Collection
Tallahassee, Florida
   Florida State University Libraries Digital Repository
      Tallahassee Civil Rights Oral History Collection
Trenton, New Jersey
   New Jersey State Library
      New Jersey State Publications Digital Library
         The Ironsides Echo
         Reports by and about the Manual Training and Industrial School for
            Colored Youth at Bordentown
Washington, DC
   Library of Congress
      Science, Technology & Business Division

PERIODICALS

Afro-American (Baltimore)
Agricultural Education Magazine
American Farm Youth
Atlanta Daily World
Chicago Defender
Cleveland Call and Post
Courier (Pittsburgh)
Faculty and Staff News (Prairie View A&M University)

Fayette County Record (La Grange, TX)
FFA New Horizons
Greensboro (NC) Daily News
Greensboro News & Record
Illinois Quarterly
Ironsides Echo
Issue Magazine
La Grange (TX) High School N.F.A. News
La Grange Journal
Mosquito Express
New Journal and Guide (Norfolk, VA)
New York Amsterdam News
New York Times
The Panther (Prairie View A&M University)
Philadelphia Tribune
Pittsburgh Courier
Port of Harlem
Prairie View Standard
School Life
Schulenburg Sticker
Southern Workman

RARE BOOKS

New Farmers of America. *N.F.A. Guide for New Farmers of America*. 1st ed. Baltimore: French-Bray Printing Company, 1938.
New Farmers of America. *N.F.A. Guide for New Farmers of America*. 2nd ed. Baltimore: French-Bray Printing Company, 1940.
New Farmers of America. *N.F.A. Guide for New Farmers of America*. 3rd ed. Baltimore: French-Bray Printing Company, 1944.
New Farmers of America. *N.F.A. Guide for New Farmers of America*. 4th ed. Baltimore: French-Bray Printing Company, 1946.
New Farmers of America. *N.F.A. Guide for New Farmers of America*. 7th ed. Baltimore: French-Bray Printing Company, 1954.
New Farmers of America. *Guide for New Farmers of America*. 12th ed. Baltimore: French-Bray Printing Company, 1963.
Norris, Ernest M. *Forty Long Years*. Langston, OK: Langston University Press, 1993.
Strickland, Cecil L., Sr. *New Farmers of America in Retrospect: The Formative Years, 1935–1965*. Hempstead, TX: Joyco Printing, 1994.

Secondary Sources

Adams, Ezola Bolden. "The Role and Function of the Manual Training and Industrial School at Bordentown as an Alternative School, 1915–1955." EdD diss., Rutgers University, 1977.

Adams, Phylis Jones. *A Place for Us: The History of the J. R. Thomas NFA-NHA Camp.* Heart 2 Pen Publishing, 2020.

Adams, Phylis Jones. "Time Remembered." *Port of Harlem* 11, no. 2 (2005): 6.

"Advance in Negro Education." *Southern Workman* 49, no. 3 (1920): 103–4.

Allen, Brandon C. M., and Levon T. Esters. "Historically Black Land Grant Universities: Overcoming Barriers and Achieving Success." CMSI Research Brief. Penn Center for Minority Serving Institutions, 2018.

Alston, Antoine J., Dexter B. Wakefield, and Netta S. Cox. *The Legacy of the New Farmers of America.* Arcadia Publishing, 2022.

Anderson, James D. *The Education of Blacks in the South, 1860–1935.* University of North Carolina Press, 1988.

Arthur, C. M. "The Vocational Summary." *School Life* 25, no. 1 (1939): 22–23.

Association of Public and Land-Grant Universities. *The Land-Grant Tradition.* Association of Public and Land-Grant Universities, 2012.

Beardall, Theresa Rocha. "Settler Simultaneity and Anti-Indigenous Racism at Land-Grant Universities." *Sociology of Race and Ethnicity* 8, no. 1 (2022): 197–212.

Beauford, E. Yvonne. "Revitalizing Rural America: Focus on Rural Youth." *Journal of Rural Social Sciences* 6, no. 1 (1989): 1–11.

Bowen, Blannie E. "Reflections on the Need for Diversity: Desegregation vs. Integration." *Agricultural Education Magazine* 66, no. 12 (1994): 6–8.

Brown, Adell, Jr. "1890 Institutions' Extension Program and Rural Development." *Journal of Rural Social Sciences* 7, no. 1 (1990): 1–7.

Brown, Adell, Jr., Ralph D. Christy, and Tesfa G. Gebremedhin. "Structural Changes in U.S. Agriculture: Implications for African American Farmers." In *Blacks in Rural America,* edited by James B. Stewart and Joyce E. Allen Smith. Transaction Publishers, 1995.

Bullock Texas State History Museum. "NAACP Youth Council Picket Line, 1955 Texas State Fair." Retrieved from www.thestoryoftexas.com/discover/artifacts /naacp-state-fair-spotlight-012315 on August 17, 2024.

Bynum, Thomas L. *NAACP Youth and the Fight for Black Freedom, 1936–1965.* University of Tennessee Press, 2013.

Carden, Hoover. "Educational Value of Livestock Shows and Fairs." Master's thesis, Prairie View A&M University, 1964.

Carrillo, Ian, Katrina Quisumbing King, and Kai A. Schafft. "Race, Ethnicity, and Twenty-First Century Rural Sociological Imaginings: A Special Issue Introduction." *Rural Sociology* 86, no. 3 (2021): 419–43.

Carter, Purvis M. "Robert Lloyd Smith and the Farmers' Improvement Society: A Self-Help Movement in Texas." *Negro History Bulletin* 29, no. 8 (1966): 175–91.

Carver, George Washington. *Nature Study and Children's Gardens.* Teacher's Leaflet No. 2. Extension Division, Department of Agriculture, Tuskegee Normal and Industrial Institute, 1904.

Carver, George Washington. *Nature Study and Gardening for Rural Schools.* Bulletin No. 18, June 1910. Experiment Station, Tuskegee Normal and Industrial Institute.

Chatelain, Marcia. *South Side Girls: Growing Up in the Great Migration.* Duke University Press, 2015.

Christy, Ralph D., and Lionel Williamson. *A Century of Service: Land-Grant Colleges and Universities, 1890–1990*. Transaction Publishers, 1992.

Clark, Caitlin. "He Made History as a Student in the '70s. Now He's Leading as an Employee." Texas A&M Stories, February 28, 2023. https://today.tamu .edu/2023/02/28/he-made-history-as-a-student-in-the-70s-now-hes-leading -as-an-employee/.

Collins, William Milton. "The Health Conditions of One Hundred Negro Households in Schulenburg, Texas, and Their Implications for Agricultural Education." Master's thesis, Prairie View A&M University, 1941.

Connors, James J. "A Historical Analysis of the Role of Music in the FFA and NFA Organizations." *Journal of Agricultural Education* 62, no. 4 (2021): 1–15.

Connors, James J., Jeremy M. Falk, and Rebekah B. Epps. "Recounting the Legacy: The History and Use of FFA Camps for Leadership and Recreation." *Journal of Agricultural Education* 51, no. 1 (2010): 32–42.

Conoly, George W. "The Program of Education for Young Negro Farmers in Florida." Master's thesis, The Ohio State University, 1936.

Conoly, George W. "Some Benefits from N.F.A. Banquets." *Agricultural Education Magazine* 21, no. 6 (1948): 126.

Conrad, Alison. *Research Brief: Identifying and Countering White Supremacy Culture in Food Systems*. World Food Policy Center, Sanford School of Public Health Policy. Duke University, September 2020. https://wfpc.sanford.duke.edu/wp -content/uploads/sites/15/2022/05/Whiteness-Food-Movements-Research-Brief -WFPC-October-2020.pdf.

Constance, Douglas H. "The Emancipatory Question: The Next Step in the Sociology of Agrifood Systems?" *Agriculture and Human Values* 25, no. 2 (2008): 151–55. doi.org/10.1007/s10460-008-9114-4.

Constance, Douglas H. "2008 AFHVS Presidential Address: The Four Questions in Agrifood Studies: A View from the Bus." *Agriculture and Human Values* 26, no. 1–2 (2009): 3–14. doi.org/10.1007/s10460-008-9187-0.

Crawford, Anthony R. *Autobiography of George Washington Owens: First African American Graduate of Kansas State University*. New Prairie Press, 2022.

Cromley, Elizabeth C. "Transforming the Food Axis: Houses, Tools, Modes of Analysis." *Material Culture Review* 44, no. 1 (1996): 8–22.

Crosby, Earl W. "The Roots of Black Agricultural Extension Work." *The Historian* 39, no. 2 (1977): 228–47.

Crosby, Earl W. "The Struggle for Existence: The Institutionalization of the Black County Agent System." *Agricultural History* 60, no. 2 (1986): 123–36.

Diani, Mario. "The Concept of Social Movement." *Sociological Review* 40, no. 1 (1992): 1–25.

Du Bois, W. E. B. "The Last Word in Caste." In *National Association for the Advancement of Colored People Fourth Annual Report, 1913*. National Association for the Advancement of Colored People, 1914.

Du Bois, W. E. B. *The Souls of Black Folk*. A. C. McClurg, 1903.

Du Bois, W. E. B. "The Talented Tenth." In *The Negro Problem: A Series of Articles by Representative American Negroes of Today*. James Pott, 1903.

Elam, William N. "New Farmers of America." In *History of Agricultural Education of Less Than College Grade in the United States: A Cooperative Project of Workers in Vocational Education in Agricultural and in Related Fields*, compiled by Rufus W. Stimson and Frank W. Lothrop. Federal Security Agency, 1942.

Farmer, Ashley D. *Remaking Black Power: How Black Women Transformed an Era*. University of North Carolina Press, 2017.

"FFA Moment: 1973." *FFA New Horizons*, Fall 2020, 43.

Fields, Marvin A. *New Farmers of America: 25 Years of Accomplishment*. Office of Education, US Department of Health, Education, and Welfare, 1959.

Flatt, Bev. "Recapturing a Lost Culture." *FFA New Horizons*, Spring/Summer 2022, 24–29.

Floyd, Arthur. "Teaching and Learning as Applied to Vocational Agriculture." *Agricultural Education Magazine* 21, no. 11 (1949): 251.

Franklin, James A. *Golden Nuggets: Experiences in the Old South*. Page Publishing, 2020.

Franklin, Sekou M. *After the Rebellion: Black Youth, Social Movement Activism, and the Post–Civil Rights Generation*. New York University Press, 2014.

Franklin, Sekou M. "Black Youth Activism and the Reconstruction of America: Leaders, Organizations, and Tactics in the Twentieth Century and Beyond." *Black History Bulletin* 79, no. 1 (2016): 5–14.

Gilbert, Jess, Gwen Sharp, and M. Sindy Felin. "The Loss and Persistence of Black-Owned Farms and Farmland: A Review of the Research Literature and Its Implications." *Journal of Rural Social Sciences* 18, no. 2 (2002): 1–30.

Gilbert, Jess, Spencer D. Wood, and Gwen Sharp. "Who Owns the Land? Agricultural Land Ownership by Race/Ethnicity." *Rural America/Rural Development Perspectives* 17, no. 4 (2002): 55–62.

Gilman, Donald F. "Examining the Merger of the NFA and FFA." PhD diss., Auburn University, 2013.

Ginwright, Shawn A. *Black Youth Rising: Activism and Radical Healing in Urban America*. Teachers College Press, 2010.

Glave, Dianne D. *Rooted in the Earth: Reclaiming the African American Environmental Heritage*. Lawrence Hill Books, 2010.

Goddard, Connie. "The Bordentown School as Institution and Idea: The Manual Training and Industrial School Honored Educational Priorities of Washington, Du Bois, and Dewey." *New Jersey Studies: An Interdisciplinary Journal* 4, no. 2 (2018): 99–128.

Goddard, Connie. "Bordentown: Where Dewey's 'Learning to Earn' Met Du Boisian Educational Priorities: The Unique Legacy of a Once Thriving but Largely Forgotten School for Black Students." *Education and Culture* 35, no. 1 (2019): 49–70.

Gomez, Michael. "From the Director: Descent into Deceit." Center for the Study of Africa and the African Diaspora, New York University, April 16, 2025. https://csaad.nyu.edu/descent-into-deceit/.

Grant, Gary R., Spencer D. Wood, and Willie J. Wright. "Black Farmers United: The Struggle Against Power and Principalities." *Journal of Pan African Studies* 5, no. 1 (2012): 3–22.

Grant, Jared, Michée A. Lachaud, and Daniel Solís. "An Overview of the History, Role, and Struggles of Agricultural Economics and Business Programs at 1890 Land-Grant Historically Black Colleges and Universities (HBCU)." *Applied Economic Perspectives and Policy* 46 (2024): 889–904.

Grim, Valerie. "African American Landlords in the Rural South, 1870–1950: A Profile." *Agricultural History* 72, no. 2 (1998): 399–416.

Grim, Valerie. "African American Rural Culture, 1900–1950." In *African American Life in the Rural South, 1900–1950*, edited by R. Douglas Hurt. University of Missouri Press, 2003.

Grim, Valerie. "The 1890 Land-Grant Colleges' Work on Behalf of Black People: A Profile from the New Deal to the Black Farmers' Class-Action Lawsuit, 1930s–2010s." In *Service as Mandate: How American Land-Grant Universities Shaped the Modern World, 1920–2015*, edited by Alan Marcus. University of Alabama Press, 2015.

Grim, Valerie. "The Impact of Mechanized Farming on Black Farm Families in the Rural South: A Study of Farm Life in the Brooks Farm Community, 1940–1970." *Agricultural History* 68, no. 2 (1994): 169–84.

Grim, Valerie. "The Politics of Inclusion: Black Farmers and the Quest for Agribusiness Participation, 1945–1990s." *Agricultural History* 69, no. 2 (1995): 257–71.

Hall, Stuart. "Constituting an Archive." *Third Text* 15, no. 54 (2001): 89–92.

Ham, Debra Newman. *The African-American Mosaic: A Library of Congress Resource Guide for the Study of Black History and Culture*. Superintendent of Documents, US Government Printing Office, 1993.

Hargraves, J. Archie. "Fifth National FFA Convention Held at Bordentown, N.J." *American Farm Youth* 5, no. 5 (1939): 19.

Harris, Carmen V. "'The Extension Service Is Not an Integration Agency': The Idea of Race in the Cooperative Extension Service." *Agricultural History* 82, no. 2 (2008): 193–219.

Harris, Carmen V. "States' Rights, Federal Bureaucrats, and Segregated 4-H Camps in the United States, 1927–1969." *Journal of African American History* 93, no. 3 (2008): 362–88.

Haunss, Sebastian, and Darcy K. Leach. "Social Movement Scenes: Infrastructures of Opposition in Civil Society." In *Civil Societies and Social Movements: Potentials and Problems*, edited by Derrick Purdue. Routledge, 2007.

Hicks, Otis. "New Farmers of America and National Defense." *American Farm Youth* 7, no. 7 (1941): 22–23.

Hickson, William F. "Needs of Farm Families." *Agricultural Education Magazine* 23, no. 2 (1950): 36.

Hightower, Jim. "Hard Tomatoes, Hard Times: Failure of the Land Grant College Complex." *Society* 10, no. 1 (1972): 10–22.

Hightower, Jim, and Agribusiness Accountability Project Task Force on the Land Grant College Complex. *Hard Tomatoes, Hard Times: A Report of the Agribusiness Accountability Project on the Failure of America's Land Grant College Complex*. Schenkman, 1973.

Hill, Walter A. "Environmental Thought and Activism: An 1890 Land-Grant University Perspective." In *Land and Power: Sustainable Agriculture and African Americans*, edited by Jeffrey L. Jordan, Edward Pennick, Walter A. Hill, and Robert Zabawa. Sustainable Agriculture Publications, 2007.

Hinson, Waymon R., and Edward Robinson. "'We Didn't Get Nothing': The Plight of Black Farmers." *Journal of African American Studies* 12 (2008): 283–302.

hooks, bell. *Talking Back: Thinking Feminist, Thinking Black*. South End Press, 1989.

Horne, Gerald. *The Rise and Fall of the Associated Negro Press: Claude Barnett's Pan-African News and the Jim Crow Paradox*. University of Illinois Press, 2017.

Hudson, Mildred J., and Barbara J. Holmes. "Missing Teachers, Impaired Communities: The Unanticipated Consequences of *Brown v. Board of Education* on the African American Teaching Force at the Precollegiate Level." *Journal of Negro Education* 63, no. 3 (1994): 388–93.

Hunt, Irvin J. *Dreaming the Present: Time, Aesthetics, and the Black Cooperative Movement*. University of North Carolina Press, 2022.

Hunte, Christopher N. "The African American Experience in Agriculture." *Agriculture and Human Values* 9 (Winter 1992): 11–14.

Hunter, Marcus Anthony, Mary Pattillo, Zandria F. Robinson, and Keeanga-Yamahtta Taylor. "Black Placemaking: Celebration, Play, and Poetry." *Theory, Culture & Society* 33, no. 7–8 (2016): 31–56.

Hurston, Zora Neale. *Their Eyes Were Watching God*. 1st HarperCollins hardcover ed. HarperCollins, 2000.

Interracial Committee of the New Jersey Conference of Social Work. *The Negro in New Jersey*. New Jersey Conference of Social Work, 1932.

Jackson, James C. "Some Aspects of Farming by Negroes Living in the LA Grange, Texas Area with Special Reference to Marketing Practices." Master's thesis, Prairie View A&M University, 1954.

Johnson, Charles S. *Growing Up in the Black Belt: Negro Youth in the Rural South*. American Council on Education, 1941.

Johnson, George M. *All Boys Aren't Blue: A Memoir-Manifesto*. Farrar, Straus and Giroux, 2020.

Johnson, James Roy. "The History and Development of the Oklahoma Association of New Farmers of America." Master's thesis, Oklahoma State University, 1961.

Johnson, Walter T. "Camping Experiences Develop Leadership." *Agricultural Education Magazine* 34, no. 11 (1962): 248–49.

Jones, Allen W. "Improving Rural Life for Blacks: The Tuskegee Negro Farmers' Conference, 1892–1915." *Agricultural History* 65, no. 2 (1991): 105–14.

Jones, Allen W. "The South's First Black Farm Agents." *Agricultural History* 50, no. 4 (1976): 636–44.

Jones, Dewitt, and Alfred L. Parks. "1890 Institutions in a Changing Socioeconomic Environment: Implications for Human Resource Development." *Journal of Agricultural and Applied Economics* 22, no. 1 (1990): 61–64.

Jones, Hezekiah S. "Federal Agricultural Policies: Do Black Farm Operators Benefit?" In *Blacks in Rural America*, edited by James B. Stewart and Joyce E. Allen Smith. Transaction Publishers, 1995.

Jones, Lewis W. "The South's Negro Farm Agent." *Journal of Negro Education* 22, no. 1 (1953): 38–45.

Jones, Lu Ann. "In Search of Jennie Booth Moton, Field Agent, AAA." *Agricultural History* 72, no. 2 (1998): 446–58.

Jones, Susan L., Barbara M. Kirby, and Wendy J. Warner. "The Role of NFA Camps in Agricultural Education for Rural African American Boys in North Carolina." *Journal of Agricultural Education* 62, no. 1 (2021): 276–90.

Jones, Wash A. "Factors Influencing Career Choice of African American and Hispanic Graduates of the College of Agriculture and Life Sciences at Texas A&M University." PhD diss., Texas A&M University, 1999.

Jones, Wash A., Douglas D. LaVergne, Curtis D. White, and Alvin Larke. "The Voices of African American Agriculture Teachers in One Southern State Regarding the NFA/FFA Merger." *Journal of Agricultural Education* 62, no. 2 (2021): 39–52.

Jones-Branch, Cherisse. "African Americans in Twentieth-Century Agriculture." In *A Companion to American Agricultural History*, edited by R. Douglas Hurt. John Wiley & Sons, 2022.

Joyner, Irving. "Pimping *Brown v. Board of Education*: The Destruction of African-American Schools and the Mis-Education of African-American Students." *North Carolina Central Law Review* 35, no. 2 (2013): 160–202.

Juris, Jeffrey S. "Spaces of Intentionality: Race, Class, and Horizontality at the United States Social Forum." In *Insurgent Encounters: Transnational Activism, Ethnography, and the Political*, edited by Jeffrey S. Juris and Alex Khasnabish. Duke University Press, 2013.

Kelley, Robin D. G. *Freedom Dreams: The Black Radical Imagination*. Beacon Press, 2002.

Kersey, G. K. "My Hopes for a Greater Development of New Farmers of America." *American Farm Youth* 5, no. 5 (1939): 18.

King, Katrina Quisumbing, Spencer D. Wood, Jess Gilbert, and Marilyn Sinkewicz. "Black Agrarianism: The Significance of African American Landownership in the Rural South." *Rural Sociology* 83, no. 3 (2018): 677–99.

Kremer, Gary R. *George Washington Carver: A Biography*. Greenwood, 2011.

Lee, Escar Robert. "Some Aspects of Activity Programs for All-Day Boys Studying Vocational Agriculture in the Crockett District of Texas." Master's thesis, Prairie View A&M University, 1949. Retrieved from https://digitalcommons.pvamu.edu/pvamu-theses/796.

Lee, John M., Jr., and Samaad W. Keys. "Land-Grant but Unequal: State One-to-One Match Funding for 1890 Land-Grant Universities." APLU Office of Access and Success publication no. 3000-PB1. Association of Public and Land-grant Universities, 2013.

Levine, Philippa. "Discipline and Pleasure: Response." *Victorian Studies* 46, no. 2 (2004): 319–25.

Luter, Buckner Sythias. "A Historical and Educational Analysis of the Administration and Curriculum of the Hempstead Negro School from 1867 to 1938: Inclusive." *A Thesis Report*, Prairie View A&M University, 1938. Retrieved from https://digitalcommons.pvamu.edu/pvamu-theses/457.

Madera, Judith. "Early Black Worldmaking: Body, Compass, and Text." *American Literary History* 33, no. 3 (2021): 481–97.

Manor, Amy, and Emily Pronovost. "4-H and Home Demonstration Among African Americans: North Carolina's African American Extension Service." NCpedia. NCSU Libraries, 2007. Retrieved from www.ncpedia.org/4-h-and-home-demonstration-among.

Martin, Oscar Baker. *A Decade of Negro Extension Work, 1914–1924.* Miscellaneous Circular No. 72, US Department of Agriculture. US Government Printing Office, 1926.

Mayberry, B. D. *A Century of Agriculture in the 1890 Land-Grant Institutions and Tuskegee University, 1890–1990.* Vantage Press, 1991.

Mclean-Meyinsse, Patricia E., and Adell Brown Jr. "Survival Strategies of Successful Farmers." In *Blacks in Rural America*, edited by James B. Stewart and Joyce E. Allen Smith. Transaction Publishers, 1995.

Minorities in Agriculture, Natural Resources, and Related Sciences. "The History of MANRRS: Our Past Helps Build the Future." Retrieved from www.manrrs.org/about/history on October 11, 2024.

Minorities in Agriculture, Natural Resources, and Related Sciences. *MANRRS Annual Report 2016–2017.* www.manrrs.org/hubfs/MANRRS%202016-2017%20Annual%20Report.pdf.

Minorities in Agriculture, Natural Resources, and Related Sciences. *MANRRS 2020 Annual Report.* www.manrrs.org/hubfs/MANRRS2020AnnReport_FINAL-1.pdf.

"Mississippi Association of N.F.A. Stresses Home Improvement Program." *American Farm Youth* 7, no. 3 (1941): 18.

"Monthly Meetings of District Association on NFA Programs of Work." *American Farm Youth* 7, no. 3 (1941): 18.

Moore, Gary. "Identifying the First Generation Leaders in Agricultural Education: The Lost Stimson Manuscript." *Journal of Agricultural Education* 59, no. 4 (2018): 137–58.

Moore, Gary. "The 'Merger' of the FFA and NFA (2/15/2019)." *The Friday Footnote: Focusing on the History of Agricultural Education and Rural America.* NCSU.edu, February 14, 2019. https://footnote.wordpress.ncsu.edu/2019/02/14/the-merger-of-the-ffa-and-nfa-2-15-2019/.

Moore, Gary. "New Farmers of America (2/8/2019)." *The Friday Footnote: Focusing on the History of Agricultural Education and Rural America.* NCSU.edu, February 8, 2019. https://footnote.wordpress.ncsu.edu/2019/02/08/the-new-farmers-of-america-2-8-2019/.

Moore, George. "North Carolina Convention." *American Farm Youth* 5, no. 4 (1939): 18–19.

Morrison, Toni. "The Site of Memory." In *Inventing the Truth: The Art and Craft of Memoir*, rev. and expanded 2nd ed., edited by Russell Baker and William Zinsser. Houghton Mifflin, 1995.

National Association of State Universities and Land-Grant Colleges. *Leadership and Learning: An Interpretive History of Historically Black Land-Grant Colleges and Universities—A Centennial Study.* NASULGC, 1990.

Nembhard, Jessica Gordon. *Collective Courage: A History of African American Cooperative Economic Thought and Practice*. Pennsylvania State University Press, 2014.

"New Farmers' Camp." *American Farm Youth* 6, no. 6 (1940): 19.

"New Farmers of America Camp for Mississippi Boys." *American Farm Youth* 7, no. 3 (1941): 18–19.

New York World's Fair. *Official Guide Book of the New York World's Fair 1939*. Exposition Publications, 1939.

Neyland, Leedell W. *Historically Black Land-Grant Institutions and the Development of Agriculture and Home Economics, 1890–1990*. Florida A&M University Foundation, 1990.

Noakes, Harold L. "The New York F.F.A. Camping Program." *Agricultural Education Magazine* 23, no. 4 (1950): 84, 90.

North Carolina FFA Association. "History of the NC FFA Center: FFA Camps in North Carolina." Retrieved from https://ncffa.org/ncffa-more/nc-ffa-center /history-of-the-nc-ffa-center#:~:text=In%201979%20othe%20Tom%20Browne, Lake%20has%20been%20in%20operation on August 3, 2024.

Okechukwu, Amaka. "Notes on Black Archival Practice: A Relationship to Evidence of Black Life." *Black Scholar* 52, no. 4 (2022): 27–42.

Owens, George W. "The New Farmers of Virginia." *Southern Workman* 58, no. 11 (1929): 512–15.

Parks, Alfred L., and Richard D. Robbins. "Human Capital Needs of Black Land-Grant Institutions." *Journal of Agricultural and Applied Economics* 17, no. 1 (1985): 61–69.

Pattillo, Mary. "Black Advantage Vision: Flipping the Script on Racial Inequality Research." *Issues in Race & Society* 10, no. 1 (2021): 5–39.

Petty, Adrienne. "I'll Take My Farm: The GI Bill, Agriculture and Veterans in North Carolina." *Journal of Peasant Studies* 35, no. 4 (2008): 742–69.

Pitre, Merline. "Robert Lloyd Smith: A Black Lawmaker in the Shadow of Booker T. Washington." *Phylon* 46, no. 3 (1985): 262–68.

Pitt County Historical Society. "A Short History of Pitt County Education." In *Chronicles of Pitt County North Carolina* (vol. 1), edited by Elizabeth H. Copeland. Hunter, 1982.

"Preliminary Announcement. Seventh World's Poultry Congress and Exposition, Cleveland, Ohio, July 20 to August 7, 1939." US Government Printing Office, 1937.

Rehder, Roberta, and Alan R. Cohen. "Eccentric Neurosurgical Virtuoso: The Life and Times of William Sharpe." *Neurosurgical Focus* 39, no. 1 (2015): 1–12.

Reid, Debra A. *Reaping a Greater Harvest : African Americans, the Extension Service, and Rural Reform in Jim Crow Texas*. Texas A&M University Press, 2007.

Reid, Ira De A. "Negro Movements and Messiahs, 1900–1949." *Phylon* 10, no. 4 (1949): 362–69.

Sanders, Crystal R. "Blue Water, Black Beach: The North Carolina Teachers Association and Hammocks Beach in the Age of Jim Crow." *North Carolina Historical Review* 92, no. 2 (2015): 145–64.

Schor, Joel. *Agriculture in the Black Land-Grant College System to 1930*. Florida A&M University, 1982.

Schor, Joel. "Anachronisms or Rising Stars: The Black Land-Grant College System." *Agriculture and Human Values* 2, no. 3 (1985): 76–79.

Schor, Joel. "The Black Presence in the US Cooperative Extension Service Since 1945: An American Quest for Service and Equity." *Agricultural History* 60, no. 2 (1986): 137–53.

Seals, Rupert Grant. "The Formation of Agricultural and Rural Development Policy with Emphasis on African-Americans: II. The Hatch-George and Smith-Lever Acts." *Agricultural History* 65, no. 2 (1991): 12–34.

Seventh World's Poultry Congress and Exposition, Cleveland, Ohio, U.S.A., July 28 to August 7, 1939. Waverly Press, 1939.

Sharpe, William. *Brain Surgeon: The Autobiography of William Sharpe.* Viking Press, 1952.

Simmons, Sidney B. "Negro Youth and the US Junior Employment Service—4-H Clubs and the New Farmers of America." *Journal of Negro Education* 11, no. 3 (1940): 408–15.

Simmons, Sidney B. "N.F.A. in Annual Convention." *Agricultural Education Magazine* 12, no. 5 (1939): 89.

Smith, Bobby J., II. "In Search of the New Farmers of America: Remembering America's Forgotten Black Youth Farm Movement." *Journal of Agriculture, Food Systems, and Community Development* 11, no. 4 (2022): 9–12. doi.org/10.5304/jafscd.2022.114.021.

Smith, Sarah. "Remembering the Walker-Gordon Dairy, an Innovator in Safe Raw Milk from 1897–1971." *Raw Milk Institute*, November 24, 2020. www.rawmilkinstitute.org/updates/remembering-the-walker-gordon-dairy-an-innovator-in-safe-raw-milk-from-1897-1971.

Spade, Dean. *Normal Life: Administrative Violence, Critical Trans Politics, and the Limits of Law.* Rev. and expanded ed. Duke University Press, 2015.

Stake, Robert E. *The Art of Case Study Research.* SAGE, 1995.

Stake, Robert E. "Case Studies." In *Strategies of Qualitative Inquiry*, 2nd ed., edited by Norman K. Denzin and Yvonna S. Lincoln. SAGE, 2003.

Stimson, Rufus W., and Frank W. Lothrop, comps. *History of Agricultural Education of Less Than College Grade in the United States: A Cooperative Project of Workers in Vocational Education in Agricultural and in Related Fields.* Federal Security Agency, 1942.

Sturdevant, Paul. "The FIS School: A Tuskegee for Texas?" *East Texas Historical Journal* 47, no. 1 (2009): 52–59.

Tabor, Alva. "Camp John Hope." *Agricultural Education Magazine* 19, no. 8 (1947): 156–57.

Te Hennepe, B. J. C. "The Seventh World's Poultry Congress and Exposition." *International Review of Poultry Science* 11, no. 1–2 (1938): 23–29.

Tenney, A. Webster. *The FFA at 50: A Golden Past, a Brighter Future.* Future Farmers of America, 1977.

Thompson, Natasha. "'Give Us a Status Above That of a Submarginal People': Racial Policies, Practices, and Activism in North Carolina 4-H." *North Carolina Historical Review* 93, no. 3 (2016): 308–38.

Trouillot, Michel-Rolph. *Silencing the Past: Power and the Production of History.* Beacon Press, 2015.

Ture, Kwame, and Charles V. Hamilton. *Black Power: The Politics of Liberation.* Vintage Books, 1992.

Turner, Clinton V. Foreword to *A Place for Us: The History of the J. R. Thomas NFA-NHA Camp,* by Phylis Jones Adams. Heart 2 Pen Publishing, 2020.

US Congress. "Second Morrill Act." US Government Publishing Office, August 30, 1890. https://www.govinfo.gov/app/details/COMPS-10284.

US Department of Health, Education, and Welfare. Office of Education. *Education Directory 1960–1961, Part 1: Federal Government and States.* US Government Printing Office, 1960. https://files.eric.ed.gov/fulltext/ED619715.pdf.

Van Slyck, Abigail Ayres. *A Manufactured Wilderness: Summer Camps and the Shaping of American Youth, 1890–1960.* University of Minnesota Press, 2006.

Wakefield, Dexter B. "Impact of the New Farmers of America (NFA) on Selected Past Members: A Historical Narrative." PhD diss., Purdue University, 2001.

Wakefield, Dexter B., and B. Allen Talbert. "A Historical Narrative on the Impact of the New Farmers of America (NFA) on Selected Past Members." *Journal of Agricultural Education* 44, no. 1 (2003): 95–104.

Walcott, Rinaldo. *The Long Emancipation: Moving Toward Black Freedom.* Duke University Press, 2021.

Washington, Booker T. *Working with the Hands: Being a Sequel to "Up From Slavery" Covering the Author's Experiences in Industrial Training at Tuskegee.* Doubleday, Page, 1904.

Watson, Elwood. "Camp Atwater (1921–)." BlackPast.org, January 25, 2011. https://blackpast.org/african-american-history/camp-atwater-1921/.

White, Monica M. "Collective Agency and Community Resilience: A Theoretical Framework to Understand Agricultural Resistance." *Journal of Agriculture, Food Systems, and Community Development* 7, no. 4 (2017): 17–21.

White, Monica M. *Freedom Farmers: Agricultural Resistance and the Black Freedom Movement.* University of North Carolina Press, 2018.

White, Monica M. "'A Pig and a Garden': Fannie Lou Hamer and the Freedom Farms Cooperative." *Food and Foodways* 25, no. 1 (2017): 20–39.

Williams, Thomas T. *The Unique Resources of the 1890 Land-Grant Institutions and Implications for International Development.* Rev. ed. Southern University, Unemployment-Underemployment Institute, 1979.

Wood, Spencer D., and Jess Gilbert. "Returning African American Farmers to the Land: Recent Trends and a Policy Rationale." *Review of Black Political Economy* 27, no. 4 (2000): 43–64.

Woodson, Carter G. *The Rural Negro.* Association for the Study of Negro Life and History, 1930.

Wright, Marion M. Thompson. *The Education of Negroes in New Jersey.* Bureau of Publications, Teachers College, Columbia University, 1941.

Young, Phoebe S. K. *Camping Grounds: Public Nature in American Life from the Civil War to the Occupy Movement.* Oxford University Press, 2021.

Zabawa, Robert, Arthur Siaway, and Ntam Baharanyi. "The Decline of Black Farmers and Strategies for Survival." *Journal of Rural Social Sciences* 7, no. 1 (1990): Article 9, 1–16.

Index

Page numbers in italics refer to illustrations.